P9-DTB-084

Date Due

172

Spirit of Flame

LESYA UKRAINKA

SPIRIT OF FLAME

A Collection of the Works of
Lesya Ukrainka

Translated by
PERCIVAL CUNDY

Foreword by
CLARENCE A. MANNING
Assistant Professor of Slavic Languages
Columbia University

GREENWOOD PRESS, PUBLISHERS
WESTPORT, CONNECTICUT

TO THE ORGANIZED UKRAINIAN WOMEN

OF THE UNITED STATES

WHO HELPED PUBLISH THIS BOOK

Table of Contents

SELECTIONS FROM THE LYRICAL POEMS

SELECTIONS FROM THE DRAMATIC POEMS AND
    DRAMAS

Foreword

With every decade the literary reputation of Lesya Ukrainka has grown and today the poetess is recognized as one of the leading figures in modern Ukrainian literature, second only to Taras Shevchenko, the incomparable master of the language, and on a par in her artistic productions with Ivan Franko. This is a remarkable tribute to a woman who died in her early forties, after a lifetime of invalidism and physical suffering.

It has been the good fortune of Lesya Ukrainka to receive the increasing homage of successive generations. In her lifetime she was compelled to live apart, to dwell in a world of books, and to avoid those close human contacts which mean so much to writers and other artists who need the inspiration of the present and an appreciation of the currents of life around them. Some of the more far-sighted critics, as Franko, welcomed her work, but it was all too often dismissed as something exotic, something alien to the Ukrainian spirit, something isolated from the Ukrainian struggle for independence and the right of national self-development.

Her critics were wrong, and they have been proved so by the march of events. She did not live to see the changes that were to take place in the political complexion of Ukrainian life, but she had an unerring instinct for the future, and the modern writers who are imbued with the love of liberty are finding it ever more easy to learn from her and to follow the path which she was the first to traverse.

To understand the significance of Lesya Ukrainka, we must appreciate the difficult position in which Ukraine was a century and a half ago. The country had lost the last vestiges of its political freedom. The last Ukrainian political institutions had been wiped out by imperial Russia about the time of the American Revolution. Before that time (and here was the great tragedy) the vernacular had been employed only for folksongs; those who

9

prided themselves upon their education employed either the artificial Church Slavic or the language of one of the occupying powers, Russia or Poland. Even such a man as the philosopher Skovoroda had contented himself with talking to the people in their own tongue while writing in the same conventional language that had been used for centuries. It was only at the very end of the eighteenth century that Ivan Kotlyarevsky, in his burlesque version of the *Aeneid*, had ventured to apply the dialect of Poltava to literature; its success and influence showed that his experiment was long overdue.

The Ukrainian language had survived because of the common people. It had survived not in the educated circles of the land but among the peasants who were tilling the fields for an alien master, and maintaining as best they could the traditions of the village. It flourished in the home, where the usually illiterate mothers and fathers talked to their children in the speech they had learned years before from their own parents. The intense conservatism of the women of Ukraine, who had remained unaffected by the fashionable trend of the times and the ambitions of those who would rise by speaking the language of the conquerors, saved the situation.

The spark lit by Kotlyarevsky was fanned into a flame by Taras Shevchenko, a genius of the first rank. From his first appearance on the Ukrainian scene, he inspired his fellow countrymen with a sense of the beauty of their language and its possibilities. Yet there was something more. From his grandfather, he had gained a first-hand knowledge of the revolt of the Haydamaki in 1768, the last uprising of the Ukrainian peasants for their liberty. Shevchenko knew from his own family tradition that there had been a free Ukraine with its own aspirations, its own hopes and struggles, and all of these he put into his poetry. The answer of the Russian government was to place him for years in a prison battalion east of the Caspian Sea. It broke his health, though not his spirit, and when he finally was released, he had not many years of active work before him.

Shevchenko's poetry dealt with the past, the present and the future of Ukraine. The fearless poet not only painted the heroism of the Cossacks and their desperate struggles for liberty but he

dared to express the hope and the confidence that there would
be again a Ukraine free from a foreign yoke, even as he was
unsparing in his attacks on the abuses of the present and in his
admonitions to his countrymen to rebuild their life on higher
ideals. Yet the hour for political action has not yet come and the
next generation of writers concentrated on the problems of the
present.

The aging poet warmly welcomed the stories of Marko Vov-
chok (Maria Markovych), when they appeared. She was a
young woman of the educated class but she understood the
problems of the peasants, their hardships and their sufferings,
especially as they concerned the fate of the village women and
the evil effects of serfdom on family life.

She was followed by a long series of talented authors and
Ukrainian literature lived on and developed. It emphasized the
sociological and ethnographical factors in Ukrainian life. It stres-
sed, often under scientific pretexts, those features of Ukrainian
village life, thought, and custom which differed from those of the
Great Russians who dominated the country. The regime at St.
Petersburg allowed this but it did everything in its power to
reduce Ukrainian letters to the status of a Little Russian provincial
literature, useful in a minor degree as the instrument of education,
but incapable of attaining independent stature. Later it put a stop
even to this humble purpose, and when Lesya Ukrainka was five
years old, an absolute prohibition was placed on the printing of
books in "Little Russian" within the territory of the Russian
Empire.

The imperial regime was banning the use of the language. It
was absorbing the gentry into the Russian system. The revolutionists, with their ideals of human liberty refracted through Russian eyes, were working as energetically to win over to the Russian
cause that part of the Ukrainian youth who were opposed to Great
Russian domination. No one can estimate the number of the
young Ukrainians who listened to the siren song of the Russian
revolutionists, and lost touch with their own native hopes and
aspirations.

The language and the literature lived on, and the ethnographic
school served its purpose. Yet there was always the danger that

it might in the end lose sight of the national interest, the feelings of the people, and sink down to what the Russians proudly proclaimed it, a mere provincial, dialect literature. There could be but one outcome for the unequal struggle, unless Ukrainian literature could establish contact with the world of ideas, with the contemporary movements of the whole of Europe, with the great classics of Western civilization throughout the ages.

The task of Ukrainian literature was to free itself from those fetters that had been voluntarily assumed by the Russian intelligentsia. The Russian demand that literature should deal only with the present, with the social evil of the day in its narrowly interpreted, realistic sense, was deadly enough to the great run of Russian writers. It was suicidal for the literature of a people whose existence was menaced by both the imperial regime and the revolutionists alike.

The danger was dimly felt by Olha Kosacheva, who wrote under the name of Olena Pchilka. She was the sister of the great Ukrainian scholar and professor, Michael Drahomaniv, who left Kiev in 1876 for a career abroad, where he could work without censorship, but Olha did not have the literary power to carry out her ideals.

Her daughter Larysa did have it, and from the days of her childhood, her mother taught the young Larysa the literatures of the world. When the girl was only twelve, Olha sent one of her poems to Lviv for publication under the pseudonym of Lesya Ukrainka, "Lesya the Ukrainian," and it was under that name that the daughter became famous. The young girl soon showed that she was well prepared by her knowledge of foreign tongues to draw upon the inherited and accumulated wealth of European civilization. Furthermore, it is to be remembered that at this period in the early eighties, there were no Russian authors who were willing to do the same thing. Those men who were later to supply the broadening influences in the themes of Russian literature had not yet begun to work, and they could have learned, had they so desired, from this educated Ukrainian girl.

Then came a blow that might have been fatal. Never robust, Lesya was stricken down with tuberculosis, first in the bones and later in the lungs. Her illness isolated her from much of the

normal activity of the young people of her own age.   It compelled
her to live with her books, to think in terms of books, and to frame
her intellectual and spiritual life on what she read, rather than on
what she saw and experienced.

The masterpieces of world literature became closer to her than
the activities of the student circles, the stormy debates of the
various intellectual groups, the ill-prepared and unrealistic dreams
of movements directed against the imperial authority.   Lesya
was compelled to ask herself the fundamental meaning of freedom,
the rights of peoples, the struggle for liberty in all ages and in all
places.   More than that, she was unable to live long at home.   Her
life was a journey from hospital to health resort.   She spent a
winter with her uncle in Sofia, Bulgaria.   She sojourned in Berlin,
in Rome, in the Crimea, in the Caucasus, in Egypt.   She went
everywhere in the vain search for health and strength.

Lesya Ukrainka was well aware that she was fighting a losing
battle against the disease which was sapping her strength and vi-
tality.   She was well aware that she could not work steadily and
consistently, that every piece of literary production was done on
her nerves, and that she could not look forward with any certainty
to the future.   Yet it is only on rare occasions that this note of
hopelessness and despair entered into her works.   She did not
waste her scanty strength on a series of laments or elegies.   Her
lyric poems are primarily a call to action and to struggle, to love of
country and to sacrifice, to the achievement of a new and just
world order, in which the poor and the downtrodden will receive
justice and mercy.

From these poems to lyric monologues, dramatic scenes, and
poetic dramas, was but a short step, and it was chiefly in these
fields that she worked during the last ten years of her life.   Her
productions were something new in Ukrainian literature.   Theatrical companies, amateur and professional, long trained to produce
plays based on the realistic life of the village, could not understand
them or find the proper technique for presenting them.   The lesser
critics could only say that they were exotic, and regret that the
poetess was not directly working for the Ukrainian cause.

They did not understand that the themes that Lesya Ukrainka
chose had a direct bearing upon the problems that they were dis-

cussing, even though Ukraine itself was not specifically men-
tioned and the characters did not act or talk like Ukrainian
peasants. The poetess drew her inspiration from the ancient
world, from the Bible, from the sufferings of the Jewish prisoners
after the fall of Jerusalem and during the Babylonian Captivity,
from the efforts of the early Christians to maintain themselves
against the power of pagan Rome, from the struggles of the
Scotch under Robert Bruce to free themselves from the power of
the English King. In almost every one of these productions, she
dealt with some aspect of the life of an enslaved nation struggling
to protect its ideals and its material existence against the encroach-
ments of a stronger and momentarily victorious power—and what
else was the Ukrainian problem as both Lesya and her critics
saw it?

Yet this assertion, which was only vaguely hidden behind the
foreign themes, was more than a clever attempt to escape the
Russian censor. It was a definite declaration of emancipation of
the Ukrainian spirit from the utter dependence upon those literary
standards, conventions, and practices that had been borrowed
from the masters of the land. It was a clear statement that the
Ukrainians as a people, as a European people, had the right to
draw upon the total literary inheritance of the continent and of
the ages. At one and the same time, Lesya Ukrainka was pleading
the cause of the oppressed nations of all ages and places, and she
was emphasizing the similarity to them of the Ukraine of her own
day.

Lesya Ukrainka died in 1913, and within five years of her death
there had been established an independent Ukrainian National
Republic which was struggling for its very existence against overwhelming force and the logical outgrowth of the ideas of the
Russian intelligentsia. The Ukrainian people learned the bitter
fact that ignorance is deeper and brutality more unregenerate
when it is combined with deliberate misuse of high-sounding
slogans and ideas. Even such Ukrainian Communists as Khvylovy
in his *Wood Snipes* was led to express the notion that Ukrainian
Communism could not depend solely upon the will of Moscow,
but that it had to knit again its broken bonds with the rest of
Europe and with the ideals of humanity. For his efforts in that

direction, Khvylovy was driven to suicide, and many of his associates who did not take that course found themselves confronted with execution, or deportation—which also meant certain death.

Yet it was such experiences that were needed to round out the picture and to complete the circle. Three centuries earlier the Hetman Khmelnytsky had learned the bitter fruit of the acceptance of Muscovite overlordship. A half-century later, the Hetman Mazepa had found the price of subservience to Peter the Great impossible to pay. Taras Shevchenko had told the bitter truth in terms of national history and tradition. Now, in the last days of the Russian monarchy Lesya Ukrainka had portrayed in literary terms the essence of conditions under the old regime, and the younger Ukrainian writers who lived under the Soviet Union could not fail, if they were honest and patriotic, to emphasize the same truths.

It is that fact, more than anything else, that has contributed to the growing popularity and understanding of Lesya Ukrainka. Events have justified her feelings, confirmed her insights. They have made her a true prophet of the future and a true historian of the past.

All this is beside the fact that she was a master of the art of poetry, a superb technician in literature, and a woman endowed with genius. With her knowledge and appreciation of European literature, she was able to sense the trend of literary development and to implant on Ukrainian soil those devices and conventions that were proving themselves abroad, without injuring her own individuality and artistic talents. She was a learned poet—in the best sense of the word. Shevchenko had the art of concealing his erudition and his literary antecedents. Lesya Ukrainka did not do this, but even the most superficial reading cannot fail to disclose the natural talent behind her literary artistry.

No one will ever be able to decide how far she was moved along these paths by her illness. With her independent spirit, had she enjoyed health and activity, she might have been swept into the conventional paths of the day. She might have been absorbed by the needs of the moment, by the struggle to improve the conditions of the people. But she could not live at home. She could not satisfy in action the instincts which might have driven her into the ranks of the Ukrainian revolutionists. She could only read and study and write and travel in a fruitless search for health. It made her a unique figure. It gave her an ever-widening point of view which allowed her to present Ukrainian hopes and desires under the aspect of their universality. It is surely not without significance that the only one of her major works which dealt with the Ukrainian scene was written at fever heat during one of her visits in Egypt.

Abroad, recognition of her work has spread rather slowly. Only a few of her poems and dramatic works have appeared in translation, and this volume, prepared by the late Dr. Percival Cundy, is the first large-scale attempt to make known to the English-speaking world a figure who is of value not only to her own people but to world literature. Her works can be read as the flowering of the Ukrainian genius, but they have a wider significance. They are the expression of the thought of a cultured and educated lady who represented that acceptance of the universal ideals of civilization which are the sole hope of humanity in the twentieth century.

CLARENCE A. MANNING

New York City
April, 1950

Introduction

SCARCELY ANY other modern literature has had to struggle against greater odds in order to survive and win recognition than has the Ukrainian. Literature is an expression of life, but when a life is cribbed, cabined, and confined by centuries of political and cultural oppression and bondage, it takes heroic efforts for a nation's literature to persist and break the fetters which have shackled the expression of a people's spirit through its writers. In this respect a parallel, historical, cultural, and political, has been drawn between the Irish and the Ukrainian peoples; but where the Irish are but a small nation, a few millions strong, the Ukrainians constitute a homogeneous nation of over forty millions which for centuries has had no sovereign independent status. Thirty-five millions of them dwelt under Tsarist rule; the rest lived under the sovereignty of adjoining states: first the Austro-Hungarian Empire and then Poland, Czecho-Slovakia, and Rumania until World War II. Even now when there is a unified Ukraine with a seat in the United Nations, there is comparatively little knowledge abroad of its distinctive culture and especially of the achievements of the Ukrainians in the field of modern literature.

Nevertheless, Ukrainian literature has some names of universal significance, although their works are at present practically unknown to the American reading public. However, the field of knowledge and appreciation of Ukrainian literary achievements is being opened up in our language. One of the pioneers in this respect, Professor C. A. Manning, of Columbia University, in his manual, *Ukrainian Literature,* remarks that "When we read the work of such men as Taras Shevchenko and Ivan Franko, we realize that we are dealing with true spiritual and intellectual leaders who show a real faith in democracy, and that these men have a message not only for their own people, but for the whole world."

To these two names must be added a third, that of a woman,

17

Lesya Ukrainka, a poetess of rare scholarship, with an expert's knowledge of poetical technique, familiar with the principal European languages and literatures (including English), an unbounded imagination, keen psychological insight, and a power and vigor of expression not surpassed by any woman writer who has made a name for herself in Western literatures. This is not fulsome praise, but sober fact; hence she is worthy of study by all who take any interest in the literary achievements of another race, especially when its literature manifests throughout its entire course two outstanding principles, namely: a keen sense of realism and an invincible faith in freedom and democracy. A fierce love of liberty, an abhorrence of tyranny and imperialism, a championship of the rights of the common people—these are some of the notes continually sounded in the works of Ukrainian authors.

In reading the work of any writer, the reader insensibly gains a general impression of his predominant traits and circumstances and so arrives at a certain conception of the personality and environment of the author whose work he is reading. After reading some of her best work, lyrical and dramatic, one would certainly conceive Lesya Ukrainka to have been a vigorous, robust person, physically as well as spiritually. Actually, nothing could be further from the fact. She had tremendous energy, but little physical strength to serve it. She was a small, frail woman, delicate as a child and, from the age of twelve or thirteen until her death some thirty years later, she was a hopeless invalid, doomed to spend months at a time in bed and compelled for the greater part of her life to live abroad from her beloved homeland, travelling from one health resort to another in search of relief and possible recovery. Unlike other writers who were able to turn out a daily stint of work, she could work only at irregular intervals, often in pain and fever and the heightened periods of activity always left her physically and mentally exhausted from the strain. An extract from one of her letters, written during her last years when she was producing her finest work, illustrates the conditions under which she had to write. She said: "My health is so precarious that I cannot guarantee to write regularly even for such periods as you suggest. For example: from Christmas until Easter this year, I have been able to write absolutely nothing except in a state bordering on delirium, as though galvanized by some invisible power. The swarm of thronging images coursing through my mind gives me no rest at night, tormenting me like another form of sickness. And then comes the demon, more brutal than any sickness, and orders me to write. Afterwards I lie back exhausted, collapsed like an empty bag. That is the way I wrote *Forest Song* and everything else I have written during the past year or so."

If ever there was a triumph of mind over matter, of the spirit over the flesh, it was in Lesya's indomitable soul. It is much more difficult to connect her poetry with specific events and stages in her life than in the case of most writers, for her mind and body seemed separate and the course of the one appears to have had little relation with the weakness of the other. In a review of her early work by Franko in 1898, there is a passage which has become a classic citation in all Ukrainian appraisals of her work: "Since Shevchenko's 'Bury me and then arise, Break your chains asunder!' Ukraine has not heard such a vigorous and vibrant message as comes from the lips of this fragile, invalid girl. It is true that the successors of Shevchenko have many a time 'broken the chains' and prophesied of liberation, but their poems were generally mere phrase-making, a re-mastication of the tropes and images of the great Kobzar and not of his thoughts. . . ." Then after an analysis of her second volume of lyrics, *Thoughts and Dreams*, he continues: "I repeat; on reading the flabby and spineless writings of our contemporary Ukrainian litterateurs and comparing them with these bold, alert, and vigorous, and at the same time simple and straightforward poems of Lesya Ukrainka, one cannot resist the feeling that this fragile, invalid girl is almost the only man in all our present-day Ukraine."

To appreciate the remarks of Franko we must remember that for over two centuries the Tsarist regime had made every effort to stamp out the Ukrainian consciousness of being a separate and distinct nationality from the all-powerful Russian. In 1863 the Russian minister, Count Valuyev, had uttered his sweeping dictum, enforced by a decree, that "There never was, is not now, and never will be a Ukrainian language." In 1876 an equally sweeping Imperial ukase prohibited in Russia the printing of Ukrainian books, excepting narratives, the importation of books in Ukrainian from abroad, all theatrical perfomances in Ukrainian, and even the printing of musical texts with Ukrainian words. The term "Little Russian" was compulsorily used for Ukrainian, and every mention of Ukraine as a territorial name was banned. This was a mortal blow to literature, and consequently Ukrainian writers were effectively debarred from printing their works at home within the bounds of the Russian Empire. Their only recourse was to get them printed and published in Western Ukraine (Galicia), then a part of the patchwork Austrian Empire, where, for political reasons the native Ukrainian population enjoyed a certain amount of cultural autonomy and freedom of spoken and written expression in their own language.

Naturally, most of the native Ukrainian gentry and educated classes succumbed to the process of Russification and were drawn into the orbit of the Tsarist aims of "One people, one language, and one religion." Yet there remained some families of the Ukrainian upper classes which still retained a consciousness of a national distinctiveness, of a separate culture, and of a glorious, if somber, past history, and who strove to preserve these values together with strivings to realise a happier national future.

Such a family was the one into which Lesya Ukrainka, or to use her real name Larysa Petrivna Kosacheva, was born February 26, 1871. Her father, Petro Antonych Kosach, a fairly well-to-do landowner, though of Yugoslav origin, was none the less a staunch supporter of Ukrainian separatism and in his earlier years had taken part in a movement to educate and uplift the Ukrainian peasantry by means of the so-called "Sunday Schools," a movement for spreading literacy among the peasants. He was a man of culture and progressive views who enjoyed a prominent position in public life, not only in the county, but in the province at large. A master of sarcasm and irony, many of his sayings became proverbial among his younger contemporaries, and were usually quoted with the introductory phrase: "As old Kosach used to say. . . ." During his university years he became a great friend of Michael Drahomaniv, the famous Ukrainian progressive thinker and leader, and married the latter's sister, Olha Petrivna.

While the father's influence on the future "Poetess of the

Ukrainian Risorgimento" is not clearly discernible, that of her mother, Olha Petrivna, is written large in the daughter's literary career. This influence was not only definitely formative in Lesya's early years, but it remained predominant all through her life. It was the mother who discovered the child's bent towards literature, cultivated it, furnished suitable reading matter, discussed ideas, smoothed rhythms, corrected words and phrases, and sent her daughter's first worthwhile efforts to be published in the Ukrainian press in Galicia beyond the Russian border. She, too, was responsible for the pseudonym by which her daughter is better known than by her personal name. Lesya began to write for publication at twelve years of age. When her mother sent these early poems to Ukrainian periodicals in Galicia, it was necessary, owing to conditions in Russia, to sign them with a pen-name. She invented one, using "Lesya," a diminutive of Larysa, together with "Ukrainka," literally "Lesya of Ukraine." The name was never replaced by her proper name in future contributions, and so it has remained. Olha Petrivna was all the better fitted to be her daughter's mentor as she herself, under the pen-name of "Olena Pchilka," was one of the outstanding figures of Ukrainian literary life up to World War I and survived her daughter by many years. With indefatigable energy she served the cause of Ukrainian literature, editing a bi-weekly family magazine and a children's monthly among other things. She waged a constant battle for the cultivation and purity of the literary language, sought for and encouraged budding talent, and many a writer who made his mark later on would acknowledge that his first efforts had originally seen the light in her somewhat old-fashioned family magazine.

Olha Petrivna took the education of the children into her own hands and, contrary to the practice even in the great majority of "Ukrainophile" families, conducted it exclusively in Ukrainian instead of in the prevalent Russian language. It was due in large measure to her mother's practice in the home that Lesya developed her literary medium; from her she learned the locutions of the people's speech, to seek out its vigorous and terse expressions, and discover the wealth of poetical images latent in the common speech and in the immense treasury of Ukrainian folksongs. Of these latter she learned a large number from her mother and gathered many more by herself in the course of time, so much so that in later years her husband published a valuable collection of them taken down from his wife's dictation.

It is possible to form a fair conception of the child's environment: a quiet provincial hamlet in the lovely woodlands (Polyssye) of Volhynia; the small river Sluch and near it "the beautiful old house with its immense garden." The tender beauty of the Volhynian forests entered into her soul, a beauty which is reflected in her masterpiece, the fairy drama, *Forest Song*. Then there was the diligent and thought-provoking study of books under her mother's guidance, as a result of which the games of the Kosach children and their companions always had something of a literary character. They dramatized episodes from the *Iliad* or the *Odyssey* or incidents from the classic romances of chivalry. One of her cousins who shared in these games recalls that "Lesya's weak limbs, on which she could not race about like the rest of us, condemned her always to take parts like that of Andromache, an embodiment of staid benevolence." There were also frequent trips to Kiev, where they stayed with the Starytsky family, and then Olha Petrivna and her host, himself a prominent literary figure with a special interest in the drama, would often read in the evenings to a gathering of old and young their latest productions, followed by discussions. All this kept the children in close touch with the currents of Ukrainian intellectual life; they learned about "stateless" peoples and struggles for national liberation, and many a time from these discussions of their elders in which the children also took part, they found good arguments to use in disputes with their young acquaintances brought up in Russified schools. Thus from their earliest years the Kosach children were "nationally-conscious," and from their mother's work they learned the importance of the cultivation of literature as a means of conserving and fostering a desire for national independence. In addition, Lesya studied foreign languages and their literatures so that by the time she reached maturity she had a first-rate mastery of Russian, French, German, Italian, English, the Greek and Latin classics, and, in later life, Spanish as well. All this gave her exceptional advantages from the point of view of a wide erudition compared to other Ukrainian poets, who, generally speaking, enjoyed no such equipment.

Her first published poem, written when she was about twelve years old, is the one called "Hope," and containing the lines:

"No more can I call liberty my own,
    There's naught remains to me but hope alone."

It was written under the deep impression made upon her by the news that her aunt Lesyna, her father's sister, had been banished to Siberia for alleged subversive activity.   Another of her early works to see the light was a translation into Ukrainian of Gogol's *Evenings at Dikanka*.   In this her brother Michael collaborated and it appeared serially in 1885 when she was about fourteen. By this time, however, the disease which was to beset her all her life had already made its appearance.   Yet, before passing to this, mention should be made of another one in addition to her mother who exercised a great influence on her literary development, an influence which, although not immediate like her mother's, nevertheless had much to do with the development of her gifts.

This was her uncle Michael Drahomaniv, the greatest Ukrainian scholar of his time.   On account of his advanced radical and democratic ideas he was deprived of his chair as professor of history at Kiev University.   He emigrated to Geneva in Switzerland the better to disseminate his propaganda for Ukrainian nationalism and liberation by infusing his people with Western European liberal and democratic ideas.   Lesya was only about five years old when he went abroad, but family conversation and news of his activities kept him very much alive in his niece's mind. When she grew older, uncle and niece commenced an active correspondence and she became an ardent convert to her uncle's views.   He wrote to her about political affairs in Galicia, sent her new books for reading, asked her to make translations for him, for example: of Carducci's philosophy, and of various European poets—in short, he helped to broaden her intellectual horizon and suggested germs of thought and ideas to be worked out later.

This correspondence culminated at last in a visit by Lesya to her uncle in 1894 in Sofia, Bulgaria, whither Drahomaniv had gone some years before to occupy a chair at the University.   At the

time he was already suffering from the malady which brought
about his death six months after his niece's arrival. This, however,
did not prevent study and teaching. The sick scholar would lie
on the couch in his study, facing the shelves of his books, with
Lesya sitting beside him, diligently engaged in study under his
direction. When the end came it was her sad duty to send the
news of her uncle's death to the relatives and friends at home.
"His passing was a heavy blow to Lesya, and left a deep scar on
her heart. All her life she preserved a great love and a sincere
admiration for her uncle and remained a faithful disciple and
propagandist of his ideas," wrote L. M. Starytska, a near relative
and friend of the family, to whom we owe many personal details
of the poetess' life.

But to return to Lesya's childhood years, so happily placed in
an environment most favorable to the development of first-rate
poetic gifts: a well-to-do cultured family where her talents were
early discerned, encouraged and trained; life among scenes of
great natural beauty, and yet kept in constant touch with all the
strivings of the national spirit in the outside world. However,
this idyllic picture was soon clouded by the onset of an implacable
disease which never gave ground until it laid her in the grave.
Tuberculosis made its appearance when Lesya was between twelve
and thirteen years of age. At first it attacked her hands. Later it
descended into her legs and condemned her to frequent spells of
immobility in bed, to long intervals of separation from home and
family. The remaining thirty years of her life are little more than
a chronology of the periods spent in various places abroad to
which she travelled in search of health, interspersed with brief intervals of activity more or less free from acute pain. The disease
seems to have commenced in the eighties and entailed frequent
trips to Kiev for treatment. She spent 1894-5 in Bulgaria, in Sofia,
until her uncle's death in June, and afterwards in the country.
The next two winters she was in Kiev, where she was able to take
some active part in literary circles. But this was followed by an
intensification of the disease which compelled her to take once
more to her bed at a time when her spirit especially yearned for
activity. After a stay in the Crimea, she was taken in 1897 to
Berlin for an operation which halted the progress of the disease

for the time being. However, a renewed series of attacks of acute pain in 1901 again shook her partially restored health, when the disease attacked her lungs. Fortunately its development was stayed by a visit to the Carpathians where she came into personal contact with Ivan Franko. The two winters following, spent on the Italian Riviera, brought some relief. Returning to Ukraine in the autumn of 1903, Lesya took a public part in the unveiling of a monument to Kotlyarevsky, "the father of modern Ukrainian literature." This was an event of particular significance in the life of the poetess who had been so largely deprived of opportunities of sharing in public manifestations of the Ukrainian national spirit. Again, however, she was compelled to leave the homeland to live under other skies in other lands. This time she was sent to the Caucasus, and returned to Kiev only twice during the winters of 1905-6 and 1906-7. It was during this latter period, in an interval of comparative immunity from suffering, that she married Klymynt B. Kvitka.

It is manifest that such a life imposed impossible conditions on her as a writer. Notwithstanding her courage and endurance, this life largely of travel from one health resort to another, with absence from home and familiar surroundings, depressed and deprived her of the proper exercise of self-expression. "Many a time she used to say," says L. M. Starytska, "that she no longer had the strength to continue to live the life of a hothouse plant, torn away from her native soil, and yet, though living thus far away from her home and native land, her thoughts were continually flying back to it." When we take into account that every thought to which she managed to give literary expression was only accomplished by a mighty effort of will and at the expense of much nervous energy, in the midst of pain and fever, we can rightly estimate the heroic note which resounds in so many of her poems, as for example, in the masterly one which begins "Yet all the same . . ." with its personal note regarding her own suffering and its wider and pointed application to the weakness of many of her too-yielding fellow-countrymen.

If life for Lesya Ukrainka up to 1907 had seemed at times to be "a sanguinary struggle," after that year it became a constant, uninterrupted warfare waged without respite between her need for literary self-expression at a time when she was at the height of her creative powers and an implacable, crippling disease, which had now taken on its severest forms. The decisive change came just after a winter spent in Kiev where she had worked enthusiastically in the society "Prosvita" (Enlightenment) without sparing herself even in the manual tasks of handling and sorting the books of the society's circulating library. This work was too heavy for her undermined physique, and in addition, she had to contend with unfavorable climatic conditions. The disease which for some time had been invading the internal organs now grew worse, and the same year in which she was married she was compelled to leave Kiev with her husband and go south. From that time on she was able to live only under southern skies, at Balaklava and Yalta in the Crimea, and other resorts on the coasts of the Black Sea and the Sea of Azov. Here she spent the next two years except for an occasional trip to Kiev and short stays in the Poltava district. Another trip to Berlin dashed all hopes of relief by a further operation. The Berlin specialists declared an operation impossible because of her condition, and advised residence in Egypt on account of its mild winters. For the next three winters she lived in Helwan, near Cairo. Egypt's mild climate revived her strength in some measure as here she was not exposed to "the bitter hostility of cold or the damp implacability of fogs."

It was during these final years of "strenuous struggle against death" that she produced some of her finest dramatic verse: *The Noblewoman* (1910), *Forest Song* (1911), and *Martianus, the Advocate* (1912). How much these splendid productions cost the writer none will ever know, but we have a few details which cast some light on the desperate conditions under which they, as well as most of her work in general, were finally put on paper. They were accomplished only by spasms of supreme exaltation followed by periods of visible exhaustion. Some things which she wrote came comparatively easily and were written in one stretch in the space of a single night or in two, three, or four successive days. Others required many periods of work with long intervals between. A few weeks of feverish literary activity would be followed by several months of exhaustion and inertia, "dead days," which depressed the poetess with nightmares of a possible com-

plete failure of her intellectual capacities. The "fearful apparitions" which such days brought find mention even in her earlier
poems, as for example, in "Foregleams of the Dawn." Later,
similar nightmares of possible intellectual sterility became more
frequent. In a letter to her friend, L. M. Starytska, undated, but
probably in 1912, she gave instructions what to do with her
papers in case of such an event. "Who can tell how long my
powers may still serve me. I am burning myself out bit by bit
and some day I must go out for ever, no candle lasts eternally.
Let my friends, however, continue to cherish the illusion that
there is no end to this candle." Notwithstanding all this, the
fecundity of her imagination during these final years was extra-
ordinary, and part of her sufferings was not due to any paucity
of ideas and images, but on the contrary, to an overwhelming
abundance of them. Turgenev, in the introduction to his *Fathers
and Sons*, says that all his characters lived an independent life of
their own in his mind and that he had to write out their experiences in order to get rid of them. Lesya Ukrainka well knew what
it was to be dominated thus, but her weakness often prevented
her from the liberative function of creative composition.

In one of her stories, *By the Sea*, we find a characteristic refer-
ence to this aspect of the creative writer's inner life. She is recalling her impression of summer life in the Crimea: "Now, when
the spots of color (that is, individual impressions) have merged
together again into that faraway picture of the whole, I feel the
urge to put that picture down in writing, and to examine it again
more closely, for it was dominating my mind overmuch and was
beginning to oppress me." In addition to an imagination over-
burdened with images and ideas, she felt a great fear of dying
before she had spoken her final word. This fear preyed upon
her, driving her to work and making her still more high-strung
and feverish. Already in 1907, from Balaklava, she had written
to her mother: "I am trying to finish not only the drama I began
a year ago, but also that one I began years ago and laid aside in a
drawer. This latter I am taking up very zealously, for somehow I
feel that if I do not finish it now, it will remain incomplete and
that would be a pity, for I attach a good deal of importance to
it." (The final phrase is in German: "Es liegt mir doch etwas
daran.")

The last piece she wrote was the beginning of a novel, *Ekbal Hanem*. The first part only was published in the Kiev "Literary and Scientific Messenger" in the same number as the announcement of the author's death. An editorial note prefixed to the fragment ran in part: "These are the last pages written by Lesya Ukrainka shortly before her death. The story was to have been one of Eastern life, and in it the author intended to present a picture of the situation and psychology of an Arab woman who has been in some measure influenced by European culture but is condemned to live in her Oriental environment. It was to have appeared serially in the "Messenger" but Lesya Ukrainka was not spared to finish it." Then the editor quotes a passage from the first page of this unfinished work which seemed to him to bear a mournful premonitory significance: "The Egyptian sunset was about to begin. The sun still shone with an air of invincibility in the last moments before its inevitable defeat. Still proud and gay, and without the slightest shadow of evening melancholy, it lavished its luminous gifts over the desert, on the great river, and on the smallest, trifling detail of its beloved land, as though somehow, in this final moment before the triumphant onrush of darkness, it refused to believe in the inevitable."

The inevitable, however, came. Not long after her last return from Egypt to attend a public gathering in Kiev, Lesya Ukrainka died August 1, 1913, at Surama, a health resort near Tiflis in the Caucasus. Within a week her remains were interred in a cemetery in Kiev and all that was left of her was in the stricken memories of her relatives and friends and the legacy of strong, vibrant verse and prose that she had bequeathed to Ukrainian literature.

In marked contrast to the vicissitudes of her physical life, the artistic life of Lesya Ukrainka was one of steady and constant development and progress. From her earliest years she was fully conscious of her vocation as a creative writer. She followed the goal set before her all through her life and literally died with pen in hand. It is clear from the testimony of her friends and from her correspondence that, as few writers have ever been, she was conscious from childhood of her calling as a poetess. Under her mother's guidance she diligently and deliberately studied to perfect herself in the technique as well as the art of poetic expression. The first influences brought to bear on her were those of Shevchenko and his successors, such as Kulish and Starytsky. This was followed by a study of Russian poetry, and next of various European poets. Among the latter she clearly shows the influence of Heine, but more and more she worked out her own independent and original style. However, Heine with his radical Romanticism and sardonic irony seems to have been most congenial to her cast of mind. She studied and translated his *Buch der Lieder*, and her work often shows a mastery of aphoristic irony and cutting epigram reminiscent of Heine at his best.

She began by writing lyrics, and at the age of twenty-one published her first volume, *On Wings of Song*, 1892. This was followed by *Thoughts and Dreams*, 1896, and *Echoes*, 1902, each collection marked by an advance in imaginative power and technical skill. The 180 pieces in these books may be roughly classified under six heads: love, nature, personal experiences, the poetic consciousness and mission, patriotism, and social justice. The theme of love occupies the smallest place in these groupings. This was undoubtedly due to her physical condition but she was always very reserved in the expression of her private feelings. Among those dealing with nature there is one on autumn which is strikingly original and forceful. Among those which deal with the poetic consciousness, there are several in which she gives expression to a keen sense of her physical inadequacy for the task laid upon her, as for example, in "The Weapon of Speech." Love of country is a theme which more or less runs through all her poetry, dramatic as well as lyrical. But the expression of this love is mingled with pain; first, because of long separations from the homeland, and second, because on returning to it from a freer atmosphere in other countries, she felt all the more the crushing weight of oppression exercised by the Tsarist government bent on blotting out her people's national consciousness, and furthermore, because she saw so many of her fellow-countrymen who yielded to the pressure. It was feelings such as these which in particular inspired the biting lines in her "Reminder to a Friend."

On account of the large place that social-humanitarian themes occupy in her lyrics, Lesya Ukrainka must be classed as a social rebel. She raises a vigorous cry on behalf of the oppressed and exploited toiling classes, and couples with it a ringing challenge to arise and wreak vengeance on the tyrants. As a true poetess, Lesya Ukrainka felt deeply the historic wrongs inflicted on the common people, and she voiced her indignation in winged words. This was a natural cry of protest, encouragement, and prophecy coming from a generous soul that hated all evil and injustice. She was also in revolt against the dogmatic, petrified type of Christianity presented by the official state church, an institution cynically manipulated by the Russian government as a police power for maintaining autocracy. This is clearly implied in many places in her writings, but it appears with especial distinctness in a few lines of the poem "Do you Remember. . . ." The poem, like many others she wrote, could not be published when written for obvious reasons. It was discovered only recently among a collection of her papers, left for safe keeping by a distant relative in the library of the Academy of Sciences in Lviv while fleeing from Kiev to a friend in Czecho-Slovakia during the German occupation of Ukraine in World War II. The original was printed for the first time in the Kiev monthly "Ukraina" in its February issue, 1946.

Great however as are Lesya Ukrainka's merits in the field of the Ukrainian lyric, her greatest achievements were in the form of "dramatic poems," a genre which she developed herself and used almost exclusively from about 1902 on. The transition between the two forms may perhaps be indicated by a series of lyric-narrative poems, all of which contained a considerable element of the dramatic. In these poems she treated such subjects as Robert Bruce, Isolde, and the like. Yet dramatic writing was not entirely new in her work, for in her volumes of lyrics we find monologues, dialogues, and single dramatic scenes such as "Iphigenia in Tauris" which appeared in her second collection, *Thoughts and Dreams*. Her bent towards the drama had been fostered in early years by her acquaintance with the Starytsky family, who were very well known for their interest in the theatre. Her first attempt in this line was a prose drama, *The Blue Rose,* which had been produced in 1896, but which had failed of success for various reasons, none the least of which was the failure of the actors to cope with the material provided. This discouraged her for some time in her dramatic writing. However, two years later, she began work on a dramatic poem in several scenes and then laid it aside for nearly ten years before completing it. It is called *In the Woods*, and the action takes place in New England during the Puritan period. The sculptor, Richard Ayron, is a believer in art for art's sake, while his fellows, the austere Puritans, demand that his art be applied to practical and utilitarian ends, out of which the conflict arises which forms the substance of the drama. It is quite probable here that Lesya Ukrainka was symbolizing the conflict of attitudes between herself and much of her public. She was often subjected to criticism for her "exoticism" in her choice of themes. There were many who could not or would not understand her aims as an artist, and who thought she ought to use domestic Ukrainian subjects instead of roaming so far afield. Some said her work was laudable but unreadable. On one occasion in reply to such criticism she said: "What people think they want is precisely what they must not have." And again: "The Muse must never do what it ought, but only what it feels impelled to do." Her first dramatic poem to appear was *The Possessed* (1901), in four scenes. The action is laid in Palestine in the time of Christ. Mariam cannot accept Jesus' doctrine of love to all, even to one's enemies, she asserts that hate also has its grounds for justification, and that it is impossible to love one's foes:

> "What! Only he can know no hate
> Who all his life has never loved."

Two more of these dramatic poems followed, *The Babylonian Captivity*, and *On the Ruins*, in 1902. Both are based on Hebrew history from the Bible. Beneath the surface there is in both a manifest symbolism of Ukrainian conditions under Tsarist Russian bondage, and it is clear that the writer intended that her readers should perceive her meaning and apply its lessons to themselves.

As she wrote still other dramas, each successive one displayed increasing power over its predecessors. *Cassandra* was begun in 1902 but not completed until 1907. Here the action is placed in ancient Troy just before the city's fall. Cassandra, the queen, is the only one who perceives the signs of decay in the social structure of Troy which will infallibly bring about its ruin. She prophesies what will come to pass, but no one believes her sufficiently to take steps to avert the disaster. *Three Moments*, (1905), is called a dialogue, but it is much more than this. It is devoted to showing the conflict in principles between a Girondist idealist and a Montagnard realist during the stormy days of the French Revolution. *Rufinus and Priscilla*, begun in 1906, completed in 1909, was one of the works for which she displayed a particular fondness. The first two acts were written at one stretch with scarcely any emendation or correction, but the remainder cost her much labor and a good deal of special reading. The action is laid in Rome in early Christian times. The conflict lies in the soul of Rufinus, who cannot accept the teachings of Christianity, but who is devotedly attached to his wife Priscilla, an enthusiastic Christian. When Priscilla is arrested and condemned to death, rather than be separated from her, Rufinus voluntarily shares her fate although he has no convictions as to the heavenly rewards for a martyr's death. Three other dramatic poems, *In the Catacombs*, *The Field of Blood*, and *Johanna, Chusa's Wife*, all indicate Lesya Ukrainka's interest in the period of early Christianity, for the subjects of all three are drawn from those times.

Somewhat apart from the rest of her dramatic poems, both in regard to subject and location, stands *The Noblewoman*, which was written in Egypt, 1910, in the space of three days. It is one of the few works in which Lesya Ukrainka frankly dealt with Ukrainian questions, using Ukrainian material, although the material here is not contemporary but historical. The Cossack maiden, Oksana, marries Stepan, who is a Ukrainian by birth but who has been brought up in Muscovy and there entered the service of the Russian Tsar. Oksana goes with her husband to live in Moscow, but it is hard for her to become accustomed to the semi-Asiatic customs of Muscovite life compared to the freedom that women enjoy in Ukraine. The situation becomes tragic when she finds that her husband has completely broken with Ukrainianism and has become "Muscovized." Stepan finally awakes to the ties that still bind him to Ukraine, but by then it is too late.

It is probable that Lesya Ukrainka chose this subject because of the not infrequent reproaches levelled at her for "disdaining" to use Ukrainian material in her dramatic poetry. The comparative absence of such material in her work may be accounted for by her long residences abroad and the consequent lack of opportunity for observing Ukrainian life at first hand. However, a better explanation is that she deliberately chose the matter of her dramatic works from non-Ukrainian sources, turning instead to the life of ancient Babylonians and Hebrews, Greeks and Romans of classical times, early Christians, medieval Spaniards, New England Puritans, and Frenchmen of the Revolution in order to gain freedom in treating the subjects about which she wished to write. After all, such persons, places, and periods were merely external details, and there is no doubt that she consciously avoided matter drawn from contemporary life in order the better to direct attention to the working out of the psychological problems and conflicts in the souls of her characters. And it is precisely in this respect, namely, that of using symbolical persons and events, that Lesya Ukrainka was more contemporary than those who then criticized her for her employment of non-Ukrainian material for analysing and illuminating the most pressing problems in the Ukrainian society of her time. Needless to say, such criticisms are now as dead as those who raised them thirty or forty years ago. Her neo-Romanticism and the heroic tone of her dramatic poems, based on themes hitherto unfamiliar to the mass of her public, did not meet with a wide response at first except from the discerning. It is now realized that she was greater than she seemed when alive, and her impact on her people's soul is being felt more and more as time goes on.

As has been pointed out, her work increased in brilliancy during the closing and most trying years of her life. In June, 1911, at Kutais, Transcaucasia, she produced her masterpiece *Forest Song* in the space of three days after having previously re-written it three times in order to condense and shorten it. All Ukrainian critics grow lyrical in praise of this "Fairy Drama in Three Acts," as it is subtitled, and with justice. To quote just one, B. Yakubsky: "In truth, this is a symbolic drama of profound psychological interest, of an extraordinarily deep and tender lyricism whose language, full of the rich treasures of native folklore, is most harmonious and musical. Without exaggeration, one can say that it is an outstanding creation, not only of Ukrainian literature, but of the world's literature. It has already been compared with the similar works of Maeterlinck and Hauptmann and has emerged from the comparison with honor." To us it also suggests some affinity with Shakespeare's *Midsummer Night's Dream.*

The classical note of Romanticism, the glorification and adoration of Mother Nature is heard in *Forest Song.* Nature and the life of nature are full of beauty, but man has become alienated from that which gives him life and significance. Man has gone his own way, created his own manner of life with its laws and canons, mean, poverty-stricken, and without uplift to higher things. When Mavka wishes to follow Lukash, the peasant, and complains that Forest Elf wants to put her under the same restraints that Water Goblin imposes on the nymph Rusalka, Forest Elf says:

> "... But I
> Respect your freedom. Go! sport with the wind;
> Play all you like with wild Will-o'-the-Wisp;
> Allure all spirits to yourself, be they
> Of water, forest, mountain, field, or air.
> But keep aloof from human pathways, child;
> You'll find no freedom there, but woes instead,
> To clog your steps and weigh you down. My child,
> Once start to tread them and your freedom's gone!"

Therefore, the indispensable condition of living life as it really should be lived is to remain true to one's own nature. Lukash was happy just so long as he lived by intuition, by that which was drawn out of his own inner being as he made music on his pipe. But by taking on the limitations of a narrow domestic existence, by succumbing to the earthy-minded dominance of his mother and his wife, he betrayed himself—lost his human form, was transformed into the semblance of a wolf and went mad until he was delivered by the one whom in his blindness he had wronged—saved by the power of Mavka's infinite love and pity. Mavka also betrayed her own nature, as Forest Elf tells her towards the end. "You have betrayed," he says. When she in surprise asks whom she has betrayed, he replies:

"Yourself.
You gave up dwelling in the high tree tops,
And came down low to walk in baser paths."

The whole drama is suffused with an atmosphere of beauty and tenderness, slightly tinged with a melancholy that comes from a reflection on nature as the action moves against the background of the changing seasons in their annual revolution, beginning with the tearing freshets of early spring and ending with the first falling snows of winter.

Three other great poetic dramas followed, which, if not in the exceptional class of *Forest Song*, in no way fall behind it— *Martianus, the Advocate*, (1911), takes us again to the period of early Christianity, the scene being laid in Puteoli, near Naples, about 300 A.D. Martianus is a secret Christian because it is so ordered by the clergy for the best interests of the Church. This gives rise to the conflict between Martianus' obedience to the Church and the interests of his wife and children, the result being that the latter become alienated from him. The role that Martianus is compelled to play is a severe test to his natural human feelings, but he plays it manfully to the end. In *The Stone Host*, written in 1912, Lesya Ukrainka took another unexpected step by working on the theme of Don Juan, a subject already treated by several outstanding figures in world literature. Here again she managed to give the subject a new and brilliant symbolical significance applicable to Ukrainian conditions. The last of her great poetic dreams was *Orgy*, which came out in the year of her death, 1913. The action takes place in Corinth during the period of the Roman domination of Greece. The conflict arises from the oppression of the older Greek culture by the younger military might of Rome. Anteus, the poet-singer, can by no means reconcile himself to the prostitution of Greek art for the delectation of the Roman conquerors, and when his wife dances for some of them, he kills her and then strangles himself with the strings of his own lyre. The writer manifestly intended her readers to substitute Russia for Rome and Ukraine for Corinth and so to perceive their own situation in the present in which they were living. On this gloomy and somber note Lesya Ukrainka was compelled by death to break off her creative work in the midst of its finest flowering.

Apart from the intrinsic value of her work, the chief merit of Lesya Ukrainka was that she exercised the function of a beneficent innovator in the field of Ukrainian poetry, an introducer of fresh new forms as well as ideas. Emerging from the imitative influences of the post-Shevchenko tradition, she labored consciously to lead Ukrainian literature out of its provincialism and the preoccupation of its writers with purely domestic themes and subjects. With the clear conviction that every national literature must needs have its own peculiar native coloring, she also was convinced that it must necessarily profit by conforming to universal standards and develop itself within the framework of the ideas common to all humanity. This point of view can be seen even in her adolescent lyrics with titles such as: "Sappho," "Mary Stuart's Last Song," "To my Piano," "Dante's Wife," and many others. Such themes were a novelty in Ukrainian poetry then. At the same time she successfully experimented with European forms hitherto unused by Ukrainian poets. These characteristics of an innovator dissatisfied with the current forms and ideas derived from tradition made her a new and vitalizing force in Ukrainian letters. Sensing that the social organism had entered on a new phase of development, and feeling that the people were sufficiently awakened to a knowledge of, and interest in the nation's past, she was profoundly convinced that it was necessary for the younger generation to create a literature that should run in the general current of universal ideas. She also introduced a new psychological attitude in her people's literature unlike the then prevailing one, which was that of looking backwards and sighing over a glorious if somber past. This, indeed, had been the dominating mood of the successors of Shevchenko, weeping tears of helplessness over what was irretrievably gone. Lesya Ukrainka's attitude, on the contrary, was one of faith in the innate strength of an indestructible nation, and consequently, the compelling necessity of battling on with a firm conviction of ultimate victory. Of course, there is at times a melancholy overtone in the bold assertions of her verse, but it is not always possible for those who enjoy rugged health continuously to maintain a mood of calm and untroubled assurance in the future, and Lesya Ukrainka had no such advantage. In any case, not to look backwards, never to lose heart, incessantly to keep on fighting, and never to doubt of eventual victory—this is the main ideological content of her poetry.

The appreciation of Lesya Ukrainka's contribution to Ukrainian literature began to be widely expressed only after her death. This, however, is usually the case with most innovators in the fields of art and literature. Their stature grows more imposing as the time goes on. The heroic tone and the neo-Romanticism of her dramatic poems based on hitherto unfamiliar themes did not meet with a wide response at first, as has been said, except among the discerning, but admiration and appreciation is steadily growing as the years go by. It is now realized that she possessed a remarkably strong poetic imagination, a universalism in her choice of themes, a profound penetration of the variations of human psychology, together with a style both highly lyrical and charged with dramatic power. She had a vast amount of energy, but unfortunately, little physical strength to support its output. In her soul she cherished an ideal of harmonious life from which all that defiles was to be swept away by human hands; to achieve the realization of this ideal she was ready to battle as far as lay in her power, if not with her hands, then by her words. The pity is that she who had the soul of a fighter was precluded by physical weakness from entering more actively and personally into the arena where the great conflict was and is still being waged.

Selections from the Lyrical Poems

1. Love

MY BURNING HEART

My heart is burning up as in a raging fire,
  Consumed within a flame of bitter grief;
Why then can I not weep and with a flood of tears
  Extinguish that fierce flame and find relief?

My soul within me weeps and cries in agony,
  While not a tear bears witness to my woe;
For tears will not well up and gush forth from my eyes
  Because the fire dries them ere they flow.

Would that I might go forth into the open field,
  And falling on earth's bosom grey and sere,
Pour out my loud lament until the stars should mark,
  And people quake to see me weeping there!

DELUSIVE SPRING

Spring again, and once more hopes
  In the sad heart germinate.
Once more am I lulled by dreams,
  Visions of a happier fate.

Spring is lovely, and as sweet
  Are the blissful dreams she brings;
How I love them, yet I know
  They are but delusive things!

41

HEBREW MELODY

No longer mine! A distant land has sundered us.
    Some alien beauty will have snared thy heart.
Thou wilt have found an unforbidden Paradise;
    A wilting flower am I—from thee apart.

And now to me remain naught else but thoughts and songs,
    Such songs as those by captive maids combined
While listening by Euphrates to the wailing made
    By Babylonian willows in the wind.

Those songs were never sung, for in those woeful days
    Our harps were put aside and hung upon
The willows where they swayed and wailed as though
    They mourned o'er happy days forever gone.

Those songs were never voiced on men's sad, silent lips,
    But flew on wings of thought, borne on the air
Far off unto the ravaged city of our God
    And wailed above the ruined Temple there:

"In ruins liest thou, O Temple of our Lord!
    The foe has made thy Holiest a pyre!
Upon thine altar to his idols vain, unclean,
    The alien has lit his sacred fire.

"Thy prophets, all forsworn, have left thee to thy fate,
    And not a Levite serves thee any more;
Who sees thy once majestic walls will shake his head
    In grief when he recalls thy days of yore."

No longer ours! But faithful unto thee will be,
    E'en though in exile, all Israel's race;
What God himself has chosen as His holy shrine,
    That shall forever be a sacred place!

My dearest one! For me thou art that ruined shrine—
    Shall I betray the Temple's sanctity,
Because it for a time is subject to its foes
    And to a false and alien deity?

A SUMMER NIGHT'S DREAM

One summer night in sleep I dreamed a blissful dream:
  Short as the summer night it swiftly sped.
My dream, brief as the dark, soon melted, disappeared,
  Ere in the east the morning sky was red.

A marvellous dream it was, ineffable and bright,
  Absorbing all my being as I slept.
I dreamed about a future of pure happiness,
  I dreamed that unknown raptures o'er me swept.

I felt that I was blest, immeasurably blest.
  I dreamed that I . . . but written words are vain!
Where is in all the world a language so divine
  Whose words could give that sense of bliss again?

The dream was brief, so brief! So swiftly did it pass,
  It died, 'twas gone almost as soon as born;
It took its flight to where the golden-crimson haze
  Gave token of the fast-approaching morn.

I looked and lo, the summer night already gone! . . .
  My soul felt burdened with a weight of grief,
And whispering in sadness to myself I said;
  "A summer night, a dream, alas, how brief!"

No happiness like that shall ever be my lot,
  For other dreams are in my heart alway.
Though I at times for such a dream may grieve, yet I
  For such a blessedness will never pray.

Let others seek in dreams for future happiness;
  I do not wish to sleep, but live and burn.
Let those who wake from sleep their blissful dreams forget,
  For to such ecstasies there's no return.

A FORGOTTEN SHADOW
(Dante's Wife)

Austere Dante, the Florentine exile,
Looms up from out the Middle Ages' gloom.
Like to those times, he also found his song
While walking through a mystical, dark wood
Amidst a chaos of wild images.
What soul would venture in his steps to go
Through those dark groves, if 'twere not for the flowers
Which bloom with hues eternal midst the thorns?
The singer plucked them with a master's hand
And wove them all into a flowery crown,
Besprinkled it with heavenly dews, and placed
It as a tribute on the early tomb
Of Portinari's lovely Beatrice,
Who once, by chance, had smiled at him,
The second time passed by without a glance.
The third time when he looked on her, she lay
Unmoving, coffined, ready for the grave.
To him she had been like the gracious sun
Which pours forth light, and with it joy and life,
Unheeding unto whom it gives its gifts.
And though that beaming sun so swiftly set,
He ne'er forgot it, neither in the gloom
Of exile, nor by friendly fireside;
Nowhere on earth, in Hell, or Paradise,
Could he forget his lovely Beatrice.
'Twas she alone who ruled him in his song,
For in the realms where he in spirit dwelt
He found no other consort like to her.
He crowned her with a chaplet glorious,
Such as no other woman e'er has worn.

Immortal pair, Dante and Beatrice!
All-powerful death has not yet sundered you.
Yet why dost thou, capricious fantasy,
Call up before my mind a wretched form

Like some vague figure seen as in a dream?
It wears no crown or shining aureole,
Its features are enshrouded with a veil
Of dense, concealing mist. Who can it be?

No poet sang a paean in her praise,
No artist tried her beauty to depict;
Somewhere, far down in history's dim depths
A hint of her still lives. Who is it then?
'Tis Dante's wife! Scarce other name remains
By which she still is known—as though she ne'er
Possessed an individual, personal name.
This woman ne'er became a guiding star,
But, like a faithful shadow, followed him
Who symbolized "Ill-fated Italy."

She shared with him sad exile's bitter bread,
She lit the household fire for him upon
An alien hearth. And, surely, many a time
The hand of Dante, seeking some support
And sympathy, would on her shoulder rest.
For her, life's path was his poetic fame,
Although she ne'er put forth her hand that it
Might be illumined by a single ray;
And when the fire in the singer's eyes
Died out, she covered them with reverent hand.
O faithful shadow! where then is thy life?
Thy personal destiny, thy griefs and joys?
Though history be silent, yet in thought,
I see how many lonely days were spent
In sadness and in dread expectancy,
How many sleepless nights as black as care,
As long as misery, I see thy tears . . .
And through thy tears into the realms of fame,
As one walks through the dew, swept—Beatrice!

2. Nature

SPRING'S VICTORY

My heart for many a day refused to yield to spring,
  Declined to lend an ear to her appeal;
I feared the magic of her mystic blandishing;
  Against her spell my heart I tried to steel.

"Nay, call thou not to me, O spring!" I said to her,
  "Thy charms and thy enchantments are in vain.
What care I for thy beauties, joyous, bright, and clear,
  When my sad heart is filled with grief and pain?"

But spring continued calling loud: "Hear me, my child!
  All things pay homage to me as their queen.
No more the gloomy wood remembers winter wild,
  But decks itself anew in garments green.

"The black cloud with its thunderbolts to me responds,
  The lightning lights all heaven with its sheen,
The dark earth robes itself with hosts of tiny fronds,
  All things submit to me as to their queen.

"Then let that burdened heart of thine once more revive,
  Let it again my joyous song repeat,
For it must surely sense that nature is alive;
  Thy heart is not yet numb—I hear it beat."

A quiet whisper came: "Put thou no faith in spring!"
  The warning failed before spring's witchery;
My former dreams awoke, my heart began to sing:
  "O spring, O spring, thine is the victory!"

SING, O MY SONG!

Long has my song been held captive in silence,
  Like bird that's encaged, shut away from its flight.
Long is it since it expanded its pinions,
  In bondage to sorrow, to grief's bitter blight.

Now is the time, O my song, to go roaming,
  To try out thy wings torn and ragged with pain.
Now is the time, O my song, to seek freedom,
  To hark how the winds freely sport o'er the main.

Roll, O my song, like the swift-ranging billow,
  Which never asks whither its course it shall trace.
Fly, O my song, like the swift-flying seagull,
  Which never is daunted by ocean's wild space.

Sing, then, O song, like the winds freely blowing,
  And roar as the billow roars back at the sky!
Have not a care that the winds leave no echo,
  And but for a moment the wave charms the eye!

AUTUMN

Autumn with fingers all bloodstained hastes on,
Longing to meet with her dear distant sun.
Blood on her garments enhances their charm,
Spattering them like brocade.

Thus for the sun is fair Autumn adorned,
Robed like a princess for festival rites.
All that the world hath of beauty she takes,
Garbing herself in its sheen.

Ah, but the days swiftly shorten and change,
Sometimes the sun gleams, then shadows his face.
Fast-fading Autumn now grieves and laments,
Hopes of the springtime are gone.

Autumn goes on, but invisible thorns
Tear at her body and wear it away;
Yet, though despairing, she smiles as she cries:
"Sun, look upon me, I smile!"

Yonder the sun sinks behind the dark hills,
Blasts of raw wind springing up bring the frost,
Massive grey clouds slowly pile in the sky,
Winter replies: "Lo, I come!"

Autumn then tears at her garments bloodstained,
Down at her feet they lie strewn in a heap;
Naked, defenceless, she stands as she groans:
"Come then, for now it is time!"

TO THE STARS

Happy are ye, all ye spotless stars!
    Brightly beaming in your converse meek;
Could I glitter tranquilly as you,
    Never would I crave a word to speak.

Happy are ye, all ye lofty stars!
    From your heights upon this world ye brood;
Were my lot like yours to dwell so high,
    All my life I'd live in solitude.

Happy are ye, all ye frigid stars!
    Firm and hard as though of crystal made;
Were I staunch as you in heaven's vault,
    Never should I be by grief dismayed.

3. Personal Experiences

A FORMER SPRING

The spring came lovely, prodigal, and sweet,
    All bathed in brilliant light and strewing flowers;

She swiftly flew, and after her there came
    A swarm of birds who piped with all their powers.

New life had come and all things had a voice:
    The greenwood rustled in a joyous mood,
In all there was a song, a smile, or ringing tone,
    But I lay sick and weak, in solitude.

I lay and thought: "The spring has come for all;
    For everyone she has a gift to bring;
But yet for me alone she has no gift,
    I am forgotten by the jocund spring."

Nay, spring did not forget!   An apple tree
    Tapped with its branches on my window pane;
The tender green leaves flashed before my eyes,
    The snowy blossoms dropped like falling rain.

Then in my narrow chamber came a breeze,
    Which sang to me of spring's broad, free domain,
And with it came the music of the birds,
    While all the forest echoed its refrain.

My soul can nevermore forget the gift
    Which lovely spring brought to me where I lay;
No other spring e'er was and e'er shall be
    Like that which in my window bloomed that day.

THE WEAPON OF THE WORD

O word, why art thou not like tempered steel,
Which in the battle gleams with vengeful zeal?
Why art thou not a keen, unsparing sword,
Which lops the foe's head from his shoulders broad?

O trusty, faithful, polished word of mine,
To draw thee from the sheath I'll ne'er decline;
But my life's blood thou drainest in the art,
Thy blade will not pierce through the hostile heart . . .

I'll whet and sharpen up thy blade until
I have exhausted all my strength and skill,
And afterwards I'll hang thee on the wall
To gladden some while I my pains recall.

O word, thou art my only armament,
And both of us should not be vainly spent!
In other, unknown hands, perhaps, who knows?
Thou'lt prove a better brand 'gainst brutal foes.

Thy blade will ring against the iron yoke,
And tyrants' fastnesses shall hear the stroke;
Then with the clang of other swords thy sound
Shall mingle with the shouts of men unbound.

Avengers strong will take my weapon bright,
And with it bravely rush into the fight . . .
O sword of mine, serve thou those warrior bands
Far better than thou servest these weak hands!

"CONTRA SPEM SPERO"

Hence, dark thoughts! Away, ye autumn mists!
    Golden spring is here, she's here today!
Should my days of youth be spent in woe,
    Drearily and sadly pass away?

Nay, through all my tears, I still will smile,
    Sing my songs though troubles round me loom;
Hopeless, still hope on against all odds,
    I will live! Away, ye thoughts of gloom!

On this hard and ingrate soil I'll sow
    Flowers that shall bloom with colors rare;
Flowers will I plant where frost doth reign,
    Water them with many a bitter tear.

And these burning tears will soften then
    All that ground so crusted, chill, malign,
Flowers, then perhaps, will bloom and bring
    Joyous spring e'en to this heart of mine.

Though the mountain side be rough and steep,
　　Onward will I bear the ponderous stone;
Struggling upwards 'neath the crushing load,
　　Still will I my joyous song intone.

Through the long, dark night inscrutable
　　Never will I close my wearied eyes,
Searching ever for that guiding star—
　　Radiant empress of the midnight skies.

Yes, through all my tears I still will smile,
　　Sing my songs though troubles round me loom;
Hopeless, still hope on against all odds,
　　I will live!　Away, ye thoughts of gloom!

DO YOU REMEMBER . . .

Do you remember that time when I spoke
　　The words: "If certainty lay in my ken
When I shall die, I'd make a will to have
　　The music played I loved while living, when

They bury me."　No sooner had the words
　　Flown from my lips than all began to laugh:
"Perhaps you'd like to see your friends compelled
　　With song and dance to write your epitaph?"

And then began a talk on funerals,
　　That would not seem worth while remembering.
But I remember every word—the jokes
　　Woke something in my soul that left a sting.

My soul seeks no repose "with all the saints,"[1]
　　No "memory perpetual"[1] wishes sung;
Those strains and words alike are strange to me
　　As are the brazen bells with clamorous tongue.

When comes the time to mourn o'er my remains,
　　Then let the music wordlessly sweep on

1. Phrases from the funeral service of the Orthodox Church.

With tears and laughter, joy and grief confused,
  Like to the song raised by the dying swan.

And let the ones who in the morning grieved,
  Go to the dance at eve in merry throng.
You think it strange—a funeral, then a dance?
  'Tis but a usual end to mournful song.

I do not wish that aught should be disturbed
  By my plunge on to unknown destiny.
I would not that my death should wound a soul
  So much as life itself has wounded me.

4. The Poetic Calling

MOODS

Why is it at times when I sit down to write,
Or else when I've finished some work that seems right,
There suddenly over my spirit will fall
A sad, heavy moodiness like a thick pall?

That mood which o'erwhelms me my hand then restrains;
Around me I see all humanity's pains,
Its tears and its miseries—straightway I think:
What use is this labor of mere pen and ink?

'Gainst evil much wiser minds cannot prevail,
Far less can my weakness and frailty avail;
I give up my task with a heart full of grief,
But then comes a second thought bringing relief.

Perhaps this my song for a moment or so
May aid in relieving some soul's bitter woe;
It may be, perchance, that because of my art,
The fire may rekindle in some unknown heart.

So therefore, some value in my task may lurk,
And someone may profit because of my work—
Then courage snaps back with reviving recoil:
With uplifted brow, I return to my toil.

THE AVENGING ANGEL

When dark enwraps the world at dead of night,
    There often visits me a doubtful guest;
    His look and speech rouse terror in my breast;
Like bloody Mars his eyes are fiercely bright.

The dreadful angel smiles at me, I know;
    I see both love and hatred in that smile:
    Red stains like blood his snowy wings defile,
Like sunset's crimson gleaming on the snow.

He speaks to me words terrible and great,
    And in his hands he holds a flaming sword;
    From out my heart there springs a warlike word,
A battle cry, wild songs of fiery hate.

"Words, words, mere words!" replies my visitor.
    "Th' avenging angel I—for deeds I long,
    Not words. Think not that thy brave song
Will others stir, but not thyself, to war.

"I give to thee my sword; though thou be weak,
    'Tis not too heavy for bold hands to swing.
    Dost thou fear death, or wounds, or suffering,
Thou, who with all thy soul, dost freedom seek?"

He tenders me the sword. I fain would take it, though
    I find my hand will not obey my will.
    My noble rage subsides, my heart grows still:
"Depart," I say, "I will not with thee go.

"I fear not for my life, but for the soul
    Which dwells in me, which I in others see;

Should I slay that, 'twould mean deep guilt for me,
For such a deed I ne'er could pay the toll.

"Thy servant Corday struck a fatal blow
  To rid her world of one tyrannic ban;
  But in the tyrant she perceived the man,
When o'er Marat she shrieked and wept for woe."

The midnight guest fades out, but leaves behind
  Within my soul a dread and bloody trace;
  By day I see the angel's smiling face;
That talk unfinished agitates my mind. . . .

THE POWER OF SONG

Nay, I am unable to subdue or vanquish
Unreasoning song which is born of deep yearning,
And neither am skilful in masking her features,
Nor know how to garb her in radiant garments.
She beats her dark pinions like ravening vulture
And wounds me whenever I fain would subdue her
By main force and strength. O tumultuous song!
With whom hast thou ever been lowly, submissive?
Behold me! I smile when my heart's inly weeping;
I'm quiet and tranquil. But thou?—like the tempest,
Thou knowest no bounds. To thee nothing matters!
A spark thou dost kindle to dread conflagration.
A ripple thou turnest to mad roaring billow.
Black clouds thou pursuest till they become chaos.
Upon some poor dwelling, a last, final shelter,
Thou loosest an avalanche till it lies buried. . . .
To thee nothing matters! Let him weep and sorrow
Who carelessly let a spark fall by the highway,
Who trusted his uncertain bark on deep waters,
Who built his poor dwelling, his final safe shelter,
Too near to the precipice high on the mountain. . . .
The winged one art thou!—thou must try thy pinions.

Yes, song is as absolute, free, self-directing:
And whether this freedom means gladness or sorrow,
I know not, for I cannot forge fetters for her.
I know not from whence I might mine out the iron,
Or where find the furnace in which I might smelt it.
But one thing is certain—whatever the effort,
The moment will come when all fetters lie shattered.
Then song liberated bursts forth into freedom,
And takes its full course unrestrained, as a weeping,
That long has been hidden but secretly seething,
Escapes the heart's dungeon.

                        O, beg not for comfort,
All ye who are burdened with song's dread endowment,
For poesy knows no indulgence or mercy.
She's born of despair, of a passionate yearning,
Seeks vengeance for all that she suffers in secret,
With fire or with venom, her two-edged weapon.
All ye who are fearful—quick, out of her pathway!
Let song take her flight, all alone, freely coursing,
Like whirlwind that sweeps o'er the sea's icy bosom.
She wishes no tears and demands no emotions,
But only an outlet to space and to freedom.
Like to a maniac who breaks from confinement
And flees in the unknown to meet with destruction . . .
So rushes unreasoning song—then beware ye.
For pity she knows not—no more than death knows it!

5. Love of Country

VAIN TEARS

Laments and groans are all around,
    Irresolute, faint challenges,
Complaints against vile destiny,
    And foreheads bowed in bitterness.

And all the time we still bewail
   Our Ukraine's ancient misery;
With tears we wait the coming day
   For chains to break and set us free.

Such tears the more inflame our wounds,
   Delay their healing, make them ache.
Our chains might rust from falling tears,
   But of themselves they'll never break.

What use are such despondent moods?
   For turning backwards 'tis too late.
Much rather let us set to work
   And strive a future to create.

From the cycle SEVEN STRINGS
(Dedicated to Uncle Michael)

For thee, O Ukraine, O our mother unfortunate, bound,
   The first string I touch is for thee.
The string will vibrate with a quiet yet deep solemn sound,
   The song from my heart will gush free.

My song o'er the earth's distant reaches will fly in its task
   With my dearest hopes as its guide;
Wherever it speeds o'er the world among mankind, 'twill ask:
   "Know ye where good fortune doth bide?"

And there somewhere yonder my song solitary will meet
   With other such wandering lays,
And then, joining in with that loud-singing swarm, will fly fleet
   Away over thorn-studded ways.

'Twill speed over ocean's blue bosom, o'er mountains will fly,
   And circle about in free air;
'Twill soar ever higher far up in the vault of the sky
   And maybe find good fortune there.

And finding it somewhere, that longed-for good fortune may greet
  And visit our dear native strand,
May visit and greet thee, Ukraine, O thou mother most sweet,
  Ill-starred and unfortunate land.

HOPE

No more can I call liberty my own,
To me there's naught remains but hope alone.

The hope to see once more my loved Ukraine,
To come back in my native land again.

To gaze once more on Dnieper's azure wave—
I care not if alive or in the grave.

To view the steppe, its ancient funeral mounds,
To sense the ardent strength which there abounds. . . .

No more can I call liberty my own,
To me there's naught remains but hope alone.

TEARS O'ER UKRAINE

Ukraine! bitter tears over thee do I weep.
  Alas! of what use is such grief unto thee?
What can I avail thee by sorrow so deep?
  Alas! thou hast small help from me.

O scalding tears! searing my soul with your flame,
  Ye leave in my eyes flaming traces of pain:
Those sharp pangs of sorrow now wither my frame,
  And all healing arts are in vain.

How many of us are shedding such tears!
  O children, how can we still laugh and be gay?
Beholding our mother in miseries and fears,
  How can we still cheerfully play?

They say that a mother's hot tears can abrade
And penetrate even the stubbornest flint;
Then should not these agonized tears of a maid
At least make a tiny imprint?

Iphigenia in Tauris

The action takes place in Tauris in the Crimea in front of the Temple of the Tauric Artemis. The scene is on the seashore. The sea has carved a bay into the rocky shores. The beach is ringed around with rugged bare cliffs, mingled red and grey in color. In the background are rising mountains, covered with abundant vegetation, and a large grove of laurel, magnolia, olive, and cypress trees. A true paradise. On the cliffs is a small semi-circular clearing. Everywhere on the mountain slopes among the trees can be seen paths leading down to the temple of Artemis, which is built with a Doric colonnade and with a broad flight of steps. Near the temple between two cypresses stands a statue of Artemis on a high double pedestal, the lower part of which projects to form an altar upon which a fire is burning. From the temple a flight of marble steps leads down to the sea. From out the temple there emerges a chorus of Tauric maidens dressed in white robes and wearing chaplets of green leaves. They are carrying flowers, round wicker baskets containing barley and salt, ewers filled with wine and oil, goblets and vials. They adorn the pedestal of the statue with garlands and wreaths of flowers. The chorus sings:

STROPHE
Goddess mysterious, great Artemis,
Praise be to thee!
Praise be to thee, unattainable one,
Bright, frigid, pure!

ANTISTROPHE
Woe unto him who should recklessly dare
To gaze on the goddess' beauty unveiled;

Woe unto him who with gross hands unclean
    Extends them to finger her garments most pure—
Shadows created by moonlight will be
    Far better and nobler than he will appear;
Mother who bore him, when gazing upon him,
    Will nevermore recognize in him her son.

STROPHE

Mighty protectress of thy loved Tauris,
    Glory to thee!
Glory to thee, implacable swift one,
    Huntress divine!

ANTISTROPHE

Woe unto him who with imprudent words
    The terrible goddess arouses to wrath!
Woe unto him who will not bend his neck
    And humbly bow down at the deity's feet!
Sooner than moonbeams can penetrate down
    To deepest recesses of ocean's dark caves,
One of her arrows will fly to its mark
    And transfix the heart of the bold, senseless wight.

IPHIGENIA, *dressed in a long robe and wearing a silver diadem
on her forehead, comes out of the temple.*

STROPHE

See, she is coming, beloved of the goddess,
    All homage pay!
All homage pay! For this priestess the goddess
    Gave us herself.

ANTISTROPHE

From far away, from an alien land,
    She hither was led by the goddess' power.
Secret as she in her virginal charms,
    Naught do we know of her race, tribe, and name.
Lo, in this grove where we ever at nighttime
    Make sacrifices to Artemis due,
Here hath the goddess in her silvery beams
    Given as priestess this maiden to us.

Meanwhile, IPHIGENIA *takes from one of the maidens a large goblet, from another a vial; a third maiden pours wine into the goblet, a fourth pours oil into the vial.* IPHIGENIA *pours the oil and the wine on the altar fire, then strews barley and salt over it, taking the latter from the baskets which the other maidens are carrying.*

IPHIGENIA
(*Offering the sacrifice*)
Hear me, O goddess bright,
Bend down thine ear to me!
The evening sacrifice we make to thee, accept!
Thou who dost light the path for sailors on the sea,
Illuminate our hearts,
That we, thy worshippers, who praise thy name, may be
In mind and heart and body pure and fit to stand
Before thine altar here!

CHORUS
All hail to thee!
Silver-throned, eternal,
Brightest radiancy,
Mighty potency,
All hail to thee!

IPHIGENIA
O thou victorious virgin, who with arrows bright,
Dost war against the shades of gloomy, hostile night,
Be gracious unto us!
The potent spells and charms which Erebus sends forth,
Assist us to repel!

CHORUS
All hail to thee!
Silver-throned, eternal,
Brightest radiancy,
Mighty potency,
All hail to thee!

IPHIGENIA *gives back the goblet and vial to the maidens, makes a sign with her hand, and the* CHORUS *goes back into the temple.*

She then stirs up the altar fire to make it burn more brightly and rearranges the flower decorations.

IPHIGENIA *(alone)*
O huntress goddess with the silver bow,
Defender of all maiden chastity,
Grant us thine aid! . . .
(She falls on her knees before the altar, and stretches out her hands despairingly towards the statue.)
Forgive me, O great goddess, that I take
Such words upon my lips while from my heart
Not one of them wells forth.
(She rises, turns her back upon the altar and gazes out at the sea.) For there alone
Art thou, my own beloved native land!
All that which makes our brief lives beautiful
In my loved Hellas have I left behind.
My kinsmen dear, my glory, youth, and love
Remain at home beyond the sounding sea.
And I alone, here in a stranger's land,
Like those dim shadows of forgotten souls
Who wander in the gloom of Hades' fields,
Live on, a grieving, strengthless, pallid shade . . .
(She walks up to the steps of the portico and leans against one of its columns.)
This chilly marble is my last resort!
And how I used to rest my head upon
A loving mother's breast and listen to
The pulsing of a heart that beat with mine . . .
How sweet it was to hold in my embrace
The slender form of my young brother dear,
Orestes, with the golden, curling hair . . .
O Leto's daughter, thou, Apollo's twin!
Forgive thy slave for these remembrances . . .
If but the wind might bear to me some news . . .
To know if my dear father there still lives,
My dearest mother . . . and Electra, too—
A bride she will be now. Orestes must

By now at the Olympic games have won
The olive crown. With what a lovely sheen
Those silvery olive leaves must have stood out
Against that mass of golden curls of his.
Yet he will scarce have won the prize for speed,
But for the discus throw, for Achilles
Was always swifter in the race. Doth he,
Achilles mine, still live? But no, not mine,
For doubtless some Greek girl or Trojan slave
Can call him hers by now. Great Artemis,
Protect me from myself, deliver me!
*(She descends again and seats herself on the lowest tread of
the steps between the cypresses.)*
How sad the rustling of these cypresses!
The autumn wind . . . and winter's blasts will soon
Come roaring through this grove like savage beast,
And snowstorms rave and swirl upon the sea,
Dissolving earth and sky in chaos wild!
Then shall I sit before a scanty fire,
Depressed and weak in body and in soul,
While there at home, in Argos far away,
Eternal lovely spring will bloom again;
And to the woods Argolian maids will wend
To pluck anemones and violets,
And maybe . . . maybe, in their songs recall
The fame of Iphigenia who gave
Herself to save her native land . . . O Fate!
Doth it beseem thee, grave and austere e'er,
To make a mockery of simple folk? . . .
Yet stay thy course, O proud and wounded heart!
What are we mortals to oppose the gods?
How can we wrestle with the mighty powers
Of those who thunders hurl, who shake the earth?
We, who are made of clay . . . Yet who made us?
Who gave to us our souls, the sacred fire?
Prometheus, thou gav'st the legacy
To us—great, unforgettable; the spark
Snatched for us from Olympian jealousy—

I feel it burst to flame within my soul.
That flame, like conflagration wild, untamed,
Dried up my maiden's tears that time I went
Courageously to die a sacrifice
In honor of my own Hellenic land.
O maids of Hellas, ye who shed your tears
When I was led to meet a glorious death,
Weep not for me, for lo, your heroine,
Ingloriously and vainly wastes away!

(She stands before the altar.)

Why didst thou, goddess great, deliver me,
And bring me hither to a distant land?
Hellenic blood was needed then by thee
To quench thy wrath against my countrymen—
Why didst thou not allow my blood to flow?
Lo, take it now, O goddess—'tis thine own!
Let it no longer course within my veins!

(She takes the sacrificial knife from the altar, throws back her upper garment and points the knife at her breast, but lets it fall to the ground.)

Nay, 'tis beneath Promethean descent!
To one who has once boldly out-faced death,
All things must needs be with like courage met.
If, for the honor of my native land,
Such sacrifice is willed by Artemis,
That Iphigenia must still dwell here,
A stranger, without glory, kin, or name—
Then be it so.

(Letting her head fall sadly, she goes towards the sea, and standing at the head of the steps which lead down to it, gazes for a long time into space.)

Argos, my own dear land!
I'd rather die a hundred times in thee
Than still live here! Nor Styx, nor Lethe's stream
Can quench remembrance of one's fatherland!
A bitter legacy, Prometheus!

At a slow, even pace, she departs from the temple.

6. *Social Justice and Human Rights*

FOREGLEAMS

Deep night wraps wearied folk in lassitude,
   Her broad, black pinions o'er them brood.
      The evening lights no longer shine,
      As all in sleep now lie supine,
   All by imperious night subdued.

Asleep, awake, all yield unto the gloom.
   Thrice happy they whom dreams illume.
      Sweet dreams flee from my sodden sleep . . .
      I'm swathed in darkness, dense and deep,
   All near me sleep as in the tomb.

My sleep's oppressed with apparitions drear,
   And vainly strives to shake off fear . . .
      When suddenly, a bright clear beam
      Arouses me from out my dream—
   The foregleams of the dawn appear!

Those foregleams solemn with victorious might
   Cleave through the darkness of the night;
      While yet the sun's rays are unseen
      The foregleams send abroad their sheen,
   And workers warn of coming light.

Let him in whom the soul still lives, arise!
   'Tis time his strength to exercise.
      Fear not the morning's gloomy shades,
      Dawn's foregleams flash with their bright blades
   Long ere the crimson lights the skies.

WHERE ARE THE STRINGS?

Where are the strings, where is the mighty voice,
   Where is the strong and wingéd word,
To sing of all these evil days—a word
   By which both joy and grief are stirred?

To carry what's immured in prison walls
 Far off into the spacious plains,
To translate into human speech the strains
 Which sound from fetters and from chains?

Jerusalem had once her Jeremy,
 Who in the deserts cried aloud;
Why have we not a Jeremy to speak
 Of our lost freedom, ravished, cowed?

With endless fires to warn posterity,
 Great Dante's Hell is still aflame;
A hell far worse burns in our native land:
 Why can we not a Dante name?

O lightning, sister of the thunderbolt,
 Where art thou? Break this evil spell!
Let us speak out and tempests prophesy,
 As clouds in spring the storms foretell!

REMINDER TO A FRIEND

My friend, who knows how soon we may resume
 Those ardent talks of ours which had no end;
No matter—while my soul's still 'neath their spell,
 Lest you forget, these somber thoughts I send.

You will recall the garden, and the porch,
 The hovering stars, the summer night unstirred,
Our conversations, songs, and then at last,
 The swiftly uttered, desperate, burning word.

I've no regrets that I to you recall
 That outburst of a hatred which I feel.
What then! Can one alone feel bitter hate
 Who all through life has ne'er known love's appeal?

When one thinks on the savage punishments
 Inflicted on all champions of the truth,
Why should not one in anger clench the fist
 And feel a thirst for vengeance without ruth?

No, I regret that this impulse seems dead,
　　As all else in our slavish souls doth die.
Ah, maybe, life would not seem so debased
　　If this same flame of hate could yet burn high!

An amiable mildness, look serene,
　　Patrician calm—all these beseem us not.
What can a slave degraded hope to do
　　When he should read his lord a lesson hot?

Yes, we are slaves, none worse are there on earth!
　　The Fellahs, Pariahs,[1] know no fate so dire,
For they have common sense, keep their thoughts close,
　　While in us lives unquenched the Titans' fire!

Yes, we are paralytics with bright eyes,
　　In spirit wealthy, but in strength there's dearth.
Behind our shoulders we feel eagles' wings
　　While still our feet are fettered to the earth.

Our land we dare not even call our own;
　　All opens for us with a jailor's key;
We, ragged captives, ne'er can proudly say:
　　"This is our home, our temple, which ye see."

Our folk is like an infant blind from birth
　　With eyes from which it ne'er had any use;
It goes through fire and water for its foes,
　　Gives up its leaders to the hangman's noose.

Our courage is like sword once stained with blood,
　　Which in its sheath now lies devoured by rust;
Whose hand, impelled by love, will draw it forth
　　Before that once proud blade becomes mere dust?

Though we be captives, mercenary slaves,
　　Dishonored, lost to shame—suppose it true!
O tell me, who were those brave fighting-men
　　Whom Spartacus[2] beneath his standard drew?

1. The peasants of Egypt and the outcasts of India.
2. Spartacus led a revolt of slaves against Rome in 73-71 B.C.

AND YET, MY MIND . . .

And yet, my mind flies back to thee again,
 My country, helpless, sunk in misery!
  When I remember thee,
My heart within me sinks from grief and pain.

Mine eyes have seen much outrage and distress,
 Yet ne'er have seen a lot that's worse than thine:
  They'd weep thy fate malign,
But shame on tears which flow from helplesssness!

Such tears have been poured forth in copious flood;
 Ukraine entire could sink and in them drown;
  Enough have trickled down—
What use are tears when there's so little blood!

"SLAV" AND "SLAVE"

The Slavic World—the magic phrase expands,
 Embracing something dark and fabulous.
So many years, and lo, so many hands
 Have built for it a shrine mysterious.

Within that shrine men set a pedestal,
 And on it placed a statue which was shaped
Like that of Isis; with a mystical,
 Protecting veil they then their idol draped.

The statue still stands there since ancient days,
 And time flows calmly on as years pass by;
But yet to none has it been given to gaze
 Upon its face with clear, courageous eye.

Why have the sons of that great Slavic race—
 Prophetic children of a mother mute—
Why have they not achieved a glorious place
 'Mongst other folk? What praise have they, what fruit?

Behold them! each by virtue of his birth
   A Slav, as strong and stubborn as the oak,
Who could on his broad shoulders bear the earth,
   With folded hands bows 'neath a paper yoke,

And humbly all the time keeps bowing down
   Before a post, surmounted by a crown
And swathed in purple. By right of descent,
   The post is called a Tsar omnipotent.

Each one is bleeding, on his face are tears,
   The knout with triple lash his body sears;
And each to save himself devises snares
   To trip and catch his brother unawares.

Once on a time it was the foreigner
   Who drove his Slavic captives o'er the plains;
But now, where'er we look, it doth appear
   That 'tis the Slav himself puts on his chains.

And so they say: "The ox deserves his yoke,
   For see how patiently he doth behave."
Nay, there is reason that with other folk
   "Slav" is the source from whence came their word "slave."

INSCRIPTION ON AN EGYPTIAN RUIN

"The king of kings, I, Aton's mighty son,
Have builded for myself this tomb so that
The nations numberless may magnify
And keep in memory perpetual
The name of . . ." Here the inscription was erased.
And all posterity's most learned men
Cannot decipher that lost royal name.
Who was it that erased the name—a foe
Victorious, or time's remorseless hand—
There's none can tell. A marvellous vignette,
With many words inscribed, beside it tells

Of all the glories of that nameless king,
With pictures of his celebrated deeds.
There sits the king, high on his lofty throne;
Before him, conquered peoples pass with gifts
Most costly, but with bowed subservient heads,
While he sits like an idol carved from stone
Beneath the gorgeous, many-colored fans.
His face resembles that of Thothmes or
Of Rameses—'tis every tyrant's face.
We see him pictured, dragging by the hair
A crowd of rebels, while o'er others' heads
He brandishes a blood-stained, dripping sword.
His face resembles that of Tirhakah,
Of Menepthah—'tis every tyrant's face.
With that same face he goes on lion hunts,
Ensnares leviathan, and slaughters birds,
And drives headlong o'er corpses of the slain,
And sends his hapless subjects into war,
And whips the remnant to their slavish toil,
That dread Egyptian labor which was meant
To glorify for aye the royal name.
The people pass, like waves upon the sea
As numberless, unto the battle field,
And fall beneath the hoofs of royal steeds,
While those who still among the folk survive,
They perish in that dread Egyptian toil:
With that huge tomb the king will make himself
A monument enduring—Let slaves die!
The slave must dig the earth, carve out the stone,
Bring slime from out the river, fashion bricks,
Cast up the walls, the giant statues raise,
And, harnessed, do it all by his main strength,
To build up something splendid and eterne,
Something unparalleled, most beautiful,
All painted, fretted with intaglio work,
So that each statue, column, painted scene,
Adornment, carven block, nay, every brick
Should ever speak with lips invisible:

"Egyptian lives created this for me!"
The king with tyrant's face is long since dead.
He left behind him: What? A name erased!
O poets, waste no dreams! O scholars, make no search
To learn who was that king and what his name!
Of his huge tomb just destiny has made
A people's monument: Let Pharoah die!

GRANDFATHER'S FAIRY TALE

When I am wearied with the cares of life,
The daily miseries I see around,
I send my thoughts into the far-away,
And peer intently in a land of dreams.
What is it that I see in that far realm?
I see the future, our posterity;
And there amidst a family group I see
An old grandsire who's telling to his brood
What seems a fairy tale about old times,
Pure fable, all about what happened once.
The family sits together round its sire,
His sons and daughters, and their children, too;
And some of them are listening intently,
While others seem enwrapped in their own dreams.
The youngest grandchild sits ensconced beside
The patriarch, and with keen shining eyes,
Notes every movement that the old man makes.
The grandsire speaks in quiet, solemn tones:
"Thrice happy children are ye who were born
In times of peace, in safe tranquility!
Ye listen as I tell of evil times
As of a fiction, awful but unreal.
Yes, children, yes! Our world so lovely, free,
Seemed like a dungeon to those old-time folk;
And verily, it was a dungeon then.
One nation crushed another 'neath the yoke,
And clamped down fetters on the spoken word.
One half the world enjoyed no human rights,

And brothers each the other slew in war.
Do you know what it was that they called war?
War was what we today call fratricide,
Waged in the name of honor, freedom, truth,
And bloodshed was to them a hero's deed.
Death by starvation they called poverty,
And stolen property·was simply wealth.
Dark ignorance was called simplicity;
Their learning was uncertain blundering.
Inhuman punishment was called the Law,
And despotism they named Rightful Rule.
The proud and haughty won the world's acclaim,
The humble poor were treated with disdain.
All mankind would have perished then for sure
If tyrants could have quenched the tiny spark
Of love to brother-man which still survived
And in the hearts of some still lived and glowed.
That spark did glow, it would not be put out,
But glimmered till it burst into a flame
Which blazed and banished all the darkness drear,
And light became the mistress of the world!
Such is the tale the old folk used to tell;
But that all happened long before my time."
So spoke the grandsire, and the youngest child,
Lifting his head, with bright and shining eyes,
A happy smile upon his lips, then said:
"Grandfather, that's a dreadful fairy tale;
I'm glad I didn't live in times like that."

Selections from the Dramatic Poems

and Dramas

On the Ruins

Dramatic Poem

During the first Babylonian Captivity. The wide plain of the Jordan. On the horizon are Mounts Moriah and Zion, whose peaks glitter in the silvery moonlight. In the valley and on the hills loom the ruins of the towns and villages around Jerusalem. Here and there fires are flickering, perhaps from ruined homes where people are still living. Other people are wandering over the plain. They have come from various places, some from Judea, some from Samaria. Others again have made themselves shelters out of stones taken from the ruins and thatched with reeds from the Jordan; some have kindled small fires in the open at which they are warming themselves or preparing food; still others are digging holes and burying therein the bones of those who fell in the recent battle. Sounds of smothered weeping, suppressed sighings and whisperings are heard from some who are not asleep, but a very large number lie sleeping, some in roofless huts, some simply in the open field, covered with rags, face downward to avoid the moonlight. The sleepers seem like corpses and thereby make the scene more dreary—like a field still covered with bodies of the slain after a battle. At one side are three figures; a woman, a maiden, and a little girl, who are sitting gloomily beside an extinguished fire. The woman is rocking a babe in her arms, the maiden is spinning wool, the little girl is weaving a basket out of reeds. TIRZAH, *the prophetess, coming from the ruins, approaches the three.*

TIRZAH

My sisters, peace to you!

WOMAN

And peace to thee!

Yea, peace to all . . . the peace of death.

75

TIRZAH
Why so?
God lives and we still live.

WOMAN
In ruins, yes!

TIRZAH
Give not thy little son thy tears to drink,
Nor suckle him with milk of bitterness.

WOMAN
Where shall forsaken ones find other food?

TIRZAH
Why should ye call yourselves forsaken ones?

MAIDEN
My brother is in far-off Nineveh.

LITTLE GIRL
Two years my father is in Babylon.

TIRZAH
But ye are three and, too, ye have a babe.
None are forsaken who still have themselves.
Relight your fire while waiting for the dawn,
So that ye may have light to do your work.

MAIDEN
(Laying her spindle down)
Our work is all for naught. Who will there be
To wear the garments when I've spun the yarn?
My brother is a soldier in Assyria's host;
Enslaving others, as a slave he'll die.
For whom have I to care?

TIRZAH
Care for thyself,
And still be free. In presence of thy foe,
Say not: Who'll give me clothes to wear?
Lest thy foe say: Come, I have clothes for thee.

The MAIDEN *picks up her spindle and goes to work again.*

TIRZAH

(*To the* LITTLE GIRL, *who has listlessly dropped her hands.*)
Why sittest thou? Hast finished all thy task?

LITTLE GIRL

What's there to finish here? My playmates weave
These baskets and in them they carry earth
To heap the grave-mounds o'er their fathers slain,
Who fell in battle, fighting for God's House.
But as for me, there is not e'en a grave!
My father is in Babylon. They say
He's working there to build a shrine for Baal.

TIRZAH

Build thou thyself a new home in this place.
Work on a dwelling, not on funeral mounds,
So thou may'st not become an alien here.
Say not: Who'll give to me a shelter now?
Lest thy foe say: I'll find a roof for thee.
Weave rushes for a roof, bring stones and clay,
And build a shelter—chilly nights draw near.

The LITTLE GIRL *swiftly falls to work again.*

TIRZAH
(*To the* WOMAN)
Why is it that thy fire no longer burns?

WOMAN

And wherefore should it burn? A woman tends
The household fire which burns in her own home.
But where's my dwelling? In the open field?
My husband's settled in far-off Phenice;
He seeks for riches in a foreign land . . .
For whom, then, should I tend a fire here?

TIRZAH
(*Pointing to the infant*)
For him and for thyself. Though in the field,
Stir up the fire for this babe of thine.
Make warmth and seek for food, lest at thy dry

And withered breasts thy little son should wail;
Lest he from hunger quiver in thy arms;
Lest thou shouldst weep in utter helplessness,
And lest thy foe should say: Come, tend my fire!

The WOMAN *begins to busy herself with the fire; after a few moments it blazes up, casting a cheerful light on the three figures at work again.*

TIRZAH
(Turning to go away from them)
My sisters, peace to you!

WOMAN
And to thee peace!
And may God bless thee, sister of good hope!

A groan is heard from amongst the sleepers lying around. TIRZAH *goes thither and stops beside a man who has just turned face upwards and is stretching his uplifted hands, clasped in despair, towards the moon.*

TIRZAH
(Bending over the man)
My brother, sufferest thou? Thy wound still pains?
I'll bind it up again, 'twill easier be.

MAN
That wound of mine can never be bound up.
The wound here on my breast is long since healed,
But that within my heart for aye will smart!
O thou, Jerusalem, Jerusalem!
My native land's forever-throbbing wound!
Unhealed, thou dost forever burn in me! . . .

He groans again, wringing his hands.

TIRZAH
But if the wound upon thy breast is healed,
Thou shouldst arise and go to work.

MAN
To work!
What work is there for me? What sort? Wherewith?
What means, what tools have I to labor with?

TIRZAH

Jerusalem's good earth was not consumed.
Thou hast a sword.

*She points to the dented sword which lies on the ground
beside the* MAN.

MAN
What use is sword to me?
A shattered ruin needeth no defence.

TIRZAH

Turn it into a share. The time is come;
The ruin needeth it for its defence,
Because the foe will come and plough the soil,
Will seed it, and therefrom will harvests reap,
And with its food will feed the people here;
A second time he'll conquer Palestine,
Not with the sword, but with the gleaming share.
Then will the widow and the orphan say:
Blessed is he, whoever gives us bread!
He hath no native land, who lies supine.
To him who sows and reaps—to him the land.
Then men will call this Babylonian soil,
And therefore those same ruins looming there
Will then be standing in a foreign land.
Who then will care about who feels the smart
Of that wound which was called Jerusalem?

The MAN *rises and picks up his sword.*

MAN
Where shall I go now to reforge this sword?

TIRZAH
(Pointing to a fire not far away)
Go thither where are living people still;
They'll gladly give thee of their living fire.
As glows and burns the wound within thy heart,
So let the iron glow and burn in fire.
There forge from this thy dented sword anew

A peasant's ploughshare and then temper it
As I have tempered, hardened now thy soul
With heat and coldness of the spoken word.

MAN

Blest be that word that can new temper give!

*He takes his sword under his arm and goes towards the fire
on the ruins.*

TIRZAH
(Singing)

Arise, O Israel, set up thy tents! . . .

*From amongst the group of sleepers, some begin to stir and
sit up. An aged man replies in a sleepy voice.*

OLD MAN

Who sings?

TIRZAH

One crying in the wilderness!
(Still singing)

Prepare the way for God who comes in strength,
Make straight paths for His Spirit which draws near!

OLD MAN

Let him be cursed who wakes the vanquished ones!
A curse on him who steals the sleep from slaves!
To rob the aged or to snatch away
The bread from starving souls is far less sin!

TIRZAH

Who is the slave? Who is the vanquished one?
'Tis he who yields unto the slavish yoke.

OLD MAN

I bear no yoke. I wish to sleep, that's all.

TIRZAH

Can anything be worse than such a yoke?
Once Jeremiah bore an iron yoke,
And thought it worse than aught else in the world.

Yet if the prophet now could see thy sleep—
The stonelike sleep of apathetic slave—
His yoke would seem to him as feather light
Compared to thy chains which no eye perceives.
Canst thou not rise from thine ingloriousness?
Canst thou not lift a hand against thy shame?

OLD MAN

Wherefore? To what, for what should I arise?

TIRZAH

To work! To counsel! Rise to life renewed!
That morning's sun should not find thee inert;
That liberation's hour should not find thee
In idleness, in shameful slumber wrapped.

OLD MAN

And what work doest thou?

TIRZAH

I rouse the folk.

OLD MAN

(He settles himself more comfortably. Then with a feigned laugh.)
Awake me when that hour of freedom strikes!

TIRZAH

For such as thee, that hour will never strike.
(Calling loudly)
Are any living on this battlefield?

Beneath the trees beside the Jordan can be heard a faint
twanging of strings and a hesitant voice which is singing with
breaks and intermissions, as though trying to recall the words and
melody of a psalm.

VOICE

'How is the fine gold changed . . . the silver, how
It has been dimmed . . . O Zion's daughter, hear! . . .
From out my eyes the tears in rivers flow . . .'

TIRZAH

(She goes towards the voice and stops before the singer who is plucking the strings of a small harp manifestly patched together. As she draws near, the singer stops and lays down his harp.)

Why singest thou in such uncertain tones?

SINGER

In vain I strive to call to mind the words
Of Jeremiah's lamentation . . . but
I scarce can do so, for my memory fails.

TIRZAH

Then try not to recall, compose thine own.

SINGER

Ah, sister, no! I would not dare presume.
Dost thou not know whose harp this is I hold?
'Twas Jeremiah's once, and he in turn
Received it from Isaiah, who, 'tis said,
Discovered it by chance in David's house.
Perhaps e'en David may have played on it,
While singing psalms unto Jehovah's praise.
Those psalms of David's I remember well,
But how may one sing them in days of shame?
Isaiah's prophecies have not come true,
Peace has not reigned, Messiah not yet appeared—
So let his songs fade in oblivion,
Let them not vex us . . . Jeremiah, though,
Was our last prophet, who 'mid ruins sang.
Let him then live again upon these strings.
If thou couldst but have heard how he wept here
With mighty voice amidst this ravaged waste!
The ruins then responded to his voice,
And e'en the stones wept as the prophet mourned.
And when that prophet, in an iron yoke,
Was led a captive from Jerusalem,
Against the ruined altar first he smote
This harp, then cast it shattered on the ground.

And so it lay there long, long years till I
Came here one day while seeking firewood,
And, hidden in cold ashes, chanced on it—
A sacred relic of that man of God.
I gathered all the fragments I could find,
Arranged and patched them up—the harp is small,
But in it there's no single piece profane.
I found the strings—a pity, not quite all—
All tangled and encrusted thick with rust.
I cleaned and straightened them as best I could,
Restrung the harp and, as you see, I play.

(He thrums the strings to demonstrate their timbre.)

They sound a little weak, but yet these strings
Once rang beneath the fingers of those saints,
Those holy prophets ne'er to be forgot.
Amongst these strings there is not one that's new:
All old . . . a shame that some of them are gone.

Tirzah

The harp lacks strings; the singer, too, lacks words!
I've heard thee say how to the prophet's voice
These ruins once replied . . . I also hear
That thou, the singer, wouldst the echo be
To these same ruins here. Give me the harp!

(She takes the harp out of the hands of the astonished Singer.*)*

These sacred ruins serve but to our shame!
Once living, these strings but give heavy groans
Beneath the dead touch from thy soul as dead.
The living words, like wind among dead leaves,
But rustle to the fruitage of thy lips.
I challenge thee, O relic sanctified!
It still may chance that by some miracle
Our God shall find for thee a worthier hand,
And wake in thee, not merely tinkling sound,
But thy eternal soul. Till then, repose!
Now let the sacred river guard thee well!

With a wide swing, she hurls the harp far into the Jordan.

SINGER

O maniac! possessed! What hast thou done?

TIRZAH

New words, new strings find for thyself, or else
Keep silence—for the graveyards cannot sing.

SINGER

Help, help! A holy relic will be lost!
*(With loud lamentations, he rushes toward the Jordan, fol-
lowed by some of the people who have started up at his cries.)*
Swim after it! Lay hold of it! Catch it!
It's sunk down to the bottom! . . . Bring a net!

FISHERMAN

It's gone right down! Too bad! No use to seek—
Thou'lt never reach the bottom here . . . too deep.
*(He shouts to the SINGER, who is preparing to plunge into the
river.)*
Stay there! Keep out, or thou wilt drown thyself!

SINGER

*(He turns and rushes at TIRZAH, followed by a crowd of
awakened people.)*
Now likewise, I'll drown thee, thou criminal!

A VOICE *from the crowd*

Come on, let's drown her! She hath dared to cast
A relic of God's Zion in the stream!

*Dragging TIRZAH towards the river, they tear her garments,
spit on her, the fisherboys throw handfuls of mud at her, while
others tie her hands.*

SAMARITAN PROPHET

*(Aroused from his prayers which he had been offering be-
neath a nearby tree, he comes rushing forward.)*
Help, men of Israel! Behold these Jews
Who fain would dare to drown a guiltless maid!

*From every direction Samaritans come running hither who
struggle with the Jews and release TIRZAH.*

SAMARITANS

Why try to drown this maid? What is her crime?

JEWS

'Tis sacrilege!

SAMARITAN PROPHET
Mere worthless wood and strings!

The Samaritans laugh, the Jews rage, and the brawl recommences more hotly than before. Standing to one side, looking calmly on, is a Levite.

SINGER

Ho, Levite, come and help us to chastize
This criminal!

LEVITE
What care I for a harp?
I've no concern with psalms and prophecies.
The Law's enough; of prophets there's no need.

The Samaritans finally get the upper hand, and having beaten off the Jews, they lead TIRZAH *beneath the tree where a little while ago their young prophet had been engaged in prayer.*

SAMARITAN PROPHET
(To TIRZAH*)*

Stand here, O prophetess; this olive tree
Will shelter thee beneath its sacred boughs.
And woe betide him who cares violate
This holy place or lay a hand on thee—
'Hear ye, O Israel!' he shall not live!
(To the SAMARITANS*)*

God hath by this maid's hands deigned to rebuke
The shameless Jews. Are ye aware what was
The relic which she cast into the stream?

SAMARITANS

Thou saidst thyself: mere worthless wood and strings . . .

SAMARITAN PROPHET

That worthless wood and strings once gave forth sound
As harp in David's hands.

SAMARITANS
O Lord our God!

SAMARITAN PROPHET
Those same malignant strings resounded once
Within the palace of our great king Saul;
They lulled him into quiet sleep the while
His throne was undermined by treacherous Jews
Like termites. Saul's throne fell; he was destroyed—
Those strings then wailed an insincere lament
Upon the deaths of Saul and Jonathan,
Played by that David who destroyed them both.
Full oft did those strings in Jerusalem
Sound for the ruin of Samaria.
Now they are gone, without a trace behind,
Like to the pride of all Jerusalem's kings.

SAMARITANS
Hail, prophetess, another Deborah!
Give unto her the timbrel! Let her play!
Let her like Miriam lead the holy dance,
As when she over Pharoah's judgment sang!
Samaria, hail! Death to Jerusalem!

A Samaritan maiden offers a timbrel to TIRZAH. *She silently
waves it away, and stands with her head sunk on her breast.*

SAMARITAN PROPHET
She hath no heart amidst these ruins to play.
A maiden's heart is pitiful, my friends.
When dawning comes, we'll leave this place and go
Away off yonder to Gerizim's mount.
There on the high place we will light again
Our holy fire in the sacred grove.
There unto us shall Tirzah prophesy
Of our Samaria.

TIRZAH
No, never, no!
I will not go up to Gerizim's mount;
And go not ye! Let us forget our feud.

Both Saul and David are together now.
What is Samaria, Jerusalem?
Both ruins, wastes!

LEVITE
(*To those who helped to deliver* TIRZAH)
The holy altar, though? . . .
It still stands whole.

TIRZAH
Without a sacrifice.

LEVITE
We have the Law and there 'tis written plain:
There's but one holy city in the world—
'Tis David's and God's dwelling place, the shrine
Of Solomon.

SAMARITANS
Where's that shrine?

LEVITE
In the Law.
(*The* SAMARITANS *laugh.*)
God brands the foolish with the foolish laugh.
No tittle of the Law shall ever pass;
What stands therein shall not be moved for aye.
Eternal is each stone of God's true house,
Because it standeth written in the Law.

SAMARITAN PROPHET
What good does that do you?

LEVITE
Take shame to ask!
What good? The Law must needs be Law for aye,
As God so is. All we are but His slaves;
Him we must serve in blind obedience.

SAMARITAN PROPHET
Serve Him with what?

LEVITE
By keeping all His rites.

To make no sacrifice outside His shrine,
So that no word be altered in the Law.

SAMARITAN PROPHET

Then we, meanwhile, will search these ruins through,
And take the stone unto Samaria!
Then on Gerizim set your altar up
And sacrifice there in the sacred grove.

GROUP OF JEWS

(Who by degrees have gathered around to listen to the dispute.)
Dogs of Samaritans! Lo, this is why
Ye have come hither like a thief by night!
Ye have but come to steal our holy shrine!
    The two factions begin to close for a fight. The LEVITE
picks up stones and aims at the SAMARITAN PROPHET.

TIRZAH

Stop, stop! The Babylonian overseer
Will else come from his tent and give his slaves
Command to have you scourged. Awake him not!

VOICES *from both sides*

That's true! Bethink yourselves! Talk not so loud!

TIRZAH

O blind unfortunates! Do ye not see
That now's the time to realize the state
Which once Isaiah prophesied? Let now
The lion with the lamb lie down in peace.
Let Judah's lion hunt the jackals down
And cease to rend the common flock of God.

SINGER

'Tis thou who hast this bitter discord sown,
And now wilt thou reap peace? Remember this:
Who sows the wind, he shall the whirlwind reap.

TIRZAH

The sowing and the reaping has been done,
Not yesterday, nor yet today—Behold

The blackened stubble from the harvest left!
(She points all around at the scene covered with ruins and
homeless people.)
The time has come to sow another seed
And look for other harvests here. But ye
Are not the ones to forge the iron yoke
Into the scythe and reaping hook. 'Tis they,
The common folk, who by their fires, in huts,
Are toiling sleeplessly ere yet 'tis dawn—
'Tis they prepare the harvest of the Lord,
While ye, like venomous serpents, in your wrath
Shoot forth at one another your fell stings
And poison each the other, like those asps
Which God once sent upon us for our sins.

Samaritan Prophet
Who set thee up to be a prophetess?
In public women ought to hold their peace.

Tirzah
Who just called me another Deborah?
Was it not some of thine own folk? Forsooth,
When all our chief men understanding lack,
A woman must stand up like Deborah
And cry: Arise, O Israel, arise!
The folk will rise like waves upon the sea,
And God's great Spirit move upon the waves,
And Zion then shall blossom like the rose,
And once again the Promised Land shall flow
With milk and honey. Yea, this very soil
Whereon we straggle, fugitives, forlorn,
Like wandering sheep lost in the wilderness.
Why should we wander here? What do we seek?
Is this not that same soil which once for us
Our fathers conquered with their blood and sweat?
The fiery pillar nowhere else doth lead,
Nor saith the cloudy pillar: Follow me.
God sends us no new manna from the skies.

The Covenant has not yet been fulfilled.
Arise, O Israel! Trench with the plough
This battlefield.   Yield not a single foot
Of this our Promised Land. Rise up and sow
O'er all its borders with good wheaten seed;
Fence it from off the wilderness with rye.
For new foundations gather up the stones,
So that no man may say: Behold this waste!
But say instead: Lo, houses shall stand here!
The years will pass, the captives will return,
And songs of Zion shall resound again.
The strong foundations will re-echo then
More loudly to the resurrection songs
Than did these ruins e'er give back the strains
Of Jeremiah's funeral laments.
Then captive unto captive shall stretch forth
The hand, and side by side will build the walls
Upon the strong foundations we have laid.
My soul prophetic sees that glorious frame,
And my heart knows how then it shall be called:
A temple new in new Jerusalem!

SAMARITANS

Jerusalem? Accurséd be the name!

LEVITE

A temple new with no old sacrifice?
Without the Ark, without the Cherubim?
Without what David, Solomon bequeathed?

TIRZAH

The old alone is holy, not the new?

SINGER

Away with her! Into the wilderness!
Let her not sow confusion in our midst!

A YOUNG JEW

From whom then shall we rear this building up?
In order that our foes should tear it down?

AN OLD JEW

Who gave permission for this building new?
The king, or who?

TIRZAH

God's Spirit doth command!
That Spirit which abideth not with you!
More surely He dwells in the wilderness,
To which ye drive me in the unknown to die,
Than in your midst!

SINGER

Thou'lt find that spirit there,
The evil spirit which hath governed thee
Since long time past! Go thou and seek it there!

TIRZAH

God's Spirit in the deserts shall find me,
But here ye are still far away from Him!

With cries of hatred, the crowd drives TIRZAH *onwards and
away until she disappears at last from the spot where the people
are dwelling.*

Babylonian Captivity

Dramatic Poem

A wide plain lying at the confluence of the rivers Tigris and Euphrates in Babylonia. The crimson of the setting sun turns the waters into the semblance of blood. Scattered all over the plain are the tents of the captive Hebrews. Naked children are searching in the sand for shellfish for food and collecting dry reeds for fuel. Women, mostly middle-aged or elderly, ragged and worn-out, are preparing the evening meal—each at her own fire—for their men-folk who, after hard toil in the near-by city of Babylon, are seated in silent groups under the willows beside the waters of Babylon. A little apart, also under the willows, are two groups: Levites in one, prophets in the other. Hanging on the willows over the prophets' heads are a number of harps; from time to time they sway as they are blown by gusts of the evening breeze and then they give forth murmuring sounds. In the near distance the walls and towers of Babylon can be seen whence sounds of the city noise and tumult are borne hither on the breezes.

WOMAN
(Calling from her fire.)
O husband, come, and eat the evening meal!

(Her husband, still young, rises from one of the groups and silently comes and sits down to the food.)
How now! Thou dost not eat?

(He makes no answer.)
'Tis bitter, eh?
It matters not, poor wretch, thou yet must eat!

He still remains silent.

MAN
(Speaking with difficulty, like a toothless old man)
I cannot eat . . .

WOMAN
What! Art thou toothless now?
Where then . . .

MAN *(Pointing to Babylon)*
'Twas there!

WOMAN
Alas! O woe, O woe!
Beside another fire

OLD MAN
(Coming up to an old woman, who is sitting motionless with sunken head beside an extinguished fire)
Give me to eat!
(She makes no reply, does not even stir.)
Why hast thou not prepared?
(She still remains silent and unmoving.)
What mean these ashes strewed upon thy head?

(Still silent, the old woman lets her head sink lower.)
Our Malka, where is she?

OLD WOMAN *(Pointing to Babylon)*
She's there!
She falls prone on the ground and strews more ashes on her head.

OLD MAN
O God!
He rends his garments and also falls to the ground.
Beside a third fire around which only very old men, grey-beards, are seated.

MIDDLE-AGED WOMAN
(She approaches them timidly, her ragged children clinging to her skirts.)
Forgive me, fathers, that I question you.
Has any one of you my husband seen?

FIRST GREYBEARD

How was he called?

MIDDLE-AGED WOMAN
Elnathan is his name.

SECOND GREYBEARD

He was called that ere thou a widow wert.

MIDDLE-AGED WOMAN

What's that thou say'st?

THIRD GREYBEARD
Don't take it so to heart.

The dead no longer suffer from the foe.

MIDDLE-AGED WOMAN

Oh, now, what shall I do?   A widow left
With little ones!
She bursts out into loud wailing.

CHILDREN
Mama, mama, mama! . . .

MADWOMAN
(Who is wandering about amongst the fires.)
Blest be the womb that never bore its fruit.
Blest be the breasts that never yet gave suck. . . .
Rejoice not, daughter of great Babylon!
Exult not, mother of a reptile brood! . . .

MAIDEN
(Pointing to the MADWOMAN *and whispering to her companion)*
She's been that way since in Jerusalem
They slew her babe.

COMPANION
O what a dreadful thing!

MAIDEN

I saw it with these very eyes of mine;
How one fierce soldier took it by the feet
And dashed its head . . .

COMPANION
Be still! Don't talk of it!
Beneath the willows.

GROUP OF LEVITES
God left the Temple for our fathers' sins!
Because they sinned, forsook His Holy Place!
And we their children, seeming prodigals
Yet innocent, must pay the fathers' debt.

GROUP OF PROPHETS
With stones Jerusalem once cast us out;
Therefore the Lord in wrath hath smitten it!
And Zion's daughter once poured scorn on us;
And so the sons of Baal now tread her down!

FIRST LEVITE
(*To a second Levite*)
Why wast thou not at daily prayers today?

SECOND LEVITE
The captain sent for me to cast accounts.
The master workmen were to get their pay
For work done on the great king's palaces.

FIRST LEVITE
Couldst thou not find at least some heathen clerk
Instead?

SECOND LEVITE
Ah, brother, this captivity—
The captain says none others have such skill
To cast accounts as have the Jews.

FIRST LEVITE
'Tis true!

SECOND LEVITE (*Softly*)
For my good work the captain gave to me
This ring of finest gold.

FIRST LEVITE
To God be praise,
That He with wisdom hath endowed His folk

Above all other peoples in the world!
  (Softly)
Maybe there's need of someone more to help?
  They whisper together.

                    SAMARITAN PROPHET
Thus saith the Lord: Lo, on Gerizim's mount
Have I established My own dwelling place.
Upon its peak My altar have I set,
But ye refused to recognise the House
Of My true glory—as a drunkard's son,
Befuddled, knoweth not his father's home,
And wandering, in the darkness lost, becomes
A laughing stock to all his enemies.

                    JEWISH PROPHET
Thus saith the Lord: Lo, in Jerusalem
I set My Temple in the people's midst,
So that as bees all swarm to one queen bee,
Unto a single hive, so also ye
Might flock to one sole Holy Place, but ye
Like wildings, flew away in wilfulness;
Therefore I loosed on you the venomous asp.

                    SAMARITAN PROPHET
The Lion of Judah rushed upon the flock
Of Israel and scattered all the sheep.

                    JEWISH PROPHET
Saul's house was merely set to guard the sheep,
And not as shepherds called to rule the flock.

                    SAMARITAN PROPHET
The God of Israel shall smite thee now,
And that by me!
        He raises his stick against the JEWISH PROPHET.

                    JEWISH PROPHET
                    O Lord, remember now
Thy servant David!
        He picks up stones and aims at the SAMARITAN PROPHET.

ELAZAR
*(A young prophet-singer, who has just come from Babylon,
rushes between the two disputants.)*

Stop! Bethink yourselves!
Bring not such shame upon the glorious names
Of Israel and Judah!

SAMARITAN PROPHET
Ah, 'tis thou,
Prophet of shame!   How hast thou glorified
Judah and Israel?

JEWISH PROPHET
Base renegade,
Why cam'st thou sneaking hither from that den?
(Pointing to Babylon)
There is thy god, thy people; go, praise them!

FIRST LEVITE
(Passing by, spits at ELAZAR.*)*
Thus may the Lord cast thee out from His lips,
And may thy name, like spittle, perish too!

Hearing the dispute, people gradually begin to gather around.

SECOND LEVITE
(He snatches one of the harps from the willows.)
Let me but smash this cursed instrument!

ELAZAR
(Seizing the LEVITE's *hand.)*
Touch not my harp, for that is innocent
Of any sins of mine!   Curse me instead,
If it seem good to thee I so deserve,
But call not thou a cursed instrument
My sacred harp.

THIRD LEVITE
What makes it sanctified?

ELAZAR
Because no single string of it hath e'er
Vibrated to a profane strain.

A YOUTH
Behold!
So that's the reason thou didst hang it there!

ELAZAR
What meanest thou, good youth, by what thou say'st?

YOUTH
Make no pretence thou dost not understand!

GREYBEARD
Elazar, this young man hath only said
To thee, what thine own conscience to thy heart
Would say—but what's been silenced cannot speak!

A MAN
What is the use to waste speech on the dumb?

A CHILD
(Stretching out its hands to ELAZAR for the harp)
Give me the plaything, please!

MOTHER
(Tugging at the CHILD)
Did I not say
Thou must not even go near to this man?
The CHILD cries and the MOTHER hastily drags it away.

OLD WOMAN
(To a maiden who is standing near by and looking on.)
'Tis plain to see that modesty has ceased
In Israel, since maidens boldly stand
Unveiled and on a traitor gaze.

MAIDEN
But I . . . .

OLD WOMAN
Take heed, my girl, 'twould be a sad mischance
If one accursed by God should steal thy heart.

MAIDEN
If he's accursed, then I will curse him, too.
She veils herself and slips away.

ELAZAR

O fathers, mothers, brethren, sisters, all!
Since when has it become the custom that
We pass a sentence ere the trial's held?
Tell me in fairness, frankly, openly,
What makes me seem a leper in your midst?

GREYBEARD

From Babylon thou bring'st the leprosy
By singing there for money in the streets
Before the sons of Baal.

ELAZAR

Have ye not caught
The same taint too, by working there for bread?

A MAN

Those toilers don't bow down to Merodach.

ELAZAR

For whose sake then are both their hands and tools?
Was it not they who built for Merodach
A splendid shrine such as the Lord our God
At no time in Jerusalem e'er had?

FIRST PROPHET

Don't blame the slave for work he has to do.

ELAZAR

And am I not a captive, too? Why then
Revile me for what I in bondage do?

SECOND PROPHET

Because the sledge, the mattock, and the spade
In human hands are slaves of men—the word
On prophet's lips by God bestowed must serve
Our God alone and no one else.

GREYBEARD

So now,
Elazar, dost thou still ask for a trial?

ELAZAR

I do demand it, though no doubt 'twill end
In death by stoning. O Thou living God!
But ye must judge me in all righteousness—
And unjust judgment will return on you!

GREYBEARD

Then let us hear him!   Ne'er let it be said
That on the ruins of Jerusalem
We left all law behind. So, tell us what
It was compelled thee thus to sell the word!

ELAZAR

Because no one would buy what I could do.
My father never taught me manual toil;
My mother brought me up indulgently.
Although my hands were skilful on the harp,
They would not serve me with the axe or spade.
I sank down when I tried to bear a load;
The overseer chased me from the task.

GREYBEARD

Then let thy parents nourish thee, because
They never taught thee how to win thy bread.

ELAZAR

Back in Jerusalem I earned my bread
In all good faith as they had taught me how.
But here . . . I cannot eat the food which burns—
The bread my father brings from Babylon.
'Tis hard to feed on parents' slavery.

FIRST LEVITE

Thy father also brings back rings of gold,
Not merely bread!

ELAZAR *(To all)*
Tell ye the Levite this:
That gold can also burn as well as gleam!

FIRST LEVITE *(Viciously)*
Why do thy father's earnings burn thee then?

ELAZAR

Am I, or is my father being tried?
If so, then bring all fathers to be judged!
All who destroy their souls for children's sake!

FIRST LEVITE

Why didst thou not apply to thine own folk,
That they might nourish thee with that same bread
With which they feed the Levite and the lame?

ELAZAR

Because I'm not a Levite, neither lame.

LITTLE BOY
(To his father in the crowd)

O father, give me bread!

FATHER
I have none, son.

A VOICE

Well, there you are!   The child hears talk of food,
Of nourishment, and straightway asks for food!

ELAZAR

The child hath spoken well!   He hath replied
For me far better than I could have done.
You all have heard the little interchange:
'O father, give me bread!' 'I have none, son!'
So long as they talk thus in Israel,
Elazar will not sink to share the bread
Of Levites and the lame.   Let him who hath
A crust of bread still left, give to this child,
And I from captives will accept a stone.
Who hath a fish, let him the children feed,
And unto me let them a serpent give,
The serpent of captivity which sucks
The blood from out the heart—I'll take it up
And carry it with me into the streets.
There with my words it shall shoot forth its sting,
And all in Babylon shall hear its hiss.

A YOUTH

But little earnings from such songs as those
Thou'lt win in Babylon!   Surely, far less
Than thou didst earn for singing Zion's songs!

ELAZAR

In ignorance, thou speakest thus.
To them I never sang our Zion songs.
Here is the truth: I hung this harp upon
Those willow trees, because its strings must ne'er
Accompany a song that's not sincere.
And songs of Zion one may never sing
Without the sacred harp.   I never sang
Those holy songs amongst our enemies.
The songs of Zion—of all songs the crown—
Were in Jerusalem like to a bride,
Were like a spouse in God's most holy place,
But here they'd seem like some base concubine.
Who'd take a captive as a wedded wife?

At these words a groan comes from the crowd standing around.

A MAN

Thou couldst have sung a captive's song to them,
Wept bitter tears about our slavery!
Continuous dripping cracks the hardest stone;
Why should not burning tears e'en penetrate
A cruel heart?

ELAZAR

The Lord our God hath set
Pride in my soul.   I never yet have wept
Before the foreigner.

MAN

Pride does not suit
Poor prisoners.

FIRST PROPHET

The horn of pride with thee
Exalts itself beyond both grief and love!

ELAZAR

Set not thyself to mete infinity;
Thou canst not fathom what may come therefrom.

YOUTH

Elazar as a prophet amongst slaves!
Why should he in the streets of Babylon
Keep silence as regards his grief and love
And pride? Perhaps there was too little space!

ELAZAR

Too little space, thou say'st? Alas, O youth!
I've measured those broad streets of Babylon,
I know their spaciousness. One day I walked
Down that broad avenue where our own folk
Are slaving on the towers of Moloch's shrine.
I checked my pace and gazed on it a while.
The marble gleamed as white as dead men's bones;
The porphyry glowed red like streaming blood;
The gold flamed like a conflagration fierce;
Still incomplete, it like a ruin seemed.
I heard the shouting of our conquerors,
I heard the groanings of our captive folk.
I felt beside myself; there in the street
I cried with mighty voice: 'Jerusalem!'
The toiling men responded with loud wails.
The overseers with a mocking laugh:
'How can a ruin still command a name,
Or desolation still be called a place?'
I went into the market where they sell
The captives into servitude. A man
Of wealth was buying there some lovely slaves . . .

A WOMAN'S VOICE (From the crowd)

O woe! O woe! O woe!

ELAZAR

To him I said:
'Consider, master, that these maidens here

Have fathers, too—Should ever child of thine
Become the prey of war, the conqueror
Would doubtless sell her as a slave like these?'
He laughed and said: 'Such is the captive's fate!'
I went on farther and beheld a slave,
A small and feeble man, on whom a tall
And robust Babylonian had piled
His purchases as if he were a mule,
And drove him with a club. I cried, 'Oh, stay!
How canst thou so abuse thy fellow-man?'
'That's what a slave is for,' the bully said.
'Lo, if thy son,' I said, 'were sold, then he
Would be a slave like this.' 'Of course, why not?'
The brute replied and laughed as he went on,
'But 'tis not I who sell my sons, for see,
'Tis yours I buy instead! . . .' Who, and wherewith,
Could penetrate such hearts? 'Twas only once
My songs brought tears into an alien's eyes—
The king himself wept o'er the fate of Saul
And Jonathan's sad death.

                A Voice *(From the crowd)*
                                Long may he live,
That king with tender heart!   On him alone
We'll rest our hopes!

                        Elazar
                That tender-hearted king
Would fain have recompensed me royally.

                    First Levite
What did he wish, Elazar, to bestow?

                        Elazar
He tendered me a chamber in his house,
With all I wished of female Jewish slaves. . . .
Since that time I have cursed the gift of song
That could move even conquerors to tears,
Such tears that crocodiles might shed.

YOUTH

Thou shouldst
Have sung to him the glories of our race,
That he might know the strength that lies in us.

ELAZAR *(Gloomily)*
I sang.

YOUTH
With what effect?
ELAZAR *does not reply.*

GREYBEARD
Elazar, how
Received the foreigners that glorious song?

ELAZAR
(Speaking slowly, as though forcing himself)
One of them smiled approvingly and wagged
His head at me. Another one burst out
And loudly asked, 'Can that be true?' A third
Demanded me as minstrel for his troops.
Then afterwards they all began to say:
'Is there no light but in Jerusalem?
Dost thou no songs of Edom's glories know?
Of Egypt's deeds? Has Amalek no fame?
Did not the Ammonites, the Amorites,
Once have a splendor like the glorious past
Of Israel?

FIRST PROPHET
O Lord our God, chastize
The lips of blasphemy and strike them dumb!

ELAZAR
So then I sang them songs of Edom's past,
Of Egypt's, and of all those Gentile tribes,
In their own tongue. And they all hearkened how
The bloody sword of Edom's treachery
Was broken by the power of Asshur's might;
How Ammon and Amor and Amalek,
From being conquerors became mere slaves;

How Egypt, once the lord of half the world,
The one-time master of the Israelites,
Was forced to bow before Eternal Strength;
How in the sea both horse and rider drowned
With all the host of Pharaoh's haughty pride;
How all the House of Bondage was laid waste
When under God's right hand the slaves escaped.

YOUTH

With what effect?

ELAZAR

There were some who turned pale.

SECOND PROPHET

Would God they all were pale and cold in death!

YOUTH

Why didst thou not tell them straight in the face
That such a day of judgment waits for them?

ELAZAR

Who could say such a thing in Babylon?
Today I sang to them of Ophir's wealth,
Of Tyre and Sidon's craftsmanship and skill,
Of all their treasures, such as Babylon
Hath not today and never will possess.

FIRST LEVITE

Didst thou obtain much treasure for thy song?

ELAZAR

Thou meanest, maybe, much of Gentile wealth?
I gained just food enough for this night's meal.

YOUTH

But, surely, for the songs which magnified
The might of Babylon, thou hast received
Full many a bracelet of the finest gold!

ELAZAR

The serpent's tongue can but with venom speak,
Yet all are not affected by its sting.

When hast thou heard that I have ever sung
The glory and the might of Babylon?
The YOUTH, *abashed, remains silent.*

GREYBEARD

Perhaps, Elazar, there in Babylon
Thy songs were suited to the time and place,
But songs of Egypt, Edom, and the rest
Recall no memories of Palestine,
Rekindle no thoughts of Jerusalem.

ELAZAR

Need we to have our memories refreshed?

GREYBEARD

Not we, but those, who in captivity,
Have learned to use the language of our foes.

ELAZAR

How shall such understand their native song,
And how can it be sung in alien speech?

GREYBEARD

Thou, too, amidst this alien speech couldst soon
Forget to utter 'O Jerusalem!'

ELAZAR

*(Standing sunk in thought, his hand begins to touch the harp.
Then he sings, his voice coming forth like that of one who is
talking in a dream.)*
The right hand of my power was strong;
Who could that right hand overcome?
Did ever I say to myself:
'I'm blest—a strong right hand I have!'
Did ever I say unto it:
'Know, right hand, thou belong'st to me!'
The cruel foe smote my forearm,
Cut off that strong right hand of mine!
Who is there now I can defeat?
Who is there cannot beat me down?
Now day and night I inly say:

'Ah, woe is me!   Where's my right hand?
I gaze upon the stump and weep:
'O right hand, who can thee forget!
    *(He gently passes his hand over the strings of the harp: a
quiet weeping is heard amongst the crowd.)*
My father had a vineyard bountiful;
My mother had a garden fair.
I used to walk therein and pluck the grapes;
I trod on leaves beneath my feet.
A wicked neighbor burnt the vineyard rare,
And ravaged all that garden fair.
The vines are withered, all the grapes destroyed,
The beauty all to ashes turned.
Could I but find one leaf beneath my feet,
I'd press it to my heart with tears.
O tell me, brethren, is there one of you
Hath still a leaf from out that garden fair?
    (The strings vibrate more sadly; the weeping grows louder.)
Of late I dreamed a fearful dream—
Who can my dream declare?
I dreamed I fell into the hands
Of my most dreaded foes.
What outrage did they do to me?
What pains did they inflict?
My hands have still their former strength;
My legs still bear me as before;
Mine eyes have still their vision clear;
My body still is whole and sound.
It was my tongue, alas! my tongue
The enemy had maimed!
I tried to speak a wingéd word,
To thought give utterance by voice—
The blood came flooding o'er my lips;
I could but mutely weep!
    A long silence. The harp falls from ELAZAR'S *hands: the
strings vibrate with a dying moan, then fade into silence. The
weeping amongst the crowd ceases as though broken off. A
tense pause.*

ELAZAR

(Speaking slowly but firmly and distinctly)
O fathers, mothers, brothers, sisters, all!
Here I await the stoning, or your words.
(Silence)
Your silence is more dreadful than a curse.

GREYBEARD

Elazar, thou shalt hear no curse from us.

YOUTH

Forgive me, brother, for my venomous speech.

ELAZAR

Ye do not curse me? Brother, I forgive
Thee every word. And yet I am accursed—
The awful curse of blood rests on me still.
Our fathers' blood, in vain for freedom shed,
Weighs down upon my head and yours as well,
And bends our foreheads to the very earth,
Down to those stones which were not lifted up
By you, my people, to be hurled at me.
The son of man inflicted his own wounds
By falling down upon the sharp-edged stones.
Despair hath made him rend his glorious robe
And strew his head with ashes of his shame!
I, too, fell down like as the Temple fell;
We all succumbed as did Jerusalem.
And just as hard as 'twould be to rebuild
The Temple so it is for us to rise
Up from the dust of slavish fear and shame.
The shame has come on us from our own hands
When we, defeated, did not lift them up
To build our life anew, but lent them to
The enemy. Dishonor's leprosy
Hath tainted all those daughters of our race
Who, rather than go down in Euphrates,
Preferred to seek the sons of wickedness
And feed upon the fruit of their disfame.

A like dishonor poisoned my own lips,
Because from hunger they would not stay closed,
But spoke and sang, too, in an alien tongue
On Babylon's broad streets, accursed by God,
Where songs of every sort are heard—save that
Which gushes from the heart, and that must die.
To suffer chains is shame unspeakable,
But to forget them is far worse disgrace.
We have two courses, death or shame, until
We find the path back to Jerusalem.
Let's seek the path back to that holy shrine
As deer seek water in the wilderness,
So that the enemy may never say:
'I have slain Israel, lo, he lies dead!'
And till we find it, let us still fight on
As wounded badger battles 'gainst the pack—
Let not this byword e'er take root and grow:
'The God of Israel sleeps in the sky!'
O Babylon, thou dost rejoice too soon!
Our harps, though on the willows, still give sound;
Tears still flow down the streams of Babylon,
And Zion's daughter still doth burn with shame;
The lion of Judah still doth roar with rage.
O Thou, the Living God, my soul yet lives!
Still Israel lives, although in Babylon!

A WATCHMAN's VOICE *(Coming from the camp)*
O Israel, to your tents!   The night comes on!

The crowd disperses, each seeking his own tent. On a distant tower, Babylonian magi, divining from the stars, can be dimly seen. The camp settles down. The uproar of the nightly orgy in Babylon grows fainter until it is scarcely heard on the breeze. The solemn night quivers over both Babylon and the captives' camp. Here and there the watchfires are kindled. Silence.

The Noblewoman

Dramatic Poem in Five Scenes

PEREBYNY, *a Cossack officer*

PEREBYNYKHA, *his wife*

OKSANA, *his daughter*

IVAN, *his son*

STEPAN, *a Cossack now in the Muscovite service*

MOTHER OF STEPAN

HANNA, *sister of* STEPAN

A COSSACK

AN ORDERLY

The action takes place in the seventeenth century

ACT I

IN UKRAINE

A garden before the house of Perebyny. The house has a spacious porch extending its entire length. There are a table and some chairs on the porch; the table is set for supper. Perebynykha is making the final preparations for the meal, while Oksana and a serving maid are helping her. Perebyny and Stepan approach the porch through the garden.

III

PEREBYNY *(To his guest)*
My wife has certainly made ready fast!
See there, she has prepared the evening meal,
While we two in the churchyard spent our time
In gossiping.

PEREBYNYKHA
(Coming a little forward on the porch to welcome her guest)
                         I pray you, noble sir,
To share with us our humble bread and salt.

STEPAN *(Bowing)*
I'd gladly do so, lady, but I fear
The older nobles might take some offence
I left their company some time ago.

PEREBYNY
Have no concern on their account. Pidny
Invited them to share this feast, while I
Begged you away from them.   "I am," I said,
"Not feeling well today and so I can't
Carouse and hold my own, while Stepan here
Because of my old friendship with his father,
I'd love to have as guest with me at home.
He's still a fledgling, and as yet not used
To play his part in banquets such as yours."
The nobles, mellowed by the fumes of wine
And vodka, were disposed to tolerance
And only said, "So be it! Let the youth
Stay at thy house—aye, even till he leaves.
What does he think we are?"

STEPAN
                         Receive my thanks
For this, my lord.
              He steps upon the porch with his host.

PEREBYNY
                    I'll tell the orderly
To transport all your baggage over here
To us and I'll hold you a prisoner,
Until the nobles free you.

STEPAN
Oh, good Lord!
I'd rather be your prisoner than free.

PEREBYNYKHA (*to* OKSANA)
Go, daughter, go and call Semen to me.
OKSANA *goes out and soon returns.*

STEPAN
I fear that I may be a nuisance here.

PEREBYNYKHA
No, not at all!   We always have a room
In our house for a guest.

PEREBYNY
My son, forget
All ceremony here. 'Twas ever thus.
Your father always took his bread and salt with us,
When we were brother Cossacks.
(*He seats* STEPAN *at the table and then sits down himself.*)
(*To* OKSANA)
Daughter, you
Shall be the first to pour out for our guest.

OKSANA *fills from a bottle two glasses, one for her father, the
other for the guest.*

OKSANA
Permit me, noble sir, to give you this.

STEPAN (*Rises, takes the glass and bows to* OKSANA)
May God grant you, young mistress, happiness
And many years!

OKSANA
And to you, sir, good health!

STEPAN *drinks and again sits down.* OKSANA *serves her father
and all begin to eat.*

PEREBYNY (*To* OKSANA)
What do you think? He did not recognize
You at the first. He asked me who she was
Who bore the standard in the foremost rank.

OKSANA (*Smiling and glancing at* STEPAN)
When was it?

PEREBYNY
Why, 'twas when on Trinity
You marched in your sodality's parade.

STEPAN
Do you the banner always bear?

OKSANA (*With an air of complacency*)
Why not?
For I'm the head of our sodality.

PEREBYNY (*Winking jovially*)
She is no longer your Oksana small,
For whom you used to weave the daisy chain.

OKSANA
I still have some of those old daisy chains. . . .
She stops suddenly with a deep blush.

STEPAN (*Joyfully*)
Is that the truth?

OKSANA (*Interrupting to change the subject which embarrasses her*)
Oh, mother, where's Ivan?

PEREBYNYKHA
Where else but on the street amongst his friends?

IVAN (*Comes out of the house*)
You're wrong, I'm here. Oh, mother, may I eat?

PEREBYNYKHA
But first of all, you ought to greet our guest.

IVAN (*Indifferently, while taking his seat*)
We have already met outside the church.

PEREBYNY
He's going to stay with us until he leaves.

IVAN (*Indifferently as before*)
Ah, so? That's good . . . Oksana, just see here,
The food's already cold. Go, get me some
That's hot.

OKSANA *(Offended by his offhand manner)*
The maid will soon be in;
Tell her yourself.

IVAN
Indeed! You're getting proud.

(To STEPAN*)*
In Moscow, I suppose, you find the girls
Are not so pert?

STEPAN
I'm not acquainted there
With any girls.

IVAN
How's that?

STEPAN
I've only been
A short time there, for while my father was
Alive, he sent me to a school in Kiev,
Most of the time to the Academy,[1]
My father dying, I to Moscow went
To help my mother there.

PEREBYNY
Why did you not
The rather bring your mother here?

STEPAN
'Twas hard.
We had naught left to live on in Ukraine.
You know it well yourselves—our whole estate
Was ravaged, plundered to the very bricks
Before the last revolt. We never were
Among the wealthy ones and then we lost
That little wealth that we had once possessed.
Before in Moscow he obtained a place,
My father had to suffer poverty;
At Pereyaslav[2] he had sworn an oath

1. The Academy of Peter Mohyla
2. The treaty of Pereyaslav between the Hetman Khmelnytsky and the Russian Tsar Alexis

To Moscow and most loyally he kept
His given word.

IVAN

Why should that oath be kept?
It was the Devil tempted them to swear.

PEREBYNY

But then, my son, there were two schools of thought
And no one knew just how things might turn out.
And after . . . one cannot betray an oath

IVAN *(Ironically)*

Of course! It's better to betray Ukraine.

STEPAN *(Flares up but restrains himself)*

My father was no traitor to Ukraine.
He served her 'neath the Tsar's hard hand no worse
Than did his enemies serve her beneath
The Polish ruthless crown.

IVAN

Of course, of course!
It makes no difference whose the boots we lick,
The Pole's or Muscovite's.

STEPAN

How many were
There then who stood up independently?

PEREBYNY *(To IVAN)*

My son, Ukraine's affairs are difficult . . .
Old Bohdan was no greater fool than I
Or even you, but yet he found that he
Could not maintain himself by his own strength.

PEREBYNY *leans over towards his son and whispers in his ear
but* IVAN *impatiently shakes his head.*

IVAN

Why beat about the bush? Let's speak the truth!
This is not private, it's a public sore.
If there were fewer in our midst of those
Who made themselves a goodly stake and fate,

Still long to kneel on Moscow's furs and stretch
Their hands out to the "treasury's money bags,"
As Muscovites are wont to say. . . .

PEREBYNY

Ivan!

Plucking at his sleeve.

STEPAN

'Twas not for "furs" nor yet for "money bags"
That my late father went to Muscovy!
Obey the alien lords in his own land
He would not; rather at the alien court
Preferred to serve his native faith, to aid,
E'en from afar, his brethren 'neath the yoke
By gaining favor for them with the Tsar.
He was too old to take up arms to fight
For Ukraine's fame and honor. . . .

IVAN

You are young—

Why did you not then take the weapon up
That fell from out your father's age-worn hand?

STEPAN

How can I make it clear to you? As child
My father taught me out of Holy Writ
And ordered me to learn by heart the place
Therefrom which tells of Cain and Abel: "Son,"
He used to say "Take heed that with an eye
Unclouded, you, not trembling as did Cain,
Can give the Heavenly Father clear reply,
When He shall ask 'Where is thy brother now?' "
With that behest, how could I in Ukraine
Lift up a weapon with the wish to strike
With it my brother-man? Can it be true
That sword and musket have a greater power
And honor than the pen and sincere words?
At least my father taught that truth to me.

PEREBYNY

We are not used to hearing things like that . . .
However . . . maybe in the world there would
Be less of sin and woe, if every one
Were of your mind. . . .

IVAN

It is those monks in Kiev
Who teach such stuff as that!

OKSANA

But you, Ivan,
Ne'er went to school in Kiev. How can you
Know anything of what they teach?

IVAN *(Sarcastically)*

Ha, ha!
Here all at once appears an advocate
For you, dear sir.

OKSANA

I simply tell the truth. . . .

*Abashed, she goes out of the porch into the garden. An
orderly comes out from the house to the porch.*

ORDERLY

My lord, I've brought the baggage of your guest.

PEREBYNY

Come then, Stepan, I'll show you where you are
To stay with us while here.

STEPAN *(To PEREBYNYKHA)*

Madame, my thanks,
For bread and salt.

PEREBYNYKHA *(Glancing sideways at her son)*

Forgive us, if perhaps
At first your welcome lacked in heartiness.

STEPAN *and* PEREBYNY *with the orderly go into the house.*

PEREBYNYKHA *(Quickly, to* IVAN*)*

You lout! Is that the way to treat a guest?

IVAN

Who cares? Let him at least once hear the truth.

PEREBYNYKHA

But you, indeed, heard what he said?

IVAN

What then?
A monkish student knows how to deceive.

PEREBYNYKHA

I like his looks. . . . A well-trained courteous youth
He seems to be. . . .

IVAN

Of course, it is not hard
To please some people with a well-oiled tongue.

PEREBYNYKHA

At any rate, another time don't dare
To treat a guest so harshly. It would seem
As though he'd been invited here for you
To pick a quarrel with. Unmannerly!

IVAN

All right! I will not pick on him again.
He goes off the porch.

PEREBYNYKHA

Where are you off to now?

IVAN

To join my friends.
*He goes through the garden, jumps over the fence and dis-
appears. The serving maid enters to clear off the table.*

PEREBYNYKHA

Oksana! Where are you?

OKSANA *(Appears with a watering can in her hand)*
Here, mother, here.
I'm watering the flowerbeds.

PEREBYNYKHA

In truth,

They need it too; they're dried up by the sun,
And water those transplanted ones as well.

> PEREBYNYKHA *and the maid finish clearing the table and go into the house.* OKSANA *sings while watering the flowers. The dusk thickens in the garden.* STEPAN *quietly climbs out of his window over the porch, drops upon it and then swiftly and gaily lowers himself to the ground and approaches* OKSANA.

OKSANA
(Breaks off her song in fright and drops her watering can)

Oh, woe! Who's there?

STEPAN
My lady, it is I.
Forgive me. Bear me no ill will for this,
For you have cast a spell o'er me and drawn
Me hither like a nightingale with song.
A greater power than mine compelled me has . . .

OKSANA *(Bashfully but proudly)*
Why say such things to me, O noble sir?
To listen to them doth not me beseem. *(Starts to go)*

STEPAN *(Takes her hand to detain her)*
No, no, you must not go . . .

OKSANA *(Offended, snatches her hand away)*
What manners these?
I am no peasant from your fatherland.

STEPAN *(Devastated)*
I had no thought of giving you offence,
For truly you are free. Is it no grief
To you that I with broken heart depart
For foreign parts, that one sweet memory
Of meeting you should leave a bitter taste?
I'm naught to you, O maiden proud and fair . . .
Yes, what am I? . . . A sort of vagabond . . .
At least that's what they call me everywhere . . .
To-morrow you'll not give a thought to me . . .

OKSANA *(Dropping her eyes)*

You leave to-morrow then?

STEPAN

Why should I stay
And be a cause of friction here to all?

OKSANA

'Twould seem as though 'twas I drive you away . . .
But yet I have not said a word to you. . . .

STEPAN

Maybe I still have that word to expect,
To hear you say: "Be on your way! Depart!"

OKSANA

*(Dismayed, plucks a leaf from a cherry tree, looks at it, and
rolls it in her hand)*

How queer and strange you are! Well, what ought I
To say to you? . . . I am not used to this. . . .
There are some youths whom I have known for years
And yet I've never heard from them the like. . . .
While you . . . you have but just arrived. . . .

STEPAN

Lady!

Those gentlemen without a care can roam
Around this garden in full liberty
And for their delectation choose a flower
And wait until it comes to fullest bloom.
But I am like a captive who escapes
From prison for a time and shortly must
Farewell say to this happy world, and so
He cannot wait until the blossom bloom.
The flower for me would not be mere delight.
I see in it the image of free life,
The beauty of my native land. For me
The corner whence I fain the flower would pluck
Would seem the world entire. True, I forgot
That you in freedom live, and that for you

There is no charm, nor can there ever be
In that place yonder, where I go to dwell.

OKSANA *(With her head bowed and almost whispering)*
Why are you in advance so sure of it?
You seem to think that I am naught else but
A flowering plant, that in me dwells no soul,
No beating heart. . . .

Her voice becomes slightly tearful. She breaks off.

STEPAN *(Again takes her hand, and this time she does not resist)*
                    Oksana, my bright star!
Forgive . . . I did not know . . . I hardly dare . . .
          (With a sudden impulse)

Nay, nay! I cannot, I have not the strength
To give you up!
          (He embraces OKSANA.)

          O, my dear heart, tell me:
Do you love me?   O, speak the blessed word!

OKSANA
Should I be otherwise now standing here?

She buries her face in his breast—silent action

STEPAN
To-morrow I shall suitors send for you;
Your father will receive them?

                    OKSANA
                    Father likes
You very much and mother does as well.

                    STEPAN
What can I give you in an alien land
To make up for the loss of your own home?
My faithful love and nothing else besides . . .

                    OKSANA
Oh, do not think that I'm a frivolous girl
With nothing in her head but gaiety

And social forms.   These times in which we live
Have taught e'en maids to think on serious things.
If you knew how the bloodshed weighs me down!

STEPAN

The bloodshed?

OKSANA
Yes, returning from campaigns,
Our knights amuse themselves with us in dance.
The soldier puts his hand out to embrace
Me in the dance, and then to me it seems
As though that hand was covered red with blood,
With brother's blood . . . Diversions such as those
Do not rejoice my heart . . . Never, perhaps,
Would I accept a ring from any knight
With hands like that . . . *(She looks at his hand.)*
That hand of yours, I see,
Is free from blood.

STEPAN
And yet not all esteem
It as an honor.

OKSANA
I at once felt drawn
To you because of your humanity.
Tell me, is all your family like you?

STEPAN
Our family's small; my mother and my sister,
And a young brother.   Yes, all those I have
Are kind and mild.

OKSANA
Mayhap your mother will
Not love a bride who comes to her unknown?
What could I then do in an alien land,
So far from all my own?

STEPAN
Oksana mine,
Be not afraid.   My mother will rejoice
That I bring back a wife from dear Ukraine,—

My father, on his deathbed, wished that I
Somewhere in my own native land might wed.
My mother will recall you as a child.

     (He embraces her again.)

And who is there who would not love my bride,
My dearest, sweet Oksana, my beloved?
'Tis but in songs that mothers-in-law are bad,
And you'll see how my mother will treat you
As though you were her own.

OKSANA
     So may God grant!

STEPAN

To me it seems that nowhere now is there
In all the wide, wide world, an alien land,
As long as we two are together. So
You'll see how we will weave a little nest,
E'en though in Muscovy. There'll nothing be
Of foreign taste in our small dwelling, eh?

OKSANA

Of course there won't. But yet I am afraid
Of living in that foreign land.

STEPAN
     With me?

OKSANA *(Smiling)*

For sure, I'll be with you. However, still
It's not so much a foreign land, is it?
Religious rites are there the same, and I
Already understand somewhat their speech.

STEPAN

It won't take long to learn the language there . . .
It's just a little difficult. But you,
Oksana dear, have such a fine, wise head,
You can learn anything.

OKSANA
     Don't boast too much,

Or you may rue it soon!

(*Somewhat gloomily*)   Yet still I fear . . .

STEPAN

What, my beloved?

OKSANA

Somehow our happiness
Has come so suddenly . . . I never knew
The like before . . . All those among my friends
Who were betrothed, experienced a lot
Of griefs and troubles ere the wedding came,
While I . . .

STEPAN

Now wait a bit; to-morrow, it
May be, your father will show me the door.

OKSANA

No, no, he'll not do that, I know full well.

STEPAN (*Jokingly*)

'Twould seem my lady is not pleased with this?
Suppose she turned me down, at least, just once?

OKSANA

Enough of this! How can you jest?

STEPAN

So then,
I cannot please you with my words. All right,
I will not speak at all, if that's the case!

*Without speaking, he embraces and fondles her. She resists
at first and then submits to his caresses.*

PEREBYNYKHA (*From the house*)

Oksana! That's enough of watering!
It's late!

OKSANA (*Breaking away*)

My mother calls!

She starts to run away.

STEPAN (*Restrains her passionately*)
                    A moment, stay!
A little moment, stay! . . .

                    OKSANA
                    I'll come to you
As soon as mother goes to bed.

                    STEPAN
                              Come, come,
My love again!   I'll wait for you till dawn!

                    PEREBYNYKHA
Oksana, where are you?

                    OKSANA
                    I'm coming, mother.

Once more she gives Stepan a parting embrace and runs into the house.

ACT II

IN MOSCOW

A parlor in STEPAN'S *house, adorned for a holy day. Outside can be heard the sound of bells.* STEPAN'S *mother and* OKSANA *enter, dressed in Ukrainian costumes; the mother wearing a headdress and a dark dress with a broad, falling collar;* OKSANA *in a Ukrainian headdress with a bodice and tunic.*

MOTHER (*Sits down on the divan, breathing heavily*)
I'll rest a little, till I can mount the stairs . . .
I'm old . . . my legs won't stand it . . .

            OKSANA (*Sits down beside her*)
                              Mother, why
Do you not have them bring your bed down here?
It's much too hard for you to climb the stairs.

MOTHER

Oh, no, my dear, let it stay where it is
Upstairs. . . . 'Tis not the custom in Moscow
That women dwell upon the lower floor.
They'll say: she's old, she doesn't know what's right.

OKSANA

But you were not born to their customs here.

MOTHER

Ah, dear Oksana, people here don't ask
Where you grew up . . . We are outsiders here.
You live with wolves—like wolves you learn to howl.

OKSANA *(Laughingly)*

And does that mean that I must learn to howl?

MOTHER

Well, what do you think, pray? . . . To-day in church
You heard the whisperings all around us there:
'Circassians, eh? . . .' 'No, Khokhols' . . .[1]

OKSANA *(Somewhat saddened)*

Yes, I heard . . .

They have no reverence. . . . In God's own church,
Instead of praying, they all buzz and talk,
Yet boast themselves of being Orthodox
Much more than we. . . .

MOTHER

So goes it in the world:

Each land, its customs; every town, its ways,
That's what the people say. To them our dress
Seems very strange. Here all the women wear
A veil while we go with our faces bare.

OKSANA

We are no Turks, are we?

MOTHER

May God forbid!

And neither are the Moscow women Turks,

---

1. A Muscovite term of derogation for Ukrainians.

But yet somehow they've introduced the style.
But as a noble dame of Muscovy
You ought to dress like them, they think.

OKSANA

                                But you?

You are the mother of a nobleman.

MOTHER

A mother's not a wife.   The people see
That I'm already on my way to God.
So why should I change my ancestral garb?
            (*With a mild but melancholy smile*)
It's not worth while for me to buy new things.
Indeed, my husband—may he rest in peace!
Wore to the end his favorite Cossack blouse
And when we laid him out, he had it on
With his embroidered shirt.

        She wipes a tear from her eye. OKSANA, *greatly moved,
gazes at her . . . A brief silence.*

OKSANA

                    But why then, now,
Does Stepan wear that nobleman's costume?
Oh, when he stood with me beneath the crown,
Dressed in a crimson Cossack vest, ah me!
That was . . . (*Blushing furiously, she stops*)

MOTHER

                    Maybe he put it on to please
Some one (*Wags her head goodnaturedly*)
(*More severely*)   However, daughter, he
Dare not the Tsar's prescribed costume neglect.

OKSANA

His father, though . . .

MOTHER

                    My husband, daughter, was
Quite old and feeble, when the Tsar made him
A noble. After that, he was too ill

To leave the house and go in company.
But Stepan goes to all the Tsar's levees,
Because he must.

OKSANA

And would it be a shame
For him, if he went dressed in Cossack style?

MOTHER

Not shame alone ... My daughter, you are strange—
Your husband is a Tsarist nobleman
And not a Cossack! Don't you comprehend?

OKSANA *(Sadly)*

Why should I not?

MOTHER

My dear, and so you see
Why I dress Hanna in the Moscow style,
For she's betrothed unto a native here,
And nevermore to Ukraine will return.

OKSANA

Why did not Stepan bring her with him, when
He was with us?

MOTHER

For maids to travel thus
Would seem a monstrous thing. The folk would say:
"She's gone off on a trip to catch a groom."
Let her stay here and wear the pantaloons,
Since she will marry here.

OKSANA

Those "pantaloons"
The girls must wear are bad enough but those
The women wear are worse, so bulging, full,
And so, so long, as long as priestly robes!
It makes me sad, when I must put them on,
And then the snood with hanging veil which goes
Upon the head! Why should one veil the face?

MOTHER

It must be done.

OKSANA *(After a moment, hesitantly)*
Dear mother, I'm afraid . . .

MOTHER
What do you fear, my daughter?   Tell me, what?

OKSANA
It's hard to say . . .

MOTHER
Come, don't be timid, child.
I take the place of your own mother here.

OKSANA *(Kisses the mother's hand)*
Yes, mother dear . . . Oh, well . . . I sometimes think
Maybe, sometimes, I might repellent be
To Stepan in such clothes. . . .

MOTHER *(Laughing)*
What an idea!
I ask you whether Stepan ever you
Repelled, when he was not in Cossack dress?

OKSANA
But I . . .

MOTHER
Do not imagine things, my dear.
Is Stepan such a child, so that he would
Not know you well, no matter what you wore?

OKSANA
There's knowing and . . .

MOTHER *(Looking out of the window)*
Look out the window, child,
Your eyes are younger; see who's coming here!

OKSANA
Maybe it's Stepan?

MOTHER
Yes, indeed, 'tis he.
And with him are two men.

MOTHER
Let's run, my child.
She rises and starts for the door.

OKSANA
What's this? For heaven' sakes, we have to flee
As if from Tartars?

MOTHER
This is no time to laugh!
'Tis not the custom here for womenfolk
To stay around when gentlemen converse.
*She opens the door and hastens up the stairs to the women's
quarters.*

OKSANA *(Following her)*
O Lord, what customs, customs have they here!
And now this one!

*The scene swiftly changes. The top floor, where the women's
quarters are in the homes of the Muscovite nobility. Beside the
mother and* OKSANA, *there is present also* HANNA, STEPAN'S *sister,
a young girl.* HANNA *is dressed as a Muscovite noblewoman.*

MOTHER *(Goes to a large wardrobe)*
Now here, my daughter, is
Your noblewoman's dress. I had it made.

OKSANA *(Politely, but without any pleasure)*
I thank you, mother.

MOTHER
Would you like to try
It on at once?

OKSANA
A little later, please.
I'm somewhat tired now. Besides, to-day,
I'm going nowhere, so I'll still have time
To change into it later.

MOTHER
As you will.
Go, rest a while. And I will do the same.
It's fitting on a holy day. *(She goes into an adjoining room.)*

HANNA

(Who up till now has been sitting quietly, cracking and eating pumpkin seeds)
What earthly use are all these holy days?

OKSANA

Why, what a question!   Your God gave them to us.

HANNA

Well, what a bore they are!

OKSANA

Why sit up here?
Alone?   Go out, enjoy some company!

HANNA

Where should I go?   And where find company?

OKSANA

But have you no companions of your age?

HANNA

Companions? . . . Well, I know a few among
The noble girls.   But how to visit them?
Our mother is not strong, she does not care
To go with me . . . And you as yet have not
Become acquainted here.   With Mama it's
A . . . Well, she's such . . .

OKSANA

Why can't you go alone?
You are no more a child.   Go by yourself.
You'll surely be more cheerful with young folks.

HANNA

In Moscow, one does not go out alone.

OKSANA

It's dangerous?

HANNA

It's not the custom here.

OKSANA

Well, they are all strange customs that you have!

HANNA

And then, what could those nobles' daughters say?
They all sit in their gardens just as I,
And never see the world. What pleasure there?

OKSANA

Why should you sit here bored? Go in a group
Somewhere out in the fields, walk in the woods,
Besides a stream and sing. At home I did
Not sit indoors to spend a holy day.

HANNA

At home, maybe! But here in Muscovy,
They never heard of anything like that—
Go singing in the woods!

OKSANA

So you don't know
How in Ukraine companions sport and play?

HANNA

I can recall but little of Ukraine,
And Vanya was born here in Muscovy.

OKSANA

Why Vanya, not Ivas?

HANNA

He's called that here,
So we use it as well. He likes it too.
There's only Mother and Stepan who still
Call me Hannusya.

OKSANA

What is then the name
The others call you?

HANNA

Annushka.

OKSANA

Indeed!
(*Laughingly tries it*)

It's Hannushka.

HANNA *(Correcting her)*
Oksana, no. Annushka.

OKSANA
I can't pronounce it right but yet it's naught
To one who speaks the Moscow language well.
How does my name, Oksana, go with them?

HANNA
Aksinya, or Aksyusha.

OKSANA
Ugly sound.
I like Oksana better. Hannusya,
You must call me Oksana all the time.

HANNA *(Nestles close to* OKSANA*)*
I'll call you what you wish. O sister, dear,
I love you, Oh so much. How glad I was,
When brother brought you hither from Ukraine!

OKSANA
You don't know me as yet, Hannusya dear.
Perhaps I'll turn out bad . . .

HANNA
No, no, you're kind!
You always say to me, "Enjoy yourself,
Come, have some fun, don't sit!" You ought to hear
How all the other noble dames keep down
Their daughters and young sisters. O good Lord!
They never let them poke their noses out.
(She nestles closer to OKSANA.*)*
Oksana . . . dearest one . . . There's something I
Should like to ask of you.

OKSANA
What is it, dear?
(Hanna is afraid to speak.)
Is there a dress of mine you'd like to have?
Choose what you like the best. A necklace too
I'll give you and I'll plait your hair in tails
And make you look just like a Hetman's bride.

HANNA (*Gloomily*)

No, mother would be sure to make a fuss.
It is not clothes . . . I wanted just to ask
If you . . . go to the garden, to call me.

OKSANA

Is that all? Why, that's nothing much to ask?
Come on, we'll go!

HANNA

No, not just now; let's wait.

OKSANA

Whene'er you like. What's in the garden, then?

HANNA

You see . . . I cannot in the garden sit
All by myself . . .

OKSANA

And what's to hinder you?

HANNA

If I with mother go—she'll talk and talk
To every one why I go there to sit.

OKSANA (*Laughing*)

You go there to divine, you crafty girl!

HANNA

No, I do not. . . . I simply go to wait
And see if maybe down the street will come
The royal guards. Towards evening they parade.

OKSANA

Perhaps one of the guards has shot a shaft
And struck your maiden heart?

HANNA

Oksana, I

Already am betrothed.

OKSANA

A royal guard?

HANNA

Why, yes.

OKSANA

Then why does he not visit us?

HANNA

E'en if he came, you think that I could see him?
I'd be upstairs, while he was down below.

OKSANA

And you don't see each other?

HANNA

How can we?

OKSANA

In public company?   By stealth, perhaps?

HANNA

What do you mean by stealth?

OKSANA

But don't you mean
You go to meet him in the garden?

HANNA

What!
No, no, I'm not already lost to shame!
How could you ever for a moment think
That I would ask you to accompany
Me to a secret tryst?   Oksana, nay,
You do not think that I could be so vile?

OKSANA

God bless us all!   What is there vile about
A maiden who in conversation stands
A while with her betrothed?   Where is the shame?

HANNA

It is so here.

OKSANA

Why then will you go out
Into the garden?

HANNA

So that I can see
Him from afar, as he rides down the street,
For otherwise I should not see him till
We meet in church.

OKSANA

Where did you talk with him?

HANNA

I never have.

OKSANA

Then how did he woo you?

HANNA

Through the matchmakers, just as all the rest.

OKSANA

I do not comprehend.

HANNA

You do not know
The customs here. Ask mother, she can tell
You all about them. I don't know the mass
Of all these fine details.

OKSANA

So it would seem
That you, without a single word exchanged,
Will marry him?

HANNA

With utmost dignity.

OKSANA

What strange young folk! *(She smiles at an unspoken thought;
a moment's silence, and then in a dreamy tone)*
At home, I used to go
And meet with Stepan every eve at dusk.

HANNA

When you had been betrothed?

OKSANA

Betrothed, of course . . .

But oft I talked with him, still unbetrothed,
For else, how could a maid be wooed?

HANNA *(Covering her face in horror)*

Oh, dreadful! Shame! (OKSANA *slumps her shoulders in silence.*)

Your mother did not know,

Still does not know, about your secret trysts?

OKSANA

Why should she know?

HANNA
So that she might forgive

And not curse you!

OKSANA
Curse me for what, Hanna?

Both she and father were once young themselves;
They know what young love is.

HANNA
Oksana, Oh!

How can you say such things?

OKSANA *(Laughing)*
You foolish dear!

STEPAN *(Entering hastily)*

Oksana dear, go change your dress at once
For Muscovite costume. A noble's come.

OKSANA

But mother said that women must not stay
Around, when men are here.

STEPAN
See here, my love,

You merely have to do the honors now
And then return to your own room.

OKSANA
Ah, so!

Then how shall I the honors pay, Stepan,
In our own manner or some other way?

STEPAN

You bring the cups of mead in on a tray—
Our mother will arrange the tray for you—
You bow, present, the nobleman will kiss
You on the lips . . .

OKSANA

Stepan, what's that you say?
The nobleman will kiss me on the lips!
Whoever dreamed the like?

STEPAN

Now, now, dear heart,
It's just a form with nothing evil meant—
A custom merely!

OKSANA

One more custom harsh!
Well, let them keep their own!   I will not come!

STEPAN *(Gloomily)*

Just as you will, but you'll destroy us all.

OKSANA

You just imagine it!

STEPAN

But you don't know
How vengeful these folk are.   This nobleman
Will be insulted, if you do not come,
And he's the brooding sort, has influence,—
His son, though young, is privy counselor.
He'll slander me before the Tsar himself
And then for us 'twould be "the word and deed"[1]

OKSANA

You're joking, are you not?

STEPAN *(Still more gloomily)*

What do you think?

OKSANA *(Horrified)*

Oh, Stepan, what's this life we have to face?
It seems to me like pagan slavery!

1. The Muscovite formula for treason.

STEPAN

I never said that you'd find freedom here,
But if in Moscow we don't crook our spine,
Then in Ukraine, maybe, the Moscow governor
Will loose a triple hell upon the backs
Of our whole family. You almost faint
With horror just because some aged fool
Is going to touch your lips, while I must stand
And let myself be called, "Stepan, good thrall!"
And kiss his hand as if I were a slave—
Is that mere nothing?

OKSANA
                    Oh, my God, Stepan!
Who'd say that it's "mere nothing?"

STEPAN
                              So you see . . .
Why do I dally here? The aged fool
Awaits me there. Oksana, what say you?
You'll come?

OKSANA
I know not . . .

MOTHER *(Coming out of her room)*
                    Go, my darling, go.
My daughter, please! For my sake, I beseech you.
Don't let me in my old age see the fate
That else will Stepan overwhelm!

HANNA
                    Sister,
If you but knew what a ferocious man
That noble is! I beg, beseech you, dear!
My sister, do not let us be destroyed!

          Weeping, she rushes to OKSANA.

     OKSANA *(Coldly and with an extraordinary outer calm)*
I'll go. Give me that Muscovite costume.

(HANNA *rushes to the wardrobe.*)
And you, my mother, can prepare the mead.
Go, Stepan, down and entertain our guest.

Stepan with bowed head, goes out. OKSANA, *deathly pale,
takes off her Ukrainian headdress.*

ACT III

THE MESSENGER

A small out-of-the-way room on the top floor of Stepan's home

STEPAN (*Bringing in a Cossack visitor*)
We'd best talk here in privacy, my friend.
Downstairs, you know . . . Well, here it's much more safe.

(*He looks up and down the passage outside, then closes and
locks the door and shuts the window. Then he takes a seat away
from the door. The conversation is carried on in low tones.*)

They're doing dreadful things down there, you say?

COSSACK
Such acts of violence you never heard.
No leeway do these Muscovitish fiends
Grant us at all. But all the time they poke
Us in the eye with that sworn oath. . . .

STEPAN
                                        Indeed,
You know, an oath is such a weighty thing.

COSSACK (*In a louder tone*)
Then why do they forget God's judgment, too?

STEPAN
Speak lower, friend; some one may overhear
Our words, if they're too loud.

Cossack

True, I forgot.

(More softly) We do not want to break our plighted word,
But let the Tsar give us protection from
These vicious rooks.

Stepan

It is a difficult
Affair. He must have some one there to keep
A watch, yet all those governors of his
Are all alike; not one is good. Of course,
When they depart, men like them will be sent.

Cossack

The Tsar should send us some Ukrainian.
In Moscow there are men—why, even you—
Who for long years have served him loyally
And who our native customs would respect.

Stepan

That won't be done.

Cossack

Why not?

Stepan

They don't trust us.

Cossack

And yet you are in highest favor here.

Stepan

Apparently, but they will not for long
Let us get out of sight. They might send us
For a short time upon a special mission
With Muscovite escort, but not alone . . .
And as for naming one a governor,
That ne'er will come to pass.

Cossack

Then wonder not,
If we rebel and Doroshenko join!

Stepan *makes a move to clap his hand over the speaker's mouth.*

STEPAN

For God's sake, brother, take heed what you say!

COSSACK (*Mastering his impulsiveness*)
Sometimes a word escapes from smothered wrath.
The worst, my friend, that vexes me is that
They won't believe our word. My relative,
Chornenko, you know him?

(STEPAN *nods his head*) Was thrashed so hard
He barely got away from them alive!

STEPAN

Chornenko? He, I think, was one who was
Most loyal to the Tsar.

COSSACK

He was, indeed!
But some one basely slandered him before
The governor that he to Chyhyryn[1]
Had sent a letter. What a blast that was!
His wife in tears cast herself at the feet
Of the cruel governor. . . .

STEPAN (*With a bitter smile*)
They say, my friend,
"Moscow believes no tears."

COSSACK

The solemn truth!
However, there were certain to give aid. . . .

STEPAN

Who?

COSSACK

Not "who," but what: cold cash!

STEPAN

Was that it?

Silence

COSSACK

That's what it was that strongly pulled the string
1. The capital of the Cossacks under Doroshenko.

To favor us . . . However, there are those
Who show no fear; by desperation moved
They will rebel, for they will stand no more.

    (*Moving very close to* STEPAN, *he continues in a whisper,*)
Our maidens—some of them were members of
The same sodality of which your wife
Was head—have sewn a standard which they sent
To Chyhyryn. . . . of course by secret ways . . .
Ivan, your brother-in-law, took it himself . . .
'Tis not known yet. But if they find it out,
I dread to think of what will happen there.

        (*He moves away and talks a little louder.*)
So now you see, how daring our folk are. . . .

    (STEPAN, *sunk in troubled meditation, twists his belt in silence.*
The COSSACK *rises.*)
So then, good friend, you think there's little hope
Of getting any mercy from the Tsar?

       STEPAN (*Starting out of his revery, also rises.*)
Oh, no, why not? I'll try it. Later on
I'll see the Tsar at his select soiree.
If he is in his cups, perhaps I may
Be able to amuse him, for he likes
To hear 'Circassian' songs and anecdotes,
All sorts of clownish chatter, and he may
Also command to have the Tropak[1] danced.

          COSSACK
You have to play the court comedian?

          STEPAN
You know the old-time saying: "Needs must when
The devil drives." . . . But I'm prepared, my friend,
To go so far as e'en to risk my head,
If that would anything obtain for you
And for Ukraine. So give me that request
Which you've drawn up to supplicate the Tsar—
If I can strike a timely chance, I'll give
It into his own hands.

1. A Ukrainian dance.

COSSACK (*Draws out of his bosom a document rolled in a cloth
with seals upon it.*)
Here, my true friend,
May God assist you! If this document
Has no effect, there will not fail to be
A shedding of your brothers' blood.

STEPAN

Good God!

May heaven forfend!

COSSACK
Farewell, I'm going now.

STEPAN

May God protect you on your homeward way.
They salute each other and the COSSACK *goes out.*

OKSANA (*Enters hastily with great steps from another door.*)
Oh, Stepan, I have sought you everywhere!

STEPAN

Why, what's the matter?

OKSANA
We've just got to talk.
Yaknenko brought a letter from a friend
In my sodality.

STEPAN *(Hurriedly)*
Where is the letter?

Burn it at once!

OKSANA
Why, why, for heaven's sake?
Why burn it up at once? She's begging me
To send her money, all that I can spare;
She has some urgent need that must be met.

STEPAN

Don't send it! God forbid! Don't dream of it!

OKSANA

But what is wrong with you? I never thought
You could be miserly. If that's the case,
I'll draw from my own dowry and send that.

STEPAN

It's not the money that I grudge, my dear.

OKSANA

Then why not let me send it?

STEPAN

Dangerous!
(He bends down close to her and whispers,)
They want it now for help to Doroshenko.

OKSANA *(She is silent for a moment from astonishment and
then smiles mysteriously.)*
Well then, there's greater need.

STEPAN

Bethink yourself!
You've always been afraid of shedding blood,
But this will mean a fratricidal war
That Doroshenko's brewing in Ukraine—
He's even won the Tartars to his aid
And pays them with the Christians they enslave.

OKSANA *(Sits down, shocked and unnerved, on the bench
and leans against the table.)*
Woe everywhere, no matter where one turns . . .
The Tartars there . . . and Tartars here. . . .

STEPAN

My dear,
What are you dreaming of? What Tartars here?

OKSANA

Why not? Don't I, like Tartar women, sit
Here in captivity? Don't you, too, when
You grovel at the feet of your own lord
As if a Khan? The whips, the stakes are here . . .
They sell and purchase slaves. . . . They're Tartars here!

STEPAN

But here's the Christian faith.

OKSANA
And what a faith!
I go to church and . . . O forgive us, Lord!
But in their Mass what do I understand?
A gibberish of this and that . . . who knows?

STEPAN
Oksana, this is sinful talk!

OKSANA
My husband,
I'm sick to death of this drear Muscovy.

She lets her head fall on the table.

STEPAN *(Standing gloomily over her)*
I knew it, wife . . . Did I not say to you
That I could give you nothing in a land
So alien from ours?

OKSANA *(Starts up and clasps him in her arms.)*
O my beloved.
'Tis I who am unkind! As though I did
Not know that you, my love, are suffering
Far worse than all of us. We ought the more
To pity you! *(She presses him to her bosom.)*
My love, tell me, how much
More shall we have to suffer in this way?

STEPAN *(Sighing)*
God only knows, dear heart.

OKSANA
Then we are doomed
To perish in the bondage?

STEPAN
Hope in God.
Perhaps, somehow, these bitter times will change.
If things should quiet down, the peace be less
Disturbed in Ukraine, I might ask the Tsar
To give me leave to make a visit there.

OKSANA

'Tis now impossible?

STEPAN

It is, my dear.
I can't e'en dream of it. You see, just now
I have a supplication to present
Unto the Tsar from persons in Ukraine—
They make complaints of arbitrary acts . . .
I must support their suit; and so for me
It's not the time to beg to leave Moscow.
They'd say: "He sings a pretty song, so he
Can fly out of the cage." Oksana, we
Have got to be most circumspect just now.
"Don't sneeze, while sifting flour," says the proverb.
If we should fail in this—which God forbid!—
We're lost, ourselves, our country's cause as well.

OKSANA

How can we be more circumspect than now?
We live as though we're treading on hot bricks!

STEPAN

Well, for example; there's that money for
Your friend at home . . .

OKSANA *(Dropping her eyes)*
I will not send it now.
She must excuse me, if it can't be done . . .
I'll write and tell her . . .

STEPAN
Better still, don't write
At all, dear heart.

OKSANA
Not write to her at all?
Why, it's but common courtesy!

STEPAN
If they
Should seize the letter—it occurs sometimes—
They would not hesitate to torture you,

When they discover Doroshenko's plot,
And you'd confess that you contributed
To your sodality. . . .

OKSANA
I'll send her word
By Yaknenko.

STEPAN
My dear, I beg of you
Not to receive him in our house at all.

OKSANA
But I've invited him to call on me!
I can't drive him away!

STEPAN
Then send a maid
To tell him you're unwell.

OKSANA
'Twould be a lie!

STEPAN
All right. But when they put you on the rack,
Do not complain.

OKSANA
What mean you: "on the rack"?

STEPAN
What do you think? To watch Yaknenko's moves,
There'll be a swarm of Muscovitish spies.
I know them well.

OKSANA (Sorely troubled)
So then I may not send
No letters and no gifts to friends at home?

STEPAN
You see, my love, that meanwhile it is best
Not to reply; and most, not to Ivan,
For he's involved in perilous affairs . . .

OKSANA
Not even to my brother send a line?
Her eyes fill with tears.

STEPAN

'Tis not forever, sweetheart, but until
Conditions there improve. . . . *(He embraces her again.)*

OKSANA *(Without responding to his caresses, dully)*
Oh, very well,
Then I won't write to any one.

STEPAN

Dear heart,
You're angry with me!

OKSANA *(In the same tone as before)*
No, why should I be?
You're right, of course. What use is there to write?
STEPAN *drops her hands.* OKSANA *walks slowly out of the room.*

ACT IV

IN THE WOMEN'S QUARTERS

Oksana is embroidering on a frame; her hands are sluggish and languid.

STEPAN *(Enters and sits down on a stool beside Oksana.)*
O Lord, how my head aches! . . .

OKSANA *(Without raising her eyes from her work)*
You got up late.

STEPAN

'Twas dawn, before the Tsar's soiree broke up.

OKSANA

Was it enjoyable?

STEPAN

The devil, no!
They're all afraid to speak an honest word. . . .
They drink and drink, until they're drunk, that's all. . . .

OKSANA

Did you succeed with that request, Stepan?

STEPAN

Not much, I fear . . . The Tsar said, "We will read
And ponder this" . . . We've heard that oft before.

OKSANA

What now will happen?

STEPAN (*Irritably*)
I don't know! Don't ask!

Silence. OKSANA *embroiders a few more stitches. Then she
lets the needle fall from her hand.*

STEPAN

Oksana, couldn't you just talk a bit?
I feel so gloomy, and my head's stuffed full
Of misery.

OKSANA (*Languidly*)
What can I talk about?
I neither see nor hear of things outside . . .
I just sit here. . . .

STEPAN (*A little more irritated*)
Don't you make anything?

OKSANA

Oh, yesterday, I stitched a crimson flower;
To-day a blue one . . . Does that interest you?

STEPAN

'Twould seem as though you're greatly vexed with me?

OKSANA (*Through her tears*)
No, no, Stepan, far from it! I'm not vexed.

STEPAN (*Examines the embroidery, then gently*)
And what's the pattern going to be, dear?

OKSANA (*Dully*)
I do not know. Something Hanna began.

STEPAN

Perhaps it's for her trousseau. 'Twill be soon
Her wedding day.

OKSANA

A month away, I think.

STEPAN

Well, at her wedding you must sing and dance,
Divert yourself.

OKSANA

Diversions such as these!
You bow and pay the honors, while behind
Your back the guests in whispers criticize:
"Circassian, eh?" "How queer she is!"

STEPAN

You pay
Too much regard to them.

OKSANA *(Indifferently)*

No, I don't care!

STEPAN

You seem to be fatigued and overwrought
To-day. You do too much about the house?

OKSANA

No, not a bit,—for mother sees to all.
Hanna and I, we simply sew.

STEPAN

Maybe,
You shouldn't sew so much?

OKSANA

What else to do?
I don't like sitting, nibbling pumpkin seeds,
As Hanna does. You need to occupy
Your hands and eyes somehow. . . .

STEPAN

My poor, dear wife!
(OKSANA *bursts into a flood of tears.*)

Oksana, what's the matter? Why these tears?
Has some one slighted you? My mother? Hanna?

OKSANA *(Controlling herself somewhat)*
No, they are kind . . . I've no complaint of them. . . .

STEPAN
Then what?

OKSANA *(Stops weeping for a moment, then despairingly)*
O Stepan, Stepan, can't you see?
I'm pining, grieving, I can't live like this!

She sinks down helplessly over her embroidery frame.

STEPAN
Too true, no flowers can in dungeons grow . . .
And I had thought . . . *(He walks around the room, pondering
gloomily and then stops in front of* OKSANA.*)*
Oksana, calm yourself.
Let's talk the matter through.

OKSANA
How so, Stepan?

STEPAN
It seems quite clear I'm ruining your life.

OKSANA
No, I . . .

STEPAN
It makes no difference. I will
No more embitter this sad fate of yours.
How hard for me it may be,—I'm prepared
To let you go back to your father.

OKSANA
How?
And what of you?

STEPAN
I'll stay on here. For me
There's no returning—that you know.

OKSANA *(Passionately)*
You mean that I should leave, abandon you?
Was it for that I stood beneath the crown
And gave my plighted word?

STEPAN
                                    Oksana, I'm
No Tartar Khan to keep a person chained
Down by an oath. You have your liberty.
I only am the slave.

OKSANA *(Shaking her head)*
No, Stepan, no.

STEPAN
Why not? I give you back your plighted word.
        (His voice breaks with emotion.)

And I beseech you . . . will you not forgive
Me for persuading you to leave your home . . .
For bringing you . . .

OKSANA *(Embracing him)*
                        Enough, don't say such things!
Do you not know? Before you said a word
To me, a single word, down there at home,
I was already yours with all my soul.
Can you not see that now, if I depart,
Go hence from you, my soul would still remain
And grieve?

STEPAN
        But what else can be done, my love?

OKSANA
Let's flee, the two of us! My father can
Assist you, till you have the means to live.
What do we care for all that Moscow gives?
Let's flee back to Ukraine!

STEPAN
                        The Tsar's long arm
Can reach his nobles all throughout Ukraine,

And vengeance wreak upon your family.
We're safe nowhere . . .

STEPAN

Let's flee to Poland, then,
Or to Wallachia!

STEPAN

What do you mean?
Exchange one exile for a different one,
Like vagabonds move on from place to place
In foreign lands . . . 'Twould be the same as here.

OKSANA

There'd be more freedom there.

STEPAN

I'd have to earn
Somehow the stranger's grace to stay with them;
And that would mean: by treason to Moscow.

OKSANA

You should do it!

STEPAN

An oath, Oksana, is
A serious thing. The Tsar will not give back
The plighted word to me as I to you.
And I cannot return to him all that
Which I, for many years, have had from him.

*Silence. The dusk gathers in the room. From somewhere
comes the muffled sound of ringing bells.*

OKSANA

Stepan, let's talk no more about such things.
No, ne'er again.

STEPAN

No, we must not, my love.
(After a moment) Why don't you sew?

OKSANA

It's much too dark to sew.
To-morrow there'll be light.

STEPAN

Sing to me, dear,
Some quiet song—that's if you can.

OKSANA

I'll try.

(Sings in a quiet tone)
"How sweet and lovely 'tis, when friend meets with a friend
They drink a cup, two cups, and for a sister send:
'O dearest, sweetest sister," *(She breaks off.)*
I cannot sing.
Perhaps I've got unused to singing songs.
I feel a soreness in my chest . . . *(She coughs.)*

STEPAN *(Alarmed)*

My dear,
Do you feel ill?

OKSANA

Oh, no! It's just a cough!

STEPAN's *mother and* HANNA *enter, followed by servants carrying packages. The servants put down the packages and leave.*

MOTHER

Good evening, children! Ha, why do you sit
Here in the dark?

STEPAN

Just talking, that is all.

MOTHER

Don't try to tell me that, my dearest children.
May God to Hanna grant a married life
As nice as yours!

HANNA *(Who meanwhile has lit the lamp and is now unwrapping the packages.)*

Oksana, look at this!
See all we've bought. *(OKSANA approaches.)*
This, for a winter cloak;
This, for a summer skirt; this, for the veil.

It's lovely, isn't it? We bought it all
Right in the foreigners' bazaar.

OKSANA *(With animation)*
How fine!
And what a charming, lovely bride you'll make!
I'll do some dancing at your wedding feast!
Who cares, though Moscow dames may think it strange?

HANNA
Oh, how I love you, when you are so gay,
Instead of sitting drooping, sunk in gloom.

MOTHER
Oh, certainly, why should you sit and grieve?
You both are young . . . and with a well-found home . . .

OKSANA *(Picking up the phrase)*
"Within the home there's wealth"

HANNA *(Not noticing the irony)*
If you had seen how many merchants there
Spread out their wares! And why did you not come
Along with us?

OKSANA
I was embroidering.
To-morrow I'll go with you everywhere
And will buy up all Moscow has to sell.
I'll get you a brocade fit for a queen.
Stepan, may I?

STEPAN
Of course you may, why not?

OKSANA *(Claps her hands and sings,)*
"O, may I such a long life find,
As I have such a husband kind!"

MOTHER *(Smiling with pleasure)*
Oh, what a witty wife you have, my son!

HANNA
And what a lovely bridal song she sang

For me.   O sister, sing that song once more,
The one they sing, while dressing the bride's hair.

OKSANA

I can't, it's sad, you'd start to cry again.
I'll play the one who makes the wedding cake
Or else the bride's attendant—listen now:

(She sings very loudly, in peasant style.)

"Fear not, mother, do not fear,
Get your scarlet boots so dear,
Put them on and click your heels,
Till the pot no longer squeals!

Hop!

(With a whoop she leaps on the divan.)

That's how the bride's maids jump over the seats!

STEPAN *(Catches her and lifts her down from the divan.)*
Now, now, Oksana, that's too much for you.

MOTHER

I hope the servants will not hear the noise . . .

OKSANA

Too bad!   But noblewomen must have fun!
Come on, Hanna, let's cut a reel and sing!

HANNA *(Laughing)*

I don't know how.

OKSANA

Come on, I'll show you how!
(She swings HANNA around her, singing the while,)
"Sing and dance, O mistress mine,
Why in sorrow should you pine?
Whether cloud or whether shine,
Sing and dance, O mistress mine?"
Stepan, why don't you join in?   Come and sing!

OKSANA'S *laughter rings out louder and louder, until it ends
in a fit of coughing.* STEPAN, *alarmed, rushes to her.*

ACT V
IN THE GARDEN

A garden in the rear of STEPAN's *house. There are seen the grated windows and the door of the women's apartments with steps leading to a gallery in front of them. At one side is an arbor covered with vines and flowers. In the arbor a large Turkish couch with cushions has been placed.* STEPAN's *mother and* OKSANA *slowly descend the steps from the women's apartments.* OKSANA *is supported by her servant-farm girls.* OKSANA *is dressed in a plain, ample housedress; her head is wrapped around with a silk kerchief in Ukrainian fashion. She is very ill; her eyes are sunken but glitter very brightly, and her cheeks are flushed.*

MOTHER
(Preceding the servants to the arbor, points out to them the couch.)
Now place her Excellency there and then
You can go back once more unto your work.
(The farm girls set OKSANA *down and go back into the women's apartments.)*
Now, daughter, here you'll feel much more at ease.
You breathe more freely?

OKSANA
Yes, indeed.

MOTHER
Lie down,
Lie down, my dove. You'd like to take a nap?

OKSANA
I'd like to, mother . . . but I am afraid . . .

MOTHER
God bless you, child! Of what are you afraid?

OKSANA
There's always such a dreadful nightmare comes.

MOTHER

Just pray to good Saint Joseph. He's the one
To ward off evil dreams and make them good.

OKSANA

Since I've been here, my dreams are not the same . . .
When I was home, I always used to dream
That I was flying . . . They were lovely dreams . . .
But here I've never had that dream.

MOTHER

See, love!
You only dream of flying, when you grow,
And that's why, when you're young, you dream such dreams,
But now your growing days are o'er. . . .

OKSANA

Oh . . . yes . . .

MOTHER *(Arranging cushions)*
Lie comfortably now and take a nap.

(She sits down beside the bed near OKSANA's *feet.)*

And I'll sit here a while and say a prayer
That God will send you health, while you're asleep.

*(She takes out a rosary with amber beads and tells them over,
her lips moving quietly. OKSANA falls asleep. STEPAN enters from
the lower floor. His MOTHER shakes her head at him, warning
him to step quietly and not to make a noise; then she gets up
cautiously and goes to meet STEPAN at the other end of the garden
away from the arbor.)*

MOTHER *(In a whisper)*
What does the German say? Does he give hope?

STEPAN

He said: "With God all things are possible."

MOTHER

Of course, but to make use of human means
Is not a sin.

STEPAN
He will use all his skill.
He is a learned man of great renown . . .
But how about an illness so severe?

MOTHER
I wonder when it first took hold of her?
Perhaps some one at Hanna's wedding put
A spell on her, for since then she's been sick.

STEPAN
It had begun, I think, much earlier . . .

MOTHER
You think so? No! She always was quite well.
'Twas something at the wedding . . . Well, what did
That German say? Whatever can it be?
Maybe the evil eye? Or fright perhaps?
Too bad, there are no peasant wizards here,
As back at home—they'd heal her with a charm.

STEPAN
No, mother, charms would be of no avail.
This is an illness.

MOTHER
What sort? What's its name?

STEPAN
He said: "Your lady's ill, she's pining for
Her native land, an illness that's well known."
And then he told me how it's called in Greek.

MOTHER
It doesn't matter what it's called in Greek,
But how to cure it, that's the thing.

STEPAN
                                He said,
"If we could take her to Ukraine again,
She might get well."

MOTHER

She might.   My son, perhaps,
The German doctor speaks in this the truth.
The poor dear's pined and longed so much for home.
Why not?   She came here from so far away.
Not everyone can stand a foreign land;
Some can and others can't, and if . . .

STEPAN

O mother,
I'm going to ask the Tsar to give me leave
To go and see my father-in-law.   Will he
Do so?

MOTHER

Perhaps he may.   There's no more war.

STEPAN

I'll say to him that I must take my wife
Who's ill, and make a pilgrimage to Kiev
To worship at the Lavra's holy shrines
  And pray for healing.   Would he let us go?

MOTHER

He ought to let you go.   It is a sin
To hinder folk from going on pilgrimage.
Yes, Stepan, that's an excellent idea—
To go and pay a pious vow, I think,
Is better far than all your medicine.

(With a sigh, she looks up to the heavens.)

But see, the sun is sinking toward the West.
You ought to go and wake Oksana up.
Sick folk should never sleep at setting sun.
Meanwhile I'll brew a healing drink from herbs,
So 'twill be ready for her, when 'tis night.

STEPAN

I thank you, mother, for the pains you take.

MOTHER

Why not, my son?   We brought her far from home,

We needs must do the best we can for her.

She goes into the women's apartments. STEPAN *approaches*
OKSANA *and quietly kisses her. She wakes up.*

OKSANA

It's you, Stepan? I just was dreaming then
About the moon which used to shine so bright
And clear above our place at home. . . .

STEPAN (*With pretended cheerfulness*)
The moon?
That's queer, for it's the sun that's shining now.

OKSANA

Maybe the moon down there more brightly shines
Than here the sun. . . .

STEPAN
Don't grieve, Oksana dear!
We soon again may see how brightly shine
Both sun and moon in your beloved Ukraine.

OKSANA

What? Am I going to die? Why then, for sure,
My soul will thither fly . . .

STEPAN
God save you, love!
Would I ever suggest a thing like that?
I merely thought we both might journey there
And visit your old home.

OKSANA (*Ironically*)
A marvellous thing
You've conjured up! The Tsar won't change his mind.

STEPAN
He'll give me leave. Conditions in Ukraine
Have settled down in peace.

OKSANA
What's that you say?
"Have settled down in peace"—And freedom's crushed.

Ukraine lies bleeding under Moscow's boots.
Is that what you call "peace?" A ruined waste?
Just as I soon will settle down in peace
Within the tomb.

STEPAN
In Ukraine you'll recover.
There Moscow cannot blot out all the sun
And blight your native groves or dry up all
The many streams.

OKSANA *(Depressed and stubborn)*
Enough, don't think of it.
I nevermore will travel anywhere.

STEPAN
Why not?

OKSANA
I've no desire.

STEPAN
Oksana, you
Seem strange to me. Why do you talk like that?

OKSANA *(Flaring up, half rising from her couch,)*
It's strange to me, how you with any face
Can dream of going back unto Ukraine!
You sat in safety here in Muscovy,
While blood flowed freely, while a struggle raged
For life and death down there in our Ukraine—
But now, when things have "settled down," you wish
To bask in its bright sunshine, to enjoy
What brutal hands have left untouched, to walk
Rejoicing through the groves unscarred by fire.
You want to see where conflagrations raged,
And gaze on places where once rivers flowed
Brimfull of blood and tears? . . .

STEPAN
You're mocking me.
Yet you yourself once told me you could not

Accept a suitor's hand, unless that hand
Was free from blood?
>   OKSANA
>   'Tis true, I did say so . . .
We're on an equal footing there. We feared
So much the bloodshed, Tartars, and the rack,
The demon's oaths, the Muscovitish spies,
And never gave a thought how it might be
When things had settled down . . . Stepan, give me
Your hand!
>   STEPAN
>   What for, I ask?
>   OKSANA
>   Why, don't you wish it?
>   STEPAN
All right.

> OKSANA (*Looking at her own and* STEPAN's *hands,*)
It seems as though these hands are clean,
Yet always in imagination they
Are covered not with blood . . . but with a rust,
Such as one sees on ancient swords, you know?
>   (*She drops his hand and sinks back again. She speaks more
>   slowly, languidly, with frequent breaks.*)
At father's there was such a sword as that . . .
It had been cast aside . . . we found it once . . .
Ivan and I . . . we wished to play at war . . .
We couldn't pull it out . . . stuck to its sheath . . .
'Twas rusted so . . . just like the two of us . . .
We have grown up . . . as that sword in its sheath . . .
Both rusted . . .
>   STEPAN
>   O Oksana, you know how
To wound with words, although you wield no sword.

>   OKSANA
That's all that I can do, and nothing more.
What else is there I ought to do instead?
>   (*Silence*)

When I am dead, don't choose another wife
From our Ukraine, find one in Muscovy . . .

STEPAN

Oksana!

OKSANA
    Yes, we all can wound with words
But here's where women fail . . . they fear too much . . .

STEPAN *(In agony)*
Have pity on yourself and me as well!

OKSANA
I've pitied all too much . . . there lies the wrong . . .
Had I had strength to vanquish pity, then
I should have broken loose from out the yoke,
And you'd have freed yourself from deadly rust . . .
We're clean, yes—but no use to any one . . .

STEPAN
Oksana dear! Let's go back to Ukraine!
See, I beseech you! With your parents there,
Your relatives, your friends, you will revive,
Divert yourself.

OKSANA *(Turning away)*
        I would not dare to look
Them in the face . . .

STEPAN
        Well, then, we'll go to Kiev,
There make our prayers, beseech God to forgive,
Restore you to your health again!

OKSANA
            What for?
What will it profit any one, if I
My health regain?

STEPAN
        'Twill profit me, my dear,
I love you so!

OKSANA

You only think you do . . .
You pity me, but as for loving me,
You have no reason to . . . I have become
So bitter, so capricious, so unkind . . .

STEPAN

No, no, my lovely wife!

OKSANA

A lovely wife?
If I had ever any loveliness,
It's long since faded from my countenance . . .

STEPAN *(Strokes her hand, bending down over her,)*
You tear and rend yourself by speaking thus.
You should not talk so much.

OKSANA

That's true enough . . .

STEPAN

And why should you reproach yourself, my love?
'Tis fate that's dealt with us so bitterly,
That certainly God must forgive our sins.
Some wipe blood from their wounds, we from our hearts,
Some are exiled, and some in prisons pant,
But we wear chains that are invisible.
Some find a moment's ecstasy in fight;
And we are cursed by dreadful lassitude
And have not been endowed with moral strength
To cast it off.

OKSANA *(Speaking more quietly and gently than before,)*
Yes, what you say is true,
But none will ever understand it, while
We still live on. Therefore, it's best to die.
You certainly will live a longer life than I—
So in your hands I leave my testament,
And you can hand it to my family
And friends, if any of them still survive.

STEPAN *(In bitter grief)*
Alas, 'tis I should say such things to you.

OKSANA *(Sits up and draws him to her.)*
No, my beloved, the world has need of you.
There's still a useful work that you can do.
No warrior can you be, but when the fight
Is o'er, you can help the defeated as
You have done many times . . . Not all the dead
Lie on the field . . . there's many wounded here . . .
Help them to stand again . . . and then, perhaps,
Some time . . . back in the ranks once more,
They may remember you with grateful hearts . . .
And if they don't—regret not that you helped.
They sit for a little while in silence, still embracing each other.

STEPAN *(Rises and extends his hand to* OKSANA.*)*
Now come. I'll lead you back into the house.
The sun is almost setting now.

OKSANA
'Tis time.

(Leaning on STEPAN'S *arm, she goes towards the house, but before reaching the steps, she pauses and turns around to look at the setting sun, which is just sinking below the horizon.)*

Dear sun, good night! Thou hastest towards the west . . .
Thou gazest on Ukraine—give her my love!

Forest Song

Fairy Drama in Three Acts

DRAMATIS PERSONAE

"HE WHO RENDS THE DIKES," *a destructive sprite dwelling in
the freshets of spring.*

LOST BABES, *water nixes*

RUSALKA, *a water nymph*

WATER GOBLIN, *guardian spirit of the lake*

LEV, *a peasant*

LUKASH, *a peasant, Lev's nephew*

FOREST ELF, *a woodland sprite*

MAVKA,[1] *a forest nymph*

WILL-O'-THE-WISP, *a fire sprite (ignis fatuus)*

KUTZ, *a malicious imp*

MOTHER of Lukash, *a peasant woman*

FIELD SPRITE, *a nymph dwelling among the grain*

KILINA, *a young peasant widow*

"HE WHO DWELLS IN ROCK," *a phantom signifying Death and
Oblivion*

STARVELINGS, *imps personifying Famine and Want*

A BOY, Kilina's *son*

FATE, *a phantom*

PROLOGUE

*A dense and hoary primeval forest in Volhynia. The scene
is a spacious glade in the heart of the forest, dotted with willows*

1. Ukrainian folklore is full of beliefs and superstitions, manifestly the
survivals from a dim ethnic past. In substance they are all connected
with natural phenomena as observed in the changing seasons as the
year runs its course, and with the activity of the manifold spirits
supposed to lie behind the visible world. This is the general background of this fairy drama. However, two remarks on the persons
of the drama will be useful. "Lost Babe" is a fairy being conceived
as coming from an unbaptized infant, the fruit of illicit love, after
having been drowned by its desperate forsaken mother. Similarly,
a "Mavka" is another sort of fairy being, whose origin is ascribed to
a female infant which dies before receiving Christian baptism.

and one very old oak. At one end the glade turns into tussocks and reedy growths, and then into a vivid green marsh, the shore of a woodland lake formed by a stream which runs through the forest. The stream emerges from a dense thicket, empties into the lake and comes out at the end of it, only to lose itself again in the undergrowth. The lake itself is a placid sheet of calm water, covered with duckweed and water lilies except for a clean open space in the center.

The spot is wild and mysterious but not gloomy, filled with the tender, pensive beauty of Polissye, the wooded part of the province of Volhynia.

It is very early spring. Along the edge of the forest and in the glade the first green is showing and hepaticas and anemones are in bloom. The trees are still leafless, but their leafbuds are about to open. A mist hangs over the lake, at times concealing it entirely, but when moved by the wind, the mist opens up, displaying the pale blue water.

*A roaring is heard from the forest; the stream begins to foam and clatter. Then, together with its waters, out of the forest there comes racing "*He Who Rends the Dikes.*" He is a youth, very blond with blue eyes, who makes expansive motions as though he were swimming. His clothing is constantly changing in color from turbid yellow to clear blue, and at times he emits swift golden sparks. Rushing with the current into the lake, he begins to circle around on the clear, open space, agitating the somnolent water. The mist dissolves and the water becomes bluer and bluer.*

"He Who Rends the Dikes"

Down from mountain into valley,
Skipping, racing, forth I sally.
All the villages are quaking,
As the dikes and dams I'm breaking.
When folk try to dam the water,
To their work I give no quarter;
For wild waters of the spring
Like wild youth, must have their fling!

He continues to agitate the water more and more, plunging and then emerging as though seeking something.

Two Lost Babes
(Tiny pale infants in scanty white shirts, who come up to the surface among the water lilies.)

1. Why do you come hither blundering?
2. Why do you disturb our slumbering?
1. Here our mother made our nest;
   Laid us gently down to rest;
   O'er the stones and o'er the gravel
   She laid reeds to make it level,
   Lily pads she gave for covering,
   And we heard her softly singing:
   "Lulla-lulla-lullaby,
   Sleep, my darlings, mother's nigh."
2. Why do you come us to scare?
1. Whom is it you're seeking here?

"He Who Rends the Dikes"
That Rusalka, blithe and kittle,
Whom I've loved since I was little;
For of water nymphs so queenly
There is none I love more keenly.
I have coursed all over mountains,
Valleys, ravines, springs, and fountains.
Lovelier spirit of the mere,
None there is than who dwells here.
Into foam this lake I'll churn,
Seeking her for whom I yearn!

He agitates the water tempestuously.

The Lost Babes
Please, oh, please! be not so savage,
Or our home you'll surely ravage.
One small cave—for there's none other
Than the one found by our mother.
Humble is the place we own—
Father's love we've never known . . .

(They seize him by the hand, beseeching him.)

We'll dive down to depths profound
Where no light or warmth is found;
There Rusalka watch is keeping
Where a fisher drowned is sleeping.

"HE WHO RENDS THE DIKES"

Let her leave him lying there!
Straightway let her come up here!

(The LOST BABES dive down into the lake.)

Come up, love, I say!

RUSALKA *comes up out of the water, smiling alluringly, joyfully clapping her hands. She is wearing two chaplets: the larger one, green; the other, small, like a crown of pearls, from which there hangs a veil.*

RUSALKA

Ah! 'tis you, my sweetheart gay.

"HE WHO RENDS THE DIKES"

(Angrily)

Why all this delay?

RUSALKA

(She starts to swim as though to meet him, but veers aside, avoiding him.)

All the night, dear, I've been yearning,
Dreaming that you were returning!
All the many tears I wept
In a silver cup I've kept.
Without you, the tears, my lover,
Filled the cup till it brimmed over.

(She claps her hands, darts forward as though to meet his embrace, but again swerves aside and avoids him.)

Some gold to the bottom fling,
And baptize the wedding ring!

She laughs in bell-like tones.

"HE WHO RENDS THE DIKES"

(Bitingly)

Ah! 'tis gold that you desire—
You, who dwell down in the mire!
Truly, my Rusalka owns
She loves best a dead man's bones.

Sitting there's her dearest wish,
Guarding him from crabs and fish
Lest they further him deface.
What a lovers' trysting place!

RUSALKA *swims closer, takes him by the hand and looks up into his face.*

RUSALKA

Why so angry? Say!
(Maliciously)
I know something, you reviler,
O you handsome heart-beguiler!
(She smiles knowingly and he becomes alarmed.)
While you were away
A miller's maid seemed fair,
So you forgot me here.
Winter nights were cruel,
Dark eyes furnished fuel—
When a maid's not cold,
Gentlemen give gold!
(She shakes her finger at him and laughs lightly.)
Well do I perceive
That you can deceive;
Yet I pardon you,
For I love you true.
(With humorous pathos)
For a lengthy second, I'll be yours most loyal;
For a moment's space, I'll give a love that's royal.
Fool me, and I'm through.
The water keeps no traces
No more than our embraces;
'Tis transient as your living,
As fleeting as my giving.

"HE WHO RENDS THE DIKES"
(With a convulsive movement, he stretches out his hand to RUSALKA.)
Anyway, 'tis spring!
O'er the lake let's take a fling!

RUSALKA

(Seizing his hand, she circles around swiftly.)

By the little lakelet,
O'er its yellow sands,
With my pearly chaplet
I fly in the dance!

*They whoop and splash and dash the water about. The
water surges and beats against the shore till the weeds and reeds
begin to thrash about, and the startled birds in swarms rise up
out of them in fright.*

WATER GOBLIN

*(He rides up from the middle of the lake. He is a very
ancient gray old man with long hair and a long white beard.
He is covered with a mass of weeds hanging down to his girdle.
His garments are the color of mud and on his head is a crown
of shells. His voice is hollow but robust.)*

Who's this who dares disturb our tranquil lake?

(RUSALKA and her partner stop, then flee asunder in haste.)

For shame, my daughter! Should the water's queen
Be romping with a stranger? Shame on you!

RUSALKA

He's not a stranger, father. Don't you see?
'Tis "He Who Rends the Dikes."

WATER GOBLIN

                    I know, I know.
He's not our kin although of watery birth.
Deceitful and malicious are his ways:
In spring he raves, he agitates, despoils,
Rips from the lake its glorious crown of green—
The year-long husbandry of water nymphs,
Affrights our guards, the wise and watchful birds,
The roots of widowed willows undermines,
Upon the poor Lost Babes he flings and pours
A stunning mass of dreadful deluges,
Destroys the smoothness of my level sands,
And wrecks the tranquil peace of my old age.
But where is he in summer? Where is he
When the insatiate sun the water drinks

From out my cup like gryphon mad with thirst;
When reeds and rushes faint for lack of drink,
And, withering, die on my arid banks;
When lilies, perishing, bend low their heads
Towards the warm water to relieve their thirst,
Where is he then?

During this harangue "HE WHO RENDS THE DIKES" *stealthily nods at* RUSALKA, *inviting her to flee with him down the stream.*

"HE WHO RENDS THE DIKES"
(With covert mockery) Why, father—in the sea.
'Tis then that Ocean calls me to his aid,
So that the sun may not drink his cup dry.
And when the Sea King calls, one must obey.
It is my duty—that you know right well.

WATER GOBLIN
Ah, so! You're in the sea . . . But as for me,
If 'twere not for the help that I receive
From my old trusty friend, the Autumn Rain,
I'd die, evaporate in mist.

RUSALKA
But, sir,
The mist can never die, for out of mist
The water comes again.

WATER GOBLIN
How wise you are!
Back down below! Enough of chattering!

RUSALKA
At once, dear father. Lo, he's disappeared!
Well, now I'll comb these tangled water plants.

Taking out of her girdle a comb made of shell, she begins to comb out and smooth the growths along the shore.

WATER GOBLIN
Yes, comb them out. I like to see things neat.
Stick to your combing. Meanwhile I'll stay here
Until you get it done. And tidy up
The water lilies so they spread out flat,

And patch the duckweed carpet that's been torn
By that bold vagabond.

RUSALKA

Yes, father, yes.

WATER GOBLIN *settles down comfortably in the reeds, following* RUSALKA'S *work with his eyes until they gradually close in sleep.*

"HE WHO RENDS THE DIKES"
(Stealthily emerging, to RUSALKA)

Hide behind the willow tree!

(After looking round at WATER GOBLIN, RUSALKA *does so.)*

Let us fly! Come, fly with me,
If you're not afraid;
Where the mill race runs so gay,
There we'll tear the dam away
And we'll drown the miller's maid!

He *seizes* RUSALKA *by the hand and speeds with her across the lake. Not far on the other side,* RUSALKA *stops.*

RUSALKA

Good grief! I've caught upon that ancient oak!

This awakens WATER GOBLIN, *who rushes after* RUSALKA *and seizes her.*

WATER GOBLIN

What's doing here? You cursed rogue, you'll learn
The cost of leading water sylphs astray!
I'll lay complaint about you to your dam,
The Mountain Snowstorm, so beware, you'll pay!

"HE WHO RENDS THE DIKES"
(Bursting into loud laughter)

Until that happens I'll just take my fling!
Good bye, Rusalka, fill your silver cup.

He rushes into the stream and disappears.

WATER GOBLIN
(To RUSALKA)

Go down below! Don't dare to rise again
Above the surface for three moonlit nights!

RUSALKA
(Rebelliously)
How long is it since all the water nymphs
Have been your slaves in this same lake? I'm free!
I'm free as water is!

WATER GOBLIN
In my domain
All waters must their limits recognize.
Go down below!

RUSALKA
I won't!

WATER GOBLIN
So, so! You won't?
Then give me back that pearly chaplet!

RUSALKA
No!
The Sea King's son gave me this pearly crown.

WATER GOBLIN
You don't deserve to wear a crown like that;
And for your disobedience, you'll go
To "Him Who Dwells in Rock."

RUSALKA *(Horror-struck)*
Oh, father, no!
I'll be obedient.

WATER GOBLIN
Then go below.

RUSALKA
(Slowly sinking in the water)
I'll go, I'll go . . . I may amuse myself
With that dead fisher lad?

WATER GOBLIN
For all I care.
(RUSALKA *reluctantly sinks in the water up to her shoulders
and, mournfully smiling, gazes up at him.*)
How strange you are! I do this for your sake.
That vagabond would simply ruin you.

He'd drag you all along the bristling bed
Of some fierce woodland stream and mutilate
Your fair white body, then abandon you
In parts unknown.

RUSALKA
But he was beautiful!

WATER GOBLIN
You're at your tricks again?

RUSALKA
No, no, I go!

She dives under.

WATER GOBLIN
(Looking up at the sky)
The young spring sun already grows quite hot . . .
It's stifling here! I must cool off a bit.

He also dives down under the water.

ACT I

The same spot, but spring is further advanced. The edge of the forest seems to be covered with a tender green veil, and in some places the top of the trees are tinted with a greenish shade. The lake is full to its brim, the green shores forming a crown of vegetation around it.

Into the glade from out the forest come UNCLE LEV *and his nephew* LUKASH. LEV *is an elderly peasant, grave, but with a very kindly face. In Polissyan style he wears his hair long, falling in a white fullness on his shoulders from beneath his square cap of grey felt. He is dressed in coarse hempen cloth, over which he wears a very light-grey smock; his high boots are made of bast; in his hand he carries a fishing net; a knife is stuck in his belt; and on a broad strap across his shoulders, he carries a basket made of woven felt.*

LUKASH *is a very young man, sturdy, black-browed, hand-some, with a still childish look in his eyes. Like his uncle he is dressed in hempen cloth but of a finer weave. His shirt, hanging outside and belted, is embroidered in white, with an open collar, fastened with red knots at both collar and cuffs. His belt is of red leather and on his head is a straw hat. A knife is stuck in his belt and there is a small pouch hanging from it on a string.*

Arriving at the shore of the lake, LUKASH *stops.*

UNCLE LEV

Why are you stopping here? This is no place
To try for fish. Too slimy, slippery.

LUKASH

I only want to cut myself a pipe;
The reeds right here are very fine for that.

UNCLE LEV

But you've got all the pipes you'll ever use.

LUKASH

No, very few—one each of cranberry,
Of willow, and of linden—that is all.
I must have one that's made of reed. That plays
The best of all.

UNCLE LEV

          All right, amuse yourself.
That's why God gave us holy days. But when
Tomorrow comes, we'll start some building here.
'Tis time to drive the cattle to the woods.
See yonder how the grass is springing up.

LUKASH

But how shall we abide here in this place?
The people say it's bad—a dangerous spot.

UNCLE LEV

Maybe for some. But I, good nephew, know
The art of dealing with such things as these:
Where one should lay a cross, where stick a twig,
Where simply spit three times, and that's enough.

We'll sow around our quarters poppy seed;
Before the threshold we'll plant gentian root.
No evil spirit then will trouble us . . .
Well, I'll be off, and you do what you please.

They separate. LUKASH *goes towards the lake and vanishes
in the reeds.* LEV *walks along by the shore and is lost to view
behind the willows.*

RUSALKA

(Comes swimming to the shore and cries out)
Grandfather! Forest Elf! There's trouble, help!

FOREST ELF

*(A tiny bearded old man appears. He is nimble in his move-
ments, but grave of countenance, dressed in dark brown, the
color of bark, and wears a shaggy fur cap.)*
Now what's the matter with you?

RUSALKA

There's a youth
Who's cutting reeds to make a pipe.

FOREST ELF

That all?
That's no great trouble. Why are you so mean?
They're going to build a dwelling here, it seems.
Forbid them I will not, provided they
Don't use live trees.

RUSALKA

Oh dear! A dwelling here?
We must have people here? Those dreadful folk
Who dwell beneath straw roofs! I can't bear them!
I can't endure that awful smell of straw!
I'll flood them and with water wash away
That hateful smell! I'll give such trespassers
Wet welcome when they come.

FOREST ELF

Stay, not so fast!
It's Uncle Lev who comes to settle here,
And he's our friend. Sometimes in jest he'll use
His simple arts to scare the forest sprites.

I love the good old man! Had it not been
For him that oak would long ago be gone,
Which has beheld our doings many a year,
Our dances, councils, and our mysteries.
Three Germans once inspected it; they stood
Around it with their arms extended wide,
And scarce their fingers touched. They offered gold,
New-minted dollars, to the folk for help.
But Uncle Lev swore by his life that none
Should touch the oak as long as he drew breath.
And so I also swore by my white beard
That Uncle Lev and all his tribe should be
Forever safe in this our forest home.

RUSALKA

Indeed! My father soon will drown them all!

FOREST ELF

Don't let him try it. If he does, I'll fill
His lake cram-full with last year's brush and leaves.

RUSALKA

Oh, dearie me! How dreadful! Ha-ha-ha!

She disappears in the water.

FOREST ELF, *muttering to himself, sits down on a fallen tree and lights his pipe.*

From the reeds there comes the sound of a pipe playing a tender, undulating air. As the melody evolves, everything in the forest gradually comes into life. First, the buds on the willows and the alders open out, then the birches commence to put forth leaves. On the lake the water lilies expand the flowers on their lily pads. The wild rose also begins to blush with its tender buds.*

From behind the trunk of an old, half-withered, tattered willow, MAVKA *emerges. She is dressed in a bright green garment, and her black hair, hanging loose, has a greenish sheen.*

*In an appendix to the original text, the authoress gives the musical notation of a number of Ukrainian folk melodies, with instructions as to when and how they are to be played by Lukash in the course of the drama.

She makes gestures with her hands and rubs them across her eyes.

MAVKA

Ah me, how long I've slept!

FOREST ELF

A long time, child.
Anemones have long since ceased to bloom;
And now the cuckoo's striking his alarm.
He's put his scarlet booties on, and soon
He'll measure off the summertime for all.
Already from the south come flying guests:
And yonder on the lake, there, where it's clear,
Like yellow balls of fluff, the ducklings swim.

MAVKA

What was it that awoke me?

FOREST ELF

Maybe spring.

MAVKA

I never heard a spring to sing the sounds
I hear today. Or did I simply dream?
    (LUKASH *plays again.*)
There, hark! . . . Is that not spring that's singing now?

FOREST ELF

Oh, no!—a youth who's playing on his pipe.

MAVKA

A youth? Maybe 'tis "He Who Rends the Dikes"?
I ne'er expected aught like that from him!

FOREST ELF

A human youth it is, nephew to Lev,
And Lukash is his name.

MAVKA

I don't know him.

FOREST ELF

Because he's not here long. He's from afar;
Not from these woods, but from the groves of pine
Where our Great Father all his winters spends.

The widowed mother and her orphaned son
Were given a home by good old Uncle Lev.

MAVKA

I'd dearly love to see what he is like.

FOREST ELF

What's he to you?

MAVKA

He must be good to see!

FOREST ELF

Beware how you gaze on these human youths:
It's perilous for wood nymphs such as you.

MAVKA

How stern you have become, grandfather dear.
You don't intend to hold me in as close
As Water Goblin holds Rusalka?

FOREST ELF

No,

My child, I don't. But Water Goblin in
His weeds has been accustomed all his life
To live by sucking other lives, while I
Respect your freedom. Go! sport with the wind,
Play all you like with wild Will-o'-the-Wisp;
Allure all spirits to yourself, be they
Of water, forest, mountain, field, or air.
But keep afar from human pathways, child;
You'll find no freedom there, but woes instead,
To clog your steps and weigh you down. My child,
Once start to tread them and your freedom's gone!

MAVKA (Laughing)

La-la! like that, my freedom would be lost?
That's just as though the wind should cease to be!

LUKASH *with his pipe suddenly emerges.* FOREST ELF *and*
MAVKA *hastily conceal themselves.*

LUKASH *is about to cut a birch to test the sap.* MAVKA
dashes out and seizes him by the hand.

MAVKA

No, no, don't touch! Don't cut the tree, you'll kill!

LUKASH

Why, girl, what's wrong? I am no murderer!
I only wanted to try out the sap
Of this tree here.

MAVKA

Don't shed it! That's its blood.
Don't draw the blood from out my sister's veins!

LUKASH

You call this birch tree "sister"? How is that?
Who are you then?

MAVKA

I'm Mavka, forest nymph.

LUKASH

(Not overly astonished, he examines her closely.)

So, you're a forest nymph! I've heard of them
From old folks many a time, but never yet
Saw one myself.

MAVKA

And did you want to see?

LUKASH

Why shouldn't I? But see, you're just the same
As any girl . . . no . . . like a lady fair!
Your hands are white, your figure's straight and slim,
Your clothes, somehow, are not the same as ours . . .
Why is it that your eyes aren't always green?

(He looks at her closely.)

Ah, now, they're green again . . . a moment since
They were as blue as heaven . . . now they're grey
As thunder clouds . . . no, now they're almost black,
Or maybe brown . . . Why, you are wonderful!

MAVKA
(Smiling)

You think me beautiful?

LUKASH
(Abashed)
How can I tell?

MAVKA
(Laughing)
Who else should tell?

LUKASH
What questions you do ask!

MAVKA
(In frank surprise)
Why should such questions be a task?
See there, doth not the wild rose ask:
"Am I not lovely?"
The ash tree nods, his branches bow,
He says: "None lovelier than thou."

LUKASH
I never knew that trees could talk like that.
I thought they were but speechless growing things.

MAVKA
In all the forest there is nothing mute.

LUKASH
And have you always lived here in the woods?

MAVKA
In all my life I've never been outside.

LUKASH
Did you live anywhere before?

MAVKA
Indeed,
I never thought on things like that at all . . .
(She ponders a moment.)
It seems to me that here I've always lived . . .

LUKASH
And were you always just the same as now?

MAVKA
I think I've been the same . . .

LUKASH

Your family,
Who are they? Or perhaps you've none at all?

MAVKA

There's Forest Elf whom I call "grandfather,"
And he calls me his "daughter," sometimes "child."

LUKASH

Well, which is he, your father, or grandsire?

MAVKA

I do not know. Is it not all the same?

LUKASH
(Laughing)

What queer folk in this wood! There's someone you
Call "mother," or "grandmother"—what you will?

MAVKA

It seems to me at times the willow tree—
That old, half-withered one—my mother is,
For during wintertime she took me in,
And spread inside a bed of something soft
On which I slept.

LUKASH

You spent the winter there!
And what work did you do the winter through?

MAVKA

Why, naught; I slept. Who works in wintertime?
The lake's asleep, the forest, and the reeds.
The willow kept on creaking: "Sleep, my dear . . ."
And always, I dreamed lovely dreams, all white:
In silver settings, I saw sparkling gems,
And carpets made of unknown grass, and flowers
Pure white and glittering. Quiet, tender stars,
Clear white, fell down from heaven, and shaped themselves
Into a white pavilion. Clean and pure
Beneath that tent it seemed. A coronet
Of crystal clear seemed glittering everywhere . . .
I slept; I breathed so freely, easily.

Through those white dreams came rosy thoughts which made
Themselves into a bright embroidery.
The dreams thus woven out of gold and blue,
Were peaceful, tranquil, not like summer dreams . . .

LUKASH
(Listening avidly)
Oh, how you talk . . .

MAVKA
You like it, do you not?
(He nods his head affirmatively.)
That pipe of yours can speak with better tongue.
Play me a tune and I will swing to it.

*She takes some of the long hanging branches of the birch,
and knotting them together, makes a seat into which she springs
and begins to rock herself gently.* LUKASH, *leaning against the
oak, plays on his reed pipe without taking his eyes off* MAVKA.
He plays spring songs and MAVKA, *listening, involuntarily joins
in singing the melodies he plays.*

"How lovely is the strain
Of mingled joy and pain;
It cuts deep in the breast
And cleaves the heart in twain."

*A cuckoo responds to the music, a nightingale follows like-
wise. The wild rose blooms more ardently, the white blossoms
of the cranberry tree expand, the hawthorn reddens bashfully,
even the black, leafless thorn bush begins to shoot forth tender
shoots.*

MAVKA, *entranced, sways quietly, smiling, while in her eyes
there is a yearning which almost overflows in tears.* LUKASH *perceiving this, stops playing.*

LUKASH
Why are you weeping, maiden?

MAVKA
(She passes her hand across her eyes.)
Did I weep?

Indeed . . . ah, no! 'Tis but the evening dew.
The sun is setting . . . See, upon the lake
The mist is rising . . .

LUKASH
Nay, 'tis early still!

MAVKA
You wouldn't like it if the day were spent?

LUKASH *(shakes his head, signifying he wouldn't.)*
Why not?

LUKASH
My uncle then would call me home.

MAVKA
You'd much prefer to stay with me?

(LUKASH *nods affirmatively.)*
You see,
You're talking now just as the ash tree did.

LUKASH
(Laughing)
I needs must learn to talk as folk do here,
Since I'm to spend the summer here.

MAVKA
(Rejoicing)
In truth?

LUKASH
Tomorrow we begin to build right here.

MAVKA
You build a house?

LUKASH
No, just a hut at first,
Together with a pen.

MAVKA
Just like the birds:
You take a lot of pains to build a nest
And then abandon it.

LUKASH
No, we shall build
For ever.

MAVKA
How for ever? You just said
You're only going to spend the summer here.

LUKASH
(Embarrassed)
Well, I don't know . . . 'Twas Uncle Lev who said
He'd give me here a piece of ground and house,
Because in autumn he wants me to wed.

MAVKA
(Alarmed)
Wed whom?

LUKASH
I don't know. Uncle did not say,
And maybe he has not yet found the girl.

MAVKA
Can you not find a partner for yourself?

LUKASH
(Gazing at her)
Maybe I could, but . . .

MAVKA
What?

LUKASH
Oh, nothing . . . but . . .
*Breaking off, he begins to play a melancholy air on his
pipe, then drops his hands and sinks into a moody train of
thought.*

MAVKA
(After a little silence)
When people mate, do they do so for long?

LUKASH
For life, of course!

MAVKA
Why, that is like the doves . . .

I've often envied them—so tenderly
They love each other . . . But I've never known
Such tender love, unless 'twas from the birch,
And that is why I call her "sister." Yet
She always seems so sorrowful, so pale,
So bowed and swaying, making mournful sounds;
It often makes me weep to gaze at her.
The alder I don't like; it is too rough.
The aspen, somehow, always frightens me;
It must feel fear, it trembles all the time.
The oak is much too stern. And the wild rose
Is prickly, like the hawthorn and the brier.
The ash, the plane, the maple, they are proud.
The cranberry so glories in her pride
Of beauty, that she cares for nothing else.
I was like her last year it seems to me,
But now, somehow, she makes me ill at ease;
For when one thinks of it, it's true that here
I'm utterly alone. . . .

She falls into a melancholy brooding.

LUKASH

              Your willow tree—
The one that you call "mother"—what of her?

MAVKA

The willow? . . . Ah! she's good to winter in;
But in the summer, oh, she is so dry!—
Forever creaking: "Winter's coming on . . ."
No! I'm alone . . . I'm utterly alone . . .

LUKASH

Here in the woods there are not only trees,
But also hosts of spirits of all sorts.

(A trifle maliciously)

Don't be so sorrowful, for we have heard
About your sports, your frolics, jollities!

MAVKA

All those are but like sudden gusts of wind,

Which start up, swirl around, then disappear.
With us there's nothing like you have—for life!

LUKASH
(Drawing nearer)
Would you like that?
Suddenly a loud shouting from UNCLE LEV is heard.

VOICE
Hey, Lukash! Where are you?

LUKASH
(Answering)   I'm here, I come!

VOICE
Well, come at once!

LUKASH
What an impatient man!
(He shouts back in response.)
I'm coming!
He starts to leave.

MAVKA
You'll come back?

LUKASH
I cannot tell.
He disappears in the bushes.
Flying out of the forest comes WILL-O'-THE-WISP, a hand-
some youth, dressed in red, with a shock of reddish hair blown
about by wind. He tries to embrace MAVKA, but she evades him.

MAVKA
Don't touch me!

WILL-O'-THE-WISP
Why not, pray?

MAVKA
Fly off and see
How in the fields the crops are getting green.

WILL-O'-THE-WISP
What care I for those crops?

MAVKA

Well, there you'll find
Your Field Sprite who is busy in the rye.
Already she's begun to plait for you
A garland of the brightest vivid green.

WILL-O'-THE-WISP

I have forgotten her.

MAVKA

Forget me too.

WILL-O'-THE-WISP

Now, don't make mock of me! Come on, let's fly!
I'll carry you to far-off mountains green.
You've always wished to see the spruce and fir.

MAVKA

Now I don't wish to.

WILL-O'-THE-WISP

What! And why not now?

MAVKA

Because I've lost desire.

WILL-O'-THE-WISP

Some mad whim!
Why have you lost desire?

MAVKA

I've no interest.

WILL-O'-THE-WISP
(Coaxingly, he circles round her.)
Let's fly, let's fly up high! and there my sisters hail,
The mountain spirits, free as is the comet's tail!.
In dizzy circling dances round you they will sail,
        As bright as lightning's trail!
From out the ferns for you I'll pluck the flowers frail;
To tear some stars from heaven I know I cannot fail:
Upon the mountain snows I'll bleach a magic veil
        To keep you from all bale.
And so that you may call the forest crown your own, .

We'll cast the Dragon-King down from his lofty throne,
And set for our defence each mountain, rock, and stone!
  Then cheer my heart forlorn!
  From evening until morn
  A garment glittering
  To you I'll always bring.
  And chaplets you shall wear,
  And in the dances share.
  On pinions I will bear
You far to crimson seas, to where the wealthy sun
His golden store in secret depths has laid.
And then we'll take a peep into the stars' abode,
And strip from them their silvery sheen, and with the load
  We'll weave ourselves for rest a velvet shade.
Then when the dawning comes, and cloudlets white are stirred
To gather in the heavens like some bright, fleecy herd,
Which drinks the clear cool water from a tranquil pool,
We'll rest like loving sweethearts on the flowery . . .

MAVKA
(Impatiently)

      Fool!

WILL-O'-THE-WISP

How pettishly you've broken off my rhyme!

(Aggrieved, and maliciously)

Have you forgotten last year's summertime?

MAVKA
(Indifferently)

Of last year's summer I no memory keep.
What was sung then died out in winter's sleep;
  No memory it provokes.

WILL-O'-THE-WISP
(Mysteriously, urgently)

  What of that grove of oaks?

MAVKA

I went to gather berries, I suppose . . .

WILL-O'-THE-WISP

Perhaps to find some trace of me, who knows?

MAVKA

I tore wild hops down from the trees, I think . . .

WILL-O'-THE-WISP

To make a couch for me in which to sink?

MAVKA

No, fragrant garlands my black hair to grace!

WILL-O'-THE-WISP

You hoped, perhaps, a lover's fond embrace?

MAVKA

No, 'tis the birch alone who cares for me.

WILL-O'-THE-WISP

Yet there was someone whom you wished to see?

MAVKA

Ha-ha-ha! I do not know.
Ask the grove if it was so!
I'll go and deck my hair with flowers today . . .

She starts off towards the forest.

WILL-O'-THE-WISP

Beware! Cold dews will smite them with decay!

MAVKA

While the breeze is blowing,
And the sun is glowing,
Who will cold dews fear?

She runs off and vanishes in the forest.

WILL-O'-THE-WISP

Stay a moment, maiden,
With longing I am laden!
Where are you, O where?

*He also rushes into the forest. For a few moments his red
garment is seen flashing amongst the trees and his voice is heard
echoing: "O where?"*

*The crimson of the setting sun bathes the forest, then dies
out. A white mist rises up over the lake.* UNCLE LEV *and* LUKASH
come out into the glade.

UNCLE LEV
(Muttering angrily)
That damned Water Goblin! May he dry up!
I'd finished catching fish and started out
To cross the lake by skiff—I only meant
To reach the other side—he up and grabbed
The bottom of my skiff and held it fast.
I couldn't stir. A bit more, I'd have sunk!
But I'm not quite a fool; I grabbed his beard
And got a twist of it around my hand,
And got my knife from out my belt—By God,
I would have sliced it off! But that damned fog—
A bump—and over went the skiff with me!
I hardly got out to the bank alive,
And lost my skiff as well . . . The dirty scamp!

(To LUKASH)
And something, too, must have caught hold of you.
I yelled and shouted, bellowed till I'm hoarse.
Where were you all the time?

LUKASH
I told you where—
Just cutting me a pipe.

UNCLE LEV
A little long,
It seems to me, it took to cut a pipe!

LUKASH
(Uncomfortably)
But, Uncle, I . . .

UNCLE LEV
(Smiling, having recovered his good humor)
Eh, lad, don't try to lie!
You're still too young for that. It hurts the tongue.
Much better hunt some dry brush in the wood

And start a fire so I can dry myself.
I wouldn't dare go home all wet like this;
Before I'd get there, I should be assailed
By one I won't name here—bad cess to her!—
And afterwards she'd rack my very soul . . .

    LUKASH *goes into the forest where a moment later he is heard cracking and breaking dry branches.*

UNCLE LEV

    (Sitting down on the gnarled roots of an oak tree, he tries to strike fire in order to light his pipe.)

Good grief! You strike and strike! The flint is wet,
The tinder's gone . . . Maybe in this old oak
I'll find a bit of punk that's dry enough
To light my pipe?

    He gropes about the trunk in search of punk.
    Out of the mist over the lake, a white female form arises, more like a wisp of vapor than a human shape. The thin fingers on its long white hands claw menacingly as the figure advances towards UNCLE LEV.

UNCLE LEV
(Aghast)

            What's this? Is it a ghost?
Aha! I know. It's well I saw it first!

    (Recovering himself, he takes some roots and herbs out of his wallet, and stretches them out towards the approaching phantom as though to ward it off. The phantom retreats somewhat. He recites a charm, speaking faster and faster as he does so.)

          Evil spirit, Fever Wraith,
          Burning fever, shivering ague!
Back into the scum you go, back into the slime;
Where good people do not walk, where the fowls don't drink,
          Where my voice you hear no more!
          Here no power you dare employ
          My white body to destroy,
          My bones' marrow to enjoy,

My red blood with which to toy,
No one's health may you annoy.
Fly, you phantom, fly!
Perish, specter, die!

*The phantom slowly retreats to the lake and dissolves in
the mist.*

Lukash *comes with an armful of brush, lays it down before
his uncle, takes out his flint and steel, strikes it and lights a fire.*

Lukash

There, Uncle, warm yourself.

Uncle Lev

Thank you, my lad.
You're good to your old uncle.
(He lights his pipe at the fire) Ah, that's good!

*Putting his wallet under his head for a pillow, he stretches
out in front of the fire and gazes at it through half-closed eyes.*

Lukash

Suppose you tell a story, Uncle.

Uncle Lev

See,
You're still a child! Which one would you prefer?
The Sorcerer? or Tromsina the Dwarf?

Lukash

I've heard those two. You know some better ones
That none can tell so well.

Uncle Lev

(After pondering a while) All right, here goes:
I'll tell about the Princess of the Wave.
(He begins to recite in a quiet, sing-song, measured tone.)
Whene'er the house is warm
And everybody's gay,
We like to tell our tales
Until the break of day.
Beyond the forest's mighty sweep,
Beyond the heaving ocean deep,

Beyond the lofty mountains steep,
There is a marvellous, enchanted strand
Where Urai rules the land.
And in that land the sun doth ne'er decline,
The moon doth always shine;
The stars that glitter in that wondrous clime
Keep dancing all the time.
Of all those stars the brightest one was he
Whose name was Silver Prodigy.
His little face so nice
Bore not a trace of vice,
His flowing hair was gilded by the sun,
His silver weapon in his small hand shone . . .

LUKASH

But what about the Princess?

UNCLE LEV
Eh? just wait! . . .
Now when young Silver Prodigy to manhood's years approached,
He pondered much about his lot and thus his thoughts
he broached:
"I've turned out handsomest of all, I guess,
And yet have not achieved my happiness.
Mother Star!" he loudly cried,
Where shall I go for a bride:
Seek among the chivalry,
Or the proud nobility,
Or perhaps the royalty,
Or the simple laity?
Is there not some princess fair,
Worthy with me life to share?"
(UNCLE LEV *begins to drowse.*)
So off he went until he reached the ocean blue,
And there upon the beach a pearly necklace threw . . .

LUKASH

Hey, Uncle! You've missed something out, I'm sure.

UNCLE LEV

You think so? . . . Well, 'tis you who don't pay heed!

... Then from the ocean rolling, a monstrous billow came,
And from the billow horses sped,
    As red as flame,
All harnessed to a chariot red,
And in the chariot was . . .
    He stops, overcome by sleep.

LUKASH

What then? A princess in the chariot sat?

UNCLE LEV
(Through his sleep)

What? . . . How? . . . What princess?

LUKASH

    Ah! he's fast asleep.
For some time LUKASH *gazes pensively at the fire, then
rises and moves away from it. He saunters about the glade, playing on his pipe, low and almost inaudibly.*

*It grows quite dark in the forest, yet the darkness is not
dense, but transparent, as it usually is just before moonrise. The
darting flames of the fire seem to be carrying on a mysterious
dance with the shadows. The flowers nearest to the fire now
gleam in full color, then fade out in the thick darkness. Along the
edge of the forest the trunks of the aspens and birches loom
strangely. The spring wind blows fitfully, running through the
trees and fluttering their branches. The mist over the lake drifts
out in white billows into the bushes, and the reeds and aspens
concealed by the floating mist whisper one to another.*

Out of the thicket MAVKA *comes running, swiftly, as
though fleeing. Her hair is dishevelled, her dress disordered. In
the glade she stops and looks around her, pressing her hands to
her bosom, then rushes to the birch and stops once more.*

MAVKA

Grateful thanks, O magic night,
For your cover in my flight,
And you paths, who helped my search
And have led me to the birch!
O my sister, shield me now!
She hides behind the birch, clasping its trunk.

LUKASH

(Coming up noiselessly to the tree)

Mavka, is that you?

MAVKA

(Quickly)

Yes.

LUKASH

You were running?

MAVKA

Like a hare.

LUKASH

You were fleeing?

MAVKA

Yes.

LUKASH

From whom?

MAVKA

From him, who's fire itself.

LUKASH

Where is he now?

MAVKA

Hush, hush! or he'll come flying round again.

Silence a moment.

LUKASH

How you tremble! And I can feel the birch
Vibrate, and all its leaves are murmuring.

MAVKA

(Moving away from the tree)

Alas! I am afraid to lean on it,
Yet thus I cannot stand.

LUKASH

Then lean on me.

I'm strong . . . I'll hold you and will you defend.

MAVKA *leans against him. They stand in close embrace.*
The moonlight creeps on, covering the forest. It spreads all over

*the glade and steals under the birch. From the forest the song
of the nightingale and all the voices of a night in spring are
heard. The breeze blows fitfully.* RUSALKA *emerges out of the
illuminated mist on the lake and silently watches the young pair.*

LUKASH *pressing* MAVKA *closer to himself, bends his face
lower and lower down to hers and suddenly kisses her.*

MAVKA
(Crying out in ecstasy)
Oh, joy! A star from heaven fell in my heart!

RUSALKA
Ha-ha!

With a laugh and a splash she dives into the water.

LUKASH
(Startled) What's that?

MAVKA
Rusalka, that was all!
My playmate—she won't harm us; have no fear!
She's wilful, and she loves to mock at folk.
But what care I . . . I care for nothing more
In all the world!

LUKASH
You care for me, don't you?

MAVKA
You are my world, more splendid, more beloved,
Than he whom hitherto I knew, and he
Is far more splendid since we two are one.

LUKASH
Then we two are now one?

MAVKA
Do you not hear
The nightingale singing the marriage song?

LUKASH
'Tis true . . . I hear that she no longer chirps
Or twitters as she always did. She sings:

"Now kiss her! Kiss her! Kiss!"
(He kisses her with a long, tremulous kiss.)
                    And her I'll kiss!
Kiss her to death!

*A gust of wind comes, blowing white blossoms like a
snowstorm all over the glade.*

                    MAVKA
                No, no, I mustn't die!
'Twould be . . .

                    LUKASH
                What's that you say? I didn't mean
To frighten you.

                    MAVKA
                And yet 'twould lovely be
To die as dies a falling star . . .

                    LUKASH
(Speaking caressingly)   Enough!
Don't talk of things like that! Don't talk at all!
Don't talk of anything! Ah, no, do talk!
The way you talk is strange, but, somehow, sweet
It is to listen to . . . Why don't you speak?
Ah, have I angered you?

                    MAVKA
                        I'm listening
To you make love.
        *She takes his head in her hands, turns his face up to the
light of the moon and scrutinizes it.*

                    LUKASH
                Don't! That makes me afraid.
Your eyes seem peering down into my soul . . .
I cannot stand it. Talk to me, make fun,
Ask questions, tell me what you like, or laugh . . .

                    MAVKA
Your voice is clear as is the running stream;
Your eyes, though, are opaque.

LUKASH

Maybe the moon's

Not bright enough.

MAVKA

(She presses her head to his breast as though fainting.)

Perhaps.

LUKASH

Oh, have you swooned?

MAVKA

No, hush! I want to hear your heart speak loud.
It talks, but faintly, like the nights in spring.

LUKASH

Why must you try to hear it? You should not!

MAVKA

You say I should not? Then I will not, love!
I should not, must not? Then I never will,
Dear heart! Instead, I will caress you, sweet!
You are not used to that?

LUKASH

I've never been

In love before, and so I never knew.
That love could be so sweet.

(She caresses him passionately until he cries out in ecstasy.)

Oh, Mavka dear,

You're drawing out my soul.

MAVKA

I'll draw it out!

I'll draw your singing soul out in these arms,
Enchant your heart with lovely words and charms . . .
    With kisses I your lips will close
        Until they yearn,
        Until they burn,
    As do the blossoms on the rose!
    I'll gaze into your deep blue eyes
        Until they blaze,
        And shoot forth rays,

As do the bright stars in the skies!
>   *(Suddenly she claps her hands.)*
But how shall I attract those eyes of yours?
With flowers I'm still unadorned.

LUKASH

>   No need!

You're lovely without flowers' help.

MAVKA

>   No, no!

I want to be adorned with flowers for you,
As suits a forest queen.
>   *She runs to the other end of the glade away from the lake,*
where there are flowering shrubs.

LUKASH

>   No, wait for me!

I'll put the flowers on myself.
>   *He runs after her.*

MAVKA

>   Alas!

The flowers at night—their colors go to sleep . . .

LUKASH

See, fireflies in the grass! I'll gather some
And put them in your hair to shine. They'll seem
Just like a crown of lovely, sparkling stars.
>   *(He puts a few fireflies in her hair.)*
No, let me take a look . . . How beautiful!
>   *(Beside himself with joy, he pulls her into his embrace, then*
looses her.)
I must collect still more. I'll dress you up
As if you were a queen in jewelled robes!
>   *He hunts around in the grass along the bushes for more*
fireflies.

MAVKA

I'll break some blossoms from the cranberry tree.
She sleeps not—nightingale, keep her awake.
>   *She breaks off the white flowers and decks her dress with*
them.

RUSALKA

*(She emerges out of the mist again. Turning back towards
the reeds, she whispers)*
> Little Lost Babes, in the night,
> Kindle now your lanterns bright!

(Two moving lights are seen in the reeds. Then the LOST
BABES *come forth, each bearing a lantern. The lights sometimes
flare up brightly and then fade out almost completely.* RUSALKA
*gathers them closely to her, whispering and pointing a little way
off to the dim figure of* LUKASH, *who is groping about in the
bushes in an intoxication of joy.)*
See there, that one who's wandering about—
He's like that father who abandoned you,
Who ruined your dead mother, let her die—
He should no longer live!

LOST BABES
> You drown him then!

RUSALKA

I do not dare; the Forest Elf forbids.

LOST BABES

But we're not strong enough; we are too small.

RUSALKA
> You are tiny,
> Light and shiny;
> With your lights in small hands sure
> You can foolish folk allure.
> Go into the rushes there
> Where no Forest Elf can hear.
> > Should he come out,
> > Put your lights out,
> > Disappear!
> Be like lights deceiving always
> > O'er the pathways;
> Burst out bright o'er reeds and rushes,
> Lead him into bogs and slushes.
> > When he's slipping,
> > Send him dipping

Down into the deepest slime . . .
Then I'll finish him this time!
Off now, like a flash!

Lost Babes
(To one another as they proceed)
You go there. This way I'll take
And we'll meet upon the lake.

Rusalka
(Elated)   They're off!
(She rushes to a marshy pool, takes water and sprinkles it
backwards over her shoulder. From behind the bushes Kutz
jumps out. He is a youthful imp, like a mannikin.)
Kutzie, Kutzie, where you stand
Here before me, kiss my hand!
With an imperious gesture she stretches out her hand. Kutz
kisses it.

Kutz
Lady, what is now your wish?

Rusalka
For you I prepare a dish
One you will like, if you don't miss your aim.
(She points to Lukash*)*
See there, you're well accustomed to such game?

Kutz
(With a wave of his hand)
Whatever's in the mud,
For the mouth is good!

Rusalka
There's the meat for you!
'Twill bring you joy and please your grandam too.
Kutz *skips into the bushes and vanishes.* Rusalka *in the*
rushes peers after the Lost Babes, *who keep flashing and dim-*
ming their lights, running forwards and backwards and weaving
in circles.

Lukash
(Still hunting for fireflies, notices the lights.)
What lovely fireflies, so swift and bright!

Such splendid ones I've never seen . . . so large!
I must get hold of them!

He chases them, first one, then the other. Imperceptibly
they lead him on towards the danger spots.

MAVKA
Don't go for them!
Sweetheart, don't go for them! It's the Lost Babes!
They'll lead you into peril!

LUKASH *absorbed in the chase, does not hear her and keeps*
right on; then with a sudden cry.

LUKASH
Lord, I'm gone!
I'm tangled in the weeds! They drag me down!

MAVKA *comes running up at his cries. She cannot, however,*
reach him because he has sunk into the mud some distance from
the solid bank. Holding her belt with one hand, she casts the
other end out towards him.

MAVKA
Now catch it!
It fails to reach him.

LUKASH
Oh, it doesn't reach! Now, what?

MAVKA
(She runs to the willow, the branches of which hang out
over the water.)
O willow dear! O mother dear, please save!

Quick as a squirrel, she climbs up the tree and, clinging
to the outmost branches, again casts out the belt. This time it
reaches. LUKASH *grasps its end,* MAVKA *pulls it back towards her-*
self, then giving him a hand, helps him to climb into the tree.

RUSALKA *in the water gives a dull groan of vexation and*
disappears in the mist. The LOST BABES *also vanish.*

UNCLE LEV
(Awakened by the outcries)
Hey, now! What's this? Some phantom here again?

Avaunt, accursed!
    (Looking around)   Hey, Lukash; where are you?

LUKASH
(From the willow)

Up here, up here!

UNCLE LEV
(Coming nearer and looking up into the tree)
What are you doing there?
Come down at once, I say!—the girl as well!

LUKASH *climbs down but* MAVKA *remains where she is.*

LUKASH

Oh dear! I nearly drowned there in those weeds.
I stepped into a hole, and she's the one
         (Pointing to MAVKA*)*
Who somehow saved my life.

UNCLE LEV
         And why do you
Go sneaking round at dead of night as though
You were a haunt?

LUKASH
         I was after fireflies . . .
He breaks off in embarrassment

UNCLE LEV
(Now noticing the fireflies in MAVKA*'s hair)*
I might have known without your telling me.
I see myself just how the matter lies!

MAVKA
Oh, Uncle, I'm the one who rescued him.

UNCLE LEV
Just hear her: "Uncle!" Now we've got a niece!
And who was it enticed him in the trap?
         (He shakes his head disapprovingly.)
You forest folk! There is your loyalty!
I'll get that Forest Elf for this, so he
Won't get away again! Inside an oak
I'll stuff that whiskered piece of trickiness,

As he'll find out! He sends his maids to do
His dirty work while he stays out of sight!

MAVKA
(She runs swiftly down from the tree.)
No, no! He's not to blame. May Dragon-King
Pour out his wrath on me, if it's not true!
And I am innocent!

UNCLE LEV
      Well—I believe
You now, for that's your greatest oath, I know.

LUKASH
Oh, Uncle! She it is who saved my life.
So help me God! without her I'd have drowned!

UNCLE LEV
Well, girl! although you don't possess a soul,
You have a good kind heart. You'll pardon me
For what I said in anger.
 (To LUKASH*)* Why were you
Out chasing fireflies in the dangerous marsh?
Were there none in the bushes on dry land?

LUKASH
But those were such big ones, such brilliant ones!

UNCLE LEV
Aha, I know them! It was those Lost Babes.
All right, just wait. Tomorrow I'll bring here
Some pups who don't fear witches—then we'll see
Who does the whining here!

VOICES OF THE LOST BABES
(Groaning miserably, almost like the grunting of frogs.)
 No, grandfather, please!
 We are not to blame.
 Out among the weeds,
 We were gathering reeds.
 We had no idea
 Visitors were here,
 Or we ne'er had come

Up above the scum.
Babes so weak and frail
Can but weep and wail!

UNCLE LEV

You notice how the treacherous mist sneaks out
To hide the witches' spawn? Well, let it try!
I'll soon find out who's guilty and who's not . . .

(To LUKASH*)*
Well, nephew, don't you think it's time for us
To start for home?

(To MAVKA*)*   Goodbye, my girl!

MAVKA

You'll come again tomorrow? I can show
You where to find good lumber for your house.

UNCLE LEV

I see you've nosed in all of our affairs.
You're smart! Well, you can come. I'm used to you,
And you folk also must get used to us.
Let's go! Goodbye!

They start off.

MAVKA

(More to LUKASH *than to* UNCLE LEV*)*
I'll be expecting you.

LUKASH *drops behind his uncle, silently squeezes* MAVKA'S
*two hands, kisses her without a sound, and overtaking his uncle,
departs with him into the forest.*

MAVKA
(Alone)

Dear night, couldst thou more swiftly pass away!
Forgive me! for I yet ne'er knew a day
So blest, so happy, such a day so bright,
So calm and tender as thou art, O night!
O birch, why must thou always mournful be?
Behold me, sister, filled with ecstasy!
O willow, no more o'er the waters weep!

Be kind, while here thy child love's watch doth keep.
And tell me, O my father, thou dark grove,
Where it were best for me this night to rove.
The night is brief, but separation's long . . .
What destiny awaits me—grief or song?

The moon sinks behind the dark mass of the forest. The darkness, velvety black, envelops the glade. Nothing is now visible except the dying coals of the fire, but by the fireflies which she is still wearing in her hair, MAVKA can be traced as she wanders among the trees. Her headdress at times shines out as a complete circlet, then again in separate sparklings until it is completely lost in the gloom. A deep midnight silence falls, broken only occasionally by the rustling of leaves in the forest, a sound as though someone were sighing in his sleep.

ACT II

Late summer. Here and there the dark, dull leaves of the trees are touched with autumn yellow. The lake has diminished in size, its beaches have broadened out; the reeds and rushes with their scanty leaves make a dry rustling.

A house has been erected in the glade and a vegetable garden planted. There are also two fields, one of rye and one of wheat. Geese are swimming on the lake. Linen is drying on the shore; household utensils hang on bushes near the house. The grass in the glade has been mowed down short, and a stack of hay is piled up under the oak. The cackle of poultry is heard among the trees and in places cattle are browsing. Nearby a pipe is heard playing a lively dance tune.

MOTHER
(Coming out of the house and calling)
Lukash, hey! Where are you?

LUKASH
(He comes out of the forest, carrying his pipe and a carved walking stick.)
Here, Mother, here!

MOTHER

Isn't it time to quit that pipe of yours?
You play and play and let the work stand still.

LUKASH

What work is there?

MOTHER

You ask, what work is there?
Whose job is it to build that cattle pen?

LUKASH

All right, all right, I'll do it right away.

MOTHER

And when will be that "right away" of yours?
You're always running off to fool around
With that bold hussy, that queer vagabond!

LUKASH

Who's running off? I drive the cattle out
To feed and Mavka helps.

MOTHER

A lot of good
Is such a help as hers!

LUKASH

You said yourself
That when she takes care of the cows, more milk
They always give.

MOTHER

Oh! Sure—by witches' tricks!

LUKASH

There's nothing that she does e'er pleases you.
When we put up the house, was it not she
Who brought the wood? And who was it who helped
You with the garden, helped to sow the fields?
Did ever you get harvest like this year's?
The lovely flowers she has planted there
Beneath the window—what a pretty sight!

MOTHER

Much good are all those flowers, since I have
No daughter in the house to marry off . . .
There's nothing on your mind but flowers and songs!
    (LUKASH *shrugs his shoulders impatiently and starts to go away.*)
Where are you off to now?

LUKASH

To build that pen.

He goes around the house and a little later the sound of a chopping axe is heard.

MAVKA *comes out of the forest, richly decked with flowers and her hair hanging loose.*

MOTHER
(Disagreeably)

Now what?

MAVKA
Where's Lukash, Auntie, do you know?

MOTHER

You're always running after him. It is
Not seemly for a maid to chase a youth.

MAVKA

No one e'er said the like of that to me!

MOTHER

Well, hear it now for once; 'twill do no harm.
(She looks at MAVKA sourly.)
Why do you always go trimmed up like that?
You're always combing, fixing up your hair.
You dress up like a witch. It isn't nice.
And what is all that rubbish you've got on?
Not practical at all for working in.
I've got some things of my dead daughter's there:
Go put them on—you'll find them hanging up;
These you can lay away inside the chest.

MAVKA

Oh, very well, I'll go and change my dress.
She goes into the house as UNCLE LEV *comes out.*

MOTHER

Not e'en a word of thanks!

UNCLE LEV

Why, sister, must
You always nag and nag the girl like that?
What has she ever done to give you cause?

MOTHER

Ah, brother, you would scarcely do a thing
Unless we pester you. You'd bring in here
Amongst us all the witches from the woods.

UNCLE LEV

If you'd talk sense—of things you understand—
I'd listen; but this talk of "witches from the woods" . . .
There are none there, for witches only dwell
In villages with folk.

MOTHER

You think that you
Are very wise, don't you? If you attract
This forest trash you'll find some day what good
You've gained by it!

UNCLE LEV

Why, sure I'll gain great good.
What comes out of the forest is not trash—
All good things from the forest come.

MOTHER

Oh yes!

(Mockingly)

UNCLE LEV

From maids like her good humans come, that's what!

MOTHER

What sort of humans? You've been drinking, eh?

UNCLE LEV

A lot you know! My dead grandfather used
To say: You only need to know the word,
And you can make a soul the same as ours
To enter into any forest sprite.

MOTHER

And will the smell that witches always have
Then also disappear?

UNCLE LEV

Ah, what's the use! . . .

I'd do much better to go back to work
Than stay here chattering with you!

MOTHER

Then go!

Who's stopping you? Am I?

UNCLE LEV *goes away, shaking his head angrily.*

MAVKA *comes out of the house, having changed her dress.*
She is wearing a blouse of coarse material, poorly made and
patched in places, a scanty skirt and a faded apron. Her hair is
now smoothly combed and made into two plaits which are
wound around her head.

MAVKA

I've changed my dress.

MOTHER

Now that is something like. All right; meanwhile
I'll go along and get the chickens fed.
I meant to do some work amongst the hemp;
But we have lots of still unfinished tasks
And you, somehow, don't give much help . . .

MAVKA

Why so?

I gladly do the work if I know how.

MOTHER

"If I know how." You're always saying that.
A pretty farmer's working girl you make!
In haying time, your head it was that ached . . .
But now you've got to reap . . .

MAVKA

I've got to reap!

You want me to go out and reap today?

MOTHER

And why not, pray? Today's no holy day.

(She gets out a sickle from behind the door and hands it to
MAVKA.)

Here is the sickle; try it. When I'm done,
I'll lend a hand.

*She goes away, taking with her a basket of grain. Soon she
is heard calling and clucking to the chickens as she scatters food
for them to eat.*

LUKASH *appears with an axe and approaches a young tree,
manifestly intending to chop it down.*

MAVKA

Sweetheart, don't touch that tree!
It's living, don't you see?

LUKASH

Leave me alone!

I haven't time!

*(*MAVKA *looks him sadly in the face.)*
All right, find me dead wood . . .

MAVKA

*(She leaves swiftly, and returns, dragging a considerable
amount of dead wood.)*

I'll find you more . . . Will you be needing much?

LUKASH

How much? Enough to make up this one pen.

MAVKA

Somehow you've turned quite disagreeable.

LUKASH

Well, see . . . Because of you my mother nags.

MAVKA

What does she want? And how is she concerned?

LUKASH

Concerned? Why, I'm her son . . .

MAVKA

Her son—so what?

LUKASH

She doesn't fancy such a daughter-in-law . . .
She has no liking for the forest folk . . .
An unkind mother-in-law she'd be to you.

MAVKA

We in the forest do not know such things.
What mean all these "in-laws" you talk about?
I don't grasp it.

LUKASH

                    She wants a daughter-in-law
Because she needs some help . . . she's getting old.
It isn't right to have to hire help;
A hired maid is not a daughter-in-law . . .
In truth, all this you'll never understand . . .
To understand these human cares and woes,
One should grow up elsewhere than in these woods.

MAVKA

(Ingenuously)
You tell me—then I'll clearly comprehend,
Because I love you. And I grasped at once
The meaning of each song I heard you play?

LUKASH

The songs I played? There's no great art in that!

MAVKA

Do not despise that flowering of your soul,
For from your music this our love was born!
Like to the magic blossom of the fern,
Which hath creative power within itself,
So in me there was born another heart
When I found that I knew your songs. Right then
A fiery miracle took place
     (Breaking off suddenly)   You laugh?

LUKASH

In truth, it did seem somewhat humorous . . .
To see you dressed in working clothes, and hear
You talk as though delivering a speech.

MAVKA

(Tearing at the dress she is wearing)

I'll burn this up!

LUKASH

Then Mother'll scold the more.

MAVKA

What care I, when this dress seems to have made
A change in me to you.

LUKASH

I knew 'twould come . . .

From now on there'll be nothing but reproach . . .

MAVKA

No, sweetheart, I am not reproaching you;
I'm only sad because you cannot bring
Your life up to the level of your soul.

LUKASH

I do not understand just what you mean.

MAVKA

Ah, that is why I love you most of all:
Because you do not understand yourself,
Although your soul sings all about what's there
So clearly and sincerely through your pipe.

LUKASH

And what is there?

MAVKA

Something more beautiful
Than all your dear and handsome manliness—
But I can not express it as I would . . .
*(Lovingly but sadly she gazes at him for a moment in
silence.)*
Play something for me, sweetheart, on your pipe,
And let it banish evil far away.

LUKASH

'Tis not the right time now for me to play.

MAVKA

Well then, embrace me, so I may forget
This conversation.

LUKASH

Hist! Mother may hear!
For see, she's always calling you a bold
And brazen girl.

MAVKA

(Flaring up)   Yes! One who's not grown up
With you will never know you! "Brazen, bold:"
What does she mean? Because I love you, eh?
Because I told you first? Is it a shame
For me to have a generous heart, which hides
No treasures it possesses, but at once
Bestows them all upon the one it loves
Without awaiting any pledges first?

LUKASH

It might have hope that they would be returned.

MAVKA

Again a strange expression, meaningless . . .
"Return?" You gave to me the gifts you wished
To give as I gave likewise unto you,
Unbounded, numberless . . .

LUKASH

So then, 'tis well,
When neither can the other blame for aught.
You said so once yourself . . . Don't you recall?

MAVKA

Why should I now recall what once I said?

MOTHER

(Coming from behind the house)
Is that the way you reap? And build the pen?

(LUKASH *hastily drags off his wood.*)
If you, my girl, have no desire to reap,
I will not force you to. Somehow, myself,

I'll get it done. But when the autumn comes,
Please God, I'll find a daughter-in-law to help.
You know, there is a widow, strong and smart;
She's sending inquiries here through the folk,
And I sent back to say that if my son
Is not against it, then . . . The sickle, dear;
Give it to me . . . I have no other one.

MAVKA

I'll reap. You go and work among the hemp.

MOTHER *crosses the glade and conceals herself in the reeds.*

MAVKA *swings the sickle and bends down over the rye.*
Suddenly out of the rye FIELD SPRITE *springs up. The green dress*
she is wearing shows in places through her long golden hair
which falls down all over her small figure. Round her head she
wears a blue fillet, and daisies and other field flowers are twined
in her hair.

FIELD SPRITE
(Rushing beseechingly to MAVKA)
O sister, stay such shameful toil!
My beauty thus do not despoil!

MAVKA

I must.

FIELD SPRITE
Already I've been sadly torn,
The flowers slain that I have borne.
Those flowers ne'er will come again,
For they were cut down with the grain.
My poppies red with fury burned,
But now to blackness they have turned.
The soil is now like blood congealed
In this my once so happy field . . .

MAVKA
I must, my sister. All your loveliness
Returns each year in still more gorgeous dress;
But if my happiness should fade today,
                'Tis gone for aye!

FIELD SPRITE

(Wringing her hands and bowing in grief as a stalk is bent by the wind.)

Woe, alas! My lovely hair!
My golden, glorious hair!
Woe, alas! My beauty fair!
Condemned to disappear!

MAVKA

Your beauty was not made with time to vie,
But merely for a time to bloom, then die.
I cannot help it, though you wail and weep;
If I do not, some other will you reap . . .

FIELD SPRITE

O grant me, sister, but a moment's grace
    In this field to sport and race.
Let me enjoy this paradise of dreams
    While still the summer beams.
    While rye stands in the field,
The hour's not yet when I at last must yield.
A moment, but a moment, dearest one,
    Ere my poor beauty must be done!
'Twill then itself lie down for ever still . . .
O sister, be not like the winter chill,
Who cannot be besought, cannot be swayed!

MAVKA

I'd gladly do as you have prayed,
But I'm no longer free, this duty I daren't shirk.

FIELD SPRITE

(Reaching up to MAVKA's *ear and whispering)*

Does it not sometimes happen in this work
That with the sickle one may wound the hand?
Such pain, O sister, you could surely stand;
Some drops of blood to save me would suffice . . .
Is not my beauty worthy such a price?

MAVKA

(She draws the sickle across her hand and the blood spurts out over FIELD SPRITE's *golden hair.)*

See, sister, I have taken your advice!

FIELD SPRITE *bows low before* MAVKA *in gratitude, then springs up and vanishes in the stalks of rye.*

LUKASH'S *mother comes from the lake accompanied by a full-faced young widow who is wearing a red kerchief with fringes, a dark red skirt with narrow and regular pleating, and a similarly pleated apron, garnished with white, blue, and yellow braid sewn on it. Her chemise is heavily embroidered in red and blue; a necklace with many trinkets attached jingles around her white, chubby neck. Her bodice is tightly laced around her plump torso, and this makes her figure appear all the more opulent. She walks with such long strides that the older woman has difficulty in keeping up with her.*

MOTHER
(Very amiably)

Come, on, Kilina; there, around the birch,
You'll find much fresher herbs. The yarrow there . . .
You'd like a boiling of it, wouldn't you?
It's very good indeed, my dear, with milk.

KILINA

I've so much milk I don't know what to do.
I wish the fair were soon, I'd buy more pails.
My cow is one of Turkish breed, a cow
My dear departed got somewhere . . . And young . . .
My Lord, you never saw the like! Somehow
I manage to get all the farm work done,
But there's the house as well. O dearie me!
A widow has to split herself in two.
She talks dolefully, making a drooping mouth.

MOTHER

And yet my dear, you did get it all done!
But then, of course, when one's industrious,
One manages . . . Yet here, with two small fields,
We have no such success.

KILINA
(Looking at the field where MAVKA is standing)

Ah, who is that
You've got a-reaping there?

MOTHER
Some orphan girl . . .
(Whispering)
Ah, God forgive me! not a bit of good.

KILINA
(Coming up with MOTHER *to* MAVKA*)*
Good day, my girl! The reaping going good?

MOTHER
Oh, goodness me! She hasn't started yet!
A plague on you! What have you done the while,
You good-for-nothing! Worthless, lazy slut!

MAVKA
(Dully)
I cut my hand . . .

MOTHER
And for what reason, pray?

KILINA
Give me the sickle . . . Let me take a swing.
MAVKA *puts the sickle behind her and stares with hostility
at* KILINA.

MOTHER
Give her the sickle now! It isn't yours!
She snatches the sickle out of MAVKA's *hand and gives it to*
KILINA, *who rushes to the rye and reaps so furiously that the
straws whistle under her strokes.*

KILINA
(Delightedly)
Ah, that's the way to reap!
(Without stopping her work) If someone here

Would twist some bands for sheaves, I'll clear this field
Off at a single stretch.

MOTHER
(Shouting) Lukash, come here!

LUKASH
(Coming up, to KILINA*)*
God give you power!

KILINA

(Without looking up) Thank you.

MOTHER

Lukash, you
Can bind the sheaves for our good visitor.
Your "helper" has already cut herself.
(LUKASH begins to bind sheaves.)
Well, keep it up, my children. I must go
And boil some dumplings for your midday meal.

She leaves, while MAVKA goes off to the birch and, leaning against it, peers through its hanging branches at the two workers.

For some time KILINA keeps up her furious reaping; then she stops, straightens up, and gazes at the bent figure of LUKASH stooping over the sheaves. She smiles, and with three long strides walks up to him and gives him a hearty slap on the back.

KILINA

Come on, young fellow! Don't crawl like a snail!
There's still a lot to do.

She bursts into a resounding laugh.

LUKASH

(Also straightening up) How fast you work!
But don't brag yet. I'm still the stronger one!

KILINA

(Throwing down the sickle, she stands with hands on hips.)
All right, just try it out! We'll see who wins!

LUKASH darts towards her but she holds him back. They then take positions "to measure strength" by placing the open palms of their hands pressed flat each against the other's and straining to see which one will first give way. For a time they are evenly matched; then KILINA yields slightly, laughing loudly and making play with her eyes. LUKASH, inflamed, pushes her hands wide apart and tries to kiss her, but at the last moment she trips him and he falls.

KILINA

(Standing over him and laughing)
Now who's the winner? Who's the stronger one?

LUKASH
(He rises, breathing heavily.)
That was a trick . . . you tripped me.

KILINA
But I won!

The door of the house slams. KILINA *again starts to reap and* LUKASH *to bind sheaves. Soon the field appears dark; only the stubble and the standing stooks of sheaves are left on its surface. Apart from these, there are some scattered piles of stalks of rye, intended for bands, lying like victims already overpowered and waiting to be bound like captives.*

MOTHER
(Calling from the open door)
You reapers, hey! 'Tis time to come and eat!

KILINA
(Shouting back)
I've finished mine, but Lukash doesn't seem
To get along so fast.

LUKASH
I won't be long.

MOTHER
Well, get done quick! Kilina, you can come.

KILINA *goes into the house and the door closes behind her.* MAVKA *comes out from underneath the birch.*

LUKASH
(Somewhat confused at seeing her, but resuming his task immediately)
Oh, so it's you? Just finish up these sheaves
So I can go.

MAVKA
I don't know how to bind.

LUKASH
Well, why did you come here to stand and look,
If you don't want to help?

He keeps on binding alone.

MAVKA
Oh, Lukash dear,
Don't let that woman come here anymore.
I don't like her . . . She's vicious and she's sly,
As otters are.

LUKASH
You don't know her at all.

MAVKA
Oh yes, I do! I've heard her voice and laugh.

LUKASH
That's not enough.

MAVKA
Nay, that is quite enough.
She's avaricious, like the lynx.

LUKASH
Worse, eh?

MAVKA
She must not come into this grove again.

LUKASH
(Straightening up)
You seem to think that you're the forest's queen,
To say who shall or shall not walk about
Here in the woods.

MAVKA
(Sadly but menacingly)   Here in the forest there
Are certain pitfalls hidden in the brush,
Of which nor beasts nor humans are aware
Until they fall therein.

LUKASH
And yet you talk
Of viciousness and slyness—Fie, for shame!
I didn't know what your true nature was
Till now.

MAVKA
Maybe I knew it not myself . . .

LUKASH

Well, listen now: if it's the case that I
Have got to ask you first who may come here
And who may not, 'twill be the best for me
To leave this forest and go back to live
Amongst my fellows, where I'll find a home.
'Twould be far better than to stay with you
Like some trapped beast.

MAVKA

     I never set a trap
For you. You came here of your own free will.

LUKASH

I'll follow my free will where'er I wish.
I will be bound by nothing, by no one!

MAVKA

Whenever have I sought to fetter you?

LUKASH

Well, what's the good of all this idle talk?
 Having finished the last sheaf, and without looking at
MAVKA, he goes into the house. MAVKA sits down in a furrow
amongst the stubble, and lets her head droop in sad meditation.

UNCLE LEV
(Coming from behind the house)
What is the matter, maiden? Why so sad?

MAVKA
(Softly and sadly)
The summer's passing, Uncle Lev.

UNCLE LEV

      For you,
That's certainly a grief. No longer can
You use the willow as your winter home.

MAVKA
Where then shall I find lodging?

UNCLE LEV

     As for me,

No house with you inside would be too cramped . . .
My sister has a nature hard to please;
No one can get along with her. If I
Were master here, I wouldn't ask, but then,
I gave them ownership of house and land,
So I've no say. Myself, I'm leaving here
To winter in the village, in my home . . .
If you could stand it there amongst us folk,
I'd gladly take you in.

MAVKA

No, no, I can't . . .

And if I could, I wouldn't go. You're good!

UNCLE LEV

'Tis bread alone that's good, not humankind.
To tell the truth, I'm downright fond of all
You forest folk. When my time comes to die,
I, like the beasts, will come back to the woods—
Here, 'neath this oak, let them lay me to rest . . .
Hey, good old oak! Will you be standing still
When my grey head shall bow itself at last?
Ah me! there never were such sturdy oaks
As those which were chopped down. As green as you,
Despite the frosts, my sturdy, shaggy friend . . .

He stands, leaning sadly on his staff. MAVKA *gathers some
half-withered flowers from among the harvested rye and makes
them into a nosegay.*
Out of the house come MOTHER, KILINA, *and* LUKASH.

MOTHER
(To KILINA)

Why must you go? Can you not stay a while?

KILINA

Eh, not a moment more; I must be off.
You see, it's getting late, and I'm afraid.

MOTHER

Why, Lukash, you could see her home?

LUKASH
Why not?

KILINA
(Looking at him)
But he's got work to do . . .

MOTHER
What sort of work,
Now evening's come? Go on, my son, go on,
And take Kilina out unto the road.
Myself, I dread these dismal woods at night;
And such a handsome girl as she might meet
Some harm, who knows?

KILINA
Oh now, you really do
Make me feel terrified to linger here!
Come on then, Lukash, ere it gets real dark,
Or both of us will be afraid.

LUKASH
Who, I?
Feel scary in the woods? Ha-ha, no fear!

MOTHER
He's such a bold and enterprising youth.
Take care, Kilina, you watch out for him!

KILINA
Oh, no, I'm joking . . .
(She notices UNCLE LEV *passing.)*
Why, here's Uncle Lev!
So you're here too?

UNCLE LEV
(Pretending not to have heard aright)
Eh? Oh, goodbye, goodbye!
He goes off into the forest.

KILINA
Now, Auntie, do take good care of yourself!
*She makes as if to kiss the older woman's hand, but the
latter does not extend it; instead, she wipes off her mouth with a*

corner of her apron and kisses KILINA *three times, "with cere-mony."*

KILINA
(Departing)
Long life to you, and don't forget us, too!

MOTHER
Don't stay away, but come another day!
    She re-enters the house and fastens the door behind her.
    MAVKA *gets up and, walking slowly as though fatigued,*
goes towards the lake. Sitting down beside the sloping birch, she
lets her head fall down between both hands and weeps softly. A
drizzling rain begins to fall, dimming the outlines of glade, house,
and forest.

RUSALKA
    (She comes swimming up to the shore and stops, gazing at
MAVKA *in surprise and curiosity.)*
You're weeping, Mavka! Why?

MAVKA
                    And have you ne'er,
Rusalka, wept yourself?

RUSALKA
                    What I? Why no!
If I should weep e'en for a moment's space,
Someone would surely laugh himself to death!

MAVKA
But ah, Rusalka, you have never loved . . .

RUSALKA
I've never loved? Nay, it is you who have
Forgotten now what real love ought to be.
Real love is like the water, rushing swift,
Which sports, caresses, draws one on, then drowns.
Where it strikes heat, it seethes; where it meets cold,
It turns dead, like a stone. So is my love!
But that of yours is like the brittle straw,
A puny child. It bends before the wind,
It cracks beneath the feet. It meets a spark
And flares without resistance, after which

There's nothing left but cinders and dead ash.
If it's despised, it lies and putrifies
Like unused straw that's in the water thrown—
The water of vain self-reproach, or else
Turns mouldy 'neath cold rains of penitence.

MAVKA
(Lifting up her head)
"Vain self-reproach" you say? Well, ask the birch
If she feels "penitence" for nights she spent
When spring's light breezes in her tresses played
And sported with her.

RUSALKA
Why then does she grieve?

MAVKA
Because she can her love no more embrace,
Clasp him eternally in her long arms.

RUSALKA
Why not?

MAVKA
Her lover is the breeze of spring.

RUSALKA
Why did she choose a lover such as that?

MAVKA
That breeze of spring was tender, gentle, mild.
It was his singing that brought out her leaves;
His fondling caused her glorious crown to spread,
And his caresses damped her hair with dew.
Yes, yes . . . it truly was the breeze of spring.
How could she help but love him and none else?

RUSALKA
Well, she should cease her grieving now and let
It fall to earth, for she will not embrace
That breeze again . . . It's fled away and gone.
     *Quietly and without a splash she swims away and vanishes
in the reeds.* MAVKA *lets her head fall down again till her long
black tresses are touching the ground.*

*A strong wind springs up, driving grey clouds before it
as well as black swarms of migrant birds which are flying south.
After this there comes a still stronger blast of wind, the dark
clouds drift asunder and the forest becomes visible in a vivid
autumnal pattern against the dark blue of the sky, betokening
thus the approaching end of the day.*

MAVKA
(Softly and in deep sorrow)
"It's fled away and gone . . ."

FOREST ELF *comes out of the thicket. He is wearing a long
gown, the color of old gold, with a dark red fringe around the
bottom, and round his cap are twined sprays of wild hops.*

FOREST ELF
My child, although
You have betrayed, do not so sorely grieve!

MAVKA
(Lifting up her head)
Betrayed? Why, whom have I betrayed?

FOREST ELF
Yourself.
You gave up dwelling in the high tree tops
And came down low to walk in baser paths.
And now you're like to some poor serving maid
Who, by the fruit of bitter toil, had hoped
A scrap of happiness to win. Then when
She's found it all in vain, a sense of shame
Allows her not a beggar to become.
Remember what you were that night in spring,
When your life flowered into glorious bloom:
That night you seemed to be a Forest Queen,
A crown of stars upon your green-black hair.
Then eagerly did happiness stretch forth
Its hands and offered you its choicest gifts!

MAVKA
What shall I do now when those stars are gone,
Extinguished in my crown and in my heart?

FOREST ELF

Not all the stars are faded out for you.
Behold, see what a festival is here!
The maple-prince has donned his golden robes,
The wild rose all her wealth of corals wears;
While innocence has changed to purple proud
Upon the cranberry, whose flowers you wore
When nightingales intoned your marriage song.
The ancient willow, e'en the mournful birch
Have put on gold and crimson, rich brocades,
For autumn's festival. And you alone
Will not cast off that beggar's garb of yours.
You seem to have forgotten that no grief
Should ever triumph over loveliness.

MAVKA

Then, grandsire, give to me my festal robes!
Once more I'll queen it as the forest's pride,
And happiness shall fall down at my feet,
Beseeching favors at my hand!

FOREST ELF

My child,
Those robes were long since ready for the queen,
But she, capriciously, has tarried long
While wearing for a jest a beggar's gown.

He throws back his gown and brings from underneath it a splendid crimson robe, embroidered with gold, together with a silvery veil. MAVKA swiftly runs to the cranberry tree and breaks off some of its sprays covered with red berries and weaves herself a chaplet. She then lets down her hair, places the chaplet on her head, and bows before FOREST ELF who throws the silvery veil over her head.

FOREST ELF

No longer now do I feel fear for you.

Gravely nodding to MAVKA, he swiftly skips off into the bushes and disappears. A moment later WILL-O'-THE-WISP comes running out of the forest.

MAVKA

What! You again?

She makes as if to flee.

WILL-O'-THE-WISP

(Contemptuously)   Fear not, I don't seek you . . .
I came to see the sprite who's in the rye,
But she's already gone to sleep. Too bad . . .
You're sadly wasted, too.

MAVKA

(Proudly)   To you, it seems!

WILL-O'-THE-WISP

"It seems," you say? Let me more closely look.
        (He draws nearer, MAVKA retreats.)
Why are you so afraid of me? I know
You are betrothed. I will not pester you.

MAVKA

Away! Hands off!

WILL-O'-THE-WISP

        Now, don't get so worked up . . .
Suppose I did wrong you? . . . Now, Mavka, come
And make it up. Let us be friends.

MAVKA

                    With you?

WILL-O'-THE-WISP

Why not with me? We're both in autumn now.
Don't you perceive the sun is growing cold
And our blood's running slow? There was a time
When we were good companions—whether then
We played or lovers were, 'tis hard to say.
But now's the time for brotherhood. Your hand!

    (MAVKA, after a momentary hesitation, gives him her hand.)
Permit me to bestow a brother kiss
On that pale face of yours.

    (MAVKA shrinks, but he kisses her all the same.)
                    O flowers on
That lovely face, again ye have bloomed out!

Autumnal, unexpected, and benign . . .
  (Without releasing her hand he looks around the glade.)
  See the spider's gossamer
  Swings and spirals in the air . . .
  And so do we . . .
  (With a sudden movement he draws her into a dance.)
    And so do we;
    As swiftly swirling,
    Circling free!
  The stars that blaze,
  Sun's golden rays,
  The clear and brilliant lights that daze
    All that glitters,
    All that flitters,
  In one unceasing mad career!
    And so do I . . .
    And so do I . . .
  Be like a spark, my love most dear!
  He whirls furiously in the dance. MAVKA's *silvery veil swirls*
up in the air like a glittering serpent, her black tresses, now
madly dishevelled, intermingle with WILL-O'-THE-WISP's *fiery*
red curls.

MAVKA

    Enough! Enough, I say!

WILL-O'-THE-WISP

    In unrestrained play
  Stay not a moment doubtfully!
    For happiness will cheat,
    And only that is sweet
  Which whirls and flies eternally!
      (The dance becomes delirious.)

    Let us whirl!
    Let us whirl!
  And like the whirlwind rise!
    Let us know
    Here below
  A frenzied, fiery paradise!

MAVKA

Enough! . . . Release me now . . . I faint . . . I swoon.

Her head falls helplessly on his shoulder, her arms hang limply, but he carries her swooning along in the dance.

Suddenly from under the earth, there rises a dark, bulky, awe-inspiring shape.

PHANTOM

Release her. Render to me what is mine.

WILL-O'-THE-WISP *stops, letting* MAVKA *fall out of his embrace. She sinks down helplessly on the ground.*

WILL-O'-THE-WISP

Ha, who are you?

PHANTOM

Do you not know me then?
I'm "He Who Dwells in Rock."

WILL-O'-THE-WISP *shudders, and with a swift turn, he dashes away and vanishes in the forest.*

MAVKA *comes to herself and sitting up she opens her eyes wide and gazes with horror at the* PHANTOM *which is stretching out its hands to lay hold of her.*

MAVKA

No, touch me not!
I do not wish to come! I'm still alive!

"HE WHO DWELLS IN ROCK"

I come to lead you to a distant land,
An unknown land, where quiet waters dark
Serenely sleep in peace; where silent rocks
Hang over them and stare with clouded eyes,
Mute witnesses of what is past and gone.
'Tis calm and tranquil there, for neither trees nor grass
E'er stir or murmur to bring on bad dreams—
Those treacherous dreams which always banish sleep.
And thither on the winds are borne no songs
Of freedoms unattainable; no fires
On altars e'er burn there. The lightning's points
Are blunted on those rocks and never can
Pierce through to that stronghold of gloom and peace.

I'll take you there. 'Tis there that you belong.
The fire has made you pale, the movement weak;
Your happiness is but a shade—you're dead.

MAVKA

No, I'm alive! I'll live eternally!
I have that in my heart which cannot die!

"HE WHO DWELLS IN ROCK"

By what are you so sure?

MAVKA
By this:

I love my pain, for I gave life to it.
If it were possible for me to wish
E'er to forget it, then I'd go with you;
But in this world there is no power so strong
That could e'en stir a longing to forget.
(The sound of human footfalls is heard in the forest.)
Lo, here he comes, the one who gave the pain!
Now vanish, Phantom, for here comes my life!

"HE WHO DWELLS IN ROCK" *retreats into the dark bushes
and there waits in ambush.* LUKASH *emerges out of the forest.*

MAVKA *goes to meet* LUKASH. *Her face with its deadly
pallor stands out in contrast against her resplendent garments.
Expiring hope distends her large dark eyes, her movements are
convulsive and faltering as though something within her is giving way.*

LUKASH
(On perceiving her)

Oh, dreadful sight! What do you want with me?
*(He rushes to the house and knocks on the door. His mother
opens but remains standing within.* LUKASH *on the threshold
cries out.)*
Hey, Mother, make the bridal loaf at once!
Tomorrow to Kilina I'll send word!
He enters and the door is shut behind him.

"HE WHO DWELLS IN ROCK" *touches* MAVKA *who with a
cry falls into his hands. He casts the skirt of his black robe over
her and both sink into the ground.*

ACT III

A cloudy, windy, autumn night. The last pallid gleams of moonlight fade out amidst the wild confusion of the forest's naked tree tops. Eerie, piercing cries of nighthawks, owls, and other nocturnal birds of prey are heard. Suddenly all these sounds are drowned out by the long-drawn mournful howling of a wolf. The howling grows louder and louder, and then suddenly breaks off. Silence follows.

A sickly, late autumn dawn soon begins to appear. The leafless trees of the forest bristle against the ashen grey sky. The white walls of LUKASH's *cottage begin to loom; and, leaning against one of the walls, the dark figure of someone apparently worn-out becomes visible. Although hardly recognizable, it is* MAVKA. *She is dressed in black, with a grey opaque veil, and her only ornament is a tiny nosegay of cranberry blossom on her bosom.*

As it grows lighter in the glade a large stump becomes visible on the spot where once stood the ancient oak, and close beside it there is a recently filled-in grave not yet overgrown with grass.

Out of the forest comes FOREST ELF. *He is wearing a grey smock and has a cap of wolf's fur on his head.*

FOREST ELF
(Peering at the figure leaning against the wall of the house)
That you, my child?

MAVKA
(Moving slightly towards him) It is.

FOREST ELF
And can it be
That "He Who Dwells in Rock" has let you go?

MAVKA
It was your crime that set me free to come.

FOREST ELF
You call it "crime," that vengeance which I took?

'Twas righteous judgment I inflicted on
That sweetheart, base and treacherous, of yours!
Was it not just that he should know what 'tis
To feel a dread, unearthly, wild despair
In roaming through the woods in wolflike form?
Now he is nothing but a savage wolf!
Then let him whine and howl—let him feel thirst
For taste of human blood—'twill not assuage
His torments and his pains!

MAVKA

               Do not exult!
For I've delivered him. Within my heart
I found the magic liberating word
Which transforms brute back into human form.

FOREST ELF

(Stamping his foot with rage, he snaps his staff in two.)
Unworthy of the name of forest child!
Your soul is no more of the forest free,
But of the slavish house!

MAVKA

            Oh, if you knew,
If you but knew how terrible it was . . .
I slept a stonelike sleep there in the rock,
In depths profound, in blackness, damp and cold,
When lo! a dreadful echo broke clean through
The rock impregnable—a long-drawn howl.
The wild despairing howl went drifting o'er
The dark and lifeless waters and aroused
Vibrations long since muted in that place . . .
And I awoke. Like subterranean fire
My ardent pity split the granite vault,
And I broke out again into the light.
The magic word gave life to my dumb lips—
I wrought a miracle . . . I only knew
I was not destined to forgetfulness.

FOREST ELF

Where is he now? Why is he not with you?

Is his ingratitude eternal as
Your deathless love?

MAVKA

Ah, grandsire, could you but
Have seen him then! He, in his human form,
Sank down before me, like a maple felled . . .
He, in abasement, lifted up to me
A countenance so anguished, full of pain,
And deepest penitence, and hopelessness . . .
None but a human face can look like that!
But yet, before I found a word to speak,
He sprang convulsively up to his feet,
And, covering his face with trembling hands,
Rushed off into the bush and disappeared.

FOREST ELF

What do you think of doing now, my child?

MAVKA

I do not know . . . I, like a shadow, roam
About this house and have no longer strength
To leave this spot . . . for in my heart I feel
'Tis hither that he will return . . .

FOREST ELF

(After a moment's silence during which MAVKA *resumes her
position leaning against the wall.)*
Poor child!
Why did you leave us for that land of gloom?
Could you not rest here in your native groves?
See how the willow is awaiting you;
Already, long ago, she spread your bed,
And mourns because of your long tarrying.
Go there and rest.

MAVKA

(Softly)   Ah, Grandsire, but I can't.

FOREST ELF *sighing deeply, betakes himself to the forest.
From the forest is heard a violent stamping as though
someone is ruthlessly riding a horse. It ceases.*

KUTZ

(He comes skipping and hopping from behind the house,
rubbing his hands, but stops on perceiving MAVKA.)
Mavka, you here?

MAVKA

And you, why are you here?

KUTZ

I got their horse out, now I've brought him back.
A glorious ride he gave me this last time.
No one will ever drive him any more!

MAVKA

O shameless one! Our forest you disgrace!
Is this how you keep faith with Uncle Lev?

KUTZ

Our compact of good faith died out with him.

MAVKA

What! Uncle Lev is dead?

KUTZ

There is his grave.
They buried him beneath the oak, but now
The old man needs must lie beside the stump.

MAVKA

So, both are gone . . . a strong presentiment
He felt that he would not see winter through . . .
(She approaches the grave.)
Alas! how shall my heart weep over thee,
My only human friend! If I could but
Shed living tears, I would bedew this ground
With them and bring forth myrtles ever green
Upon thy grave. But now I'm destitute;
My grief has no more weight than withered leaves . . .

KUTZ

Pity beseems me not, yet still I must
Confess, I feel regret for that old man,
For he knew how to live on terms with us.
With all his horses he was wont to keep

A goat so I could ride on it at night.
As lightning flies, I'd ride on that black goat,
His horses meanwhile left alone in peace.
Those women don't know how to live on terms
With us at all. They sold the goat; they had
The oak chopped down; they broke good faith with us.
Well, I have paid them back! I rode to death
Their working horses; they buy more—I ride.
I asked the witch who acts as midwife for
Old Nick to use her arts upon their cows,
And she did well. Oh, yes, they'll surely learn!
The Water Goblin waterlogged their ricks;
The Lost Babes dusted rust amongst their grain;
And now the Fever Wraith is thrashing them,
Because with offal they defiled the lake.
They'll never thrive now in this forest glade,
The Starvelings round their house already lurk!

STARVELINGS

(Small wizened creatures, in rags, their faces seamed with the signs of eternal hunger, suddenly appear from around the corner of the house.)
We're here! Who's calling us!

MAVKA

Go, disappear!

No one was calling you!

ONE STARVELING

The word went forth,

Can't be recalled.

STARVELINGS

(Besieging the threshold)   Hey, open up the door,
At once, at once! We're starving, famishing!

MAVKA

I will not let you in!

STARVELINGS

Give us to eat!

MAVKA

I haven't anything . . .

STARVELINGS
The cranberries
You're wearing on your bosom! Give us those!

MAVKA

But that's my blood.

STARVELINGS
No matter! We love blood.
One of them rushes at her and tears the nosegay from her breast. The others snatch at it to get a piece, fighting among themselves and yelping like dogs.

KUTZ
Hey, Starvelings, stop it! . . . She's not humankind!
They desist, gnashing their teeth and whimpering from hunger.

STARVELINGS
(To KUTZ)
Well, you give us to eat or we'll eat you!
They rush at KUTZ who jumps backwards.

KUTZ

Now, now, go slow!

STARVELINGS
Give us to eat! We starve!

KUTZ
Just wait a while; I'll wake those women up.
You'll all get food, and I'll have sport besides.
He picks up a clod of earth and hurls it at the window, smashing in the glass.

VOICE OF MOTHER
(From inside)
Oy! What was that? Some evil sprites again!

KUTZ
(Whispering to the STARVELINGS)
Now, now, you see, she is awake; and soon
You'll hear your name. But sit here still,
Or else the dame will put a curse on you

And you'll sink through the ground. She knows the word.

The STARVELINGS *crouch in a dark corner at the threshold.*
From inside the house through the broken window panes
are heard the movements of MOTHER *getting up; then her voice,*
next that of KILINA.

MOTHER
It's nearly broad daylight and still she sleeps.
Kilina! Hey, Kilina! Still she sleeps.
(Would that she slept for good!) . . .Get up, get up!
(Would that she never rose!) . . .

KILINA
(Sleepily)
What now? What's wrong!

MOTHER
(Spitefully)
Get up and go and milk that cow of yours,
That fine young cow, that one of Turkish breed,
Which your departed hubby got for you.

KILINA
(Now fully awake)
I'll go and milk the one that I found here;
She'll give me just about three drops of milk—
A pound of butter, eh?

MOTHER
You'd best not talk!
Who is to blame if we don't get more milk,
With such a famous dairymaid? . . . Oy, woe!
A daughter-in-law like this! What have we done
To merit such bad luck?

KILINA
Who was it, pray,
Sent me the invitation? What about
That slattern you had here? Why didn't you
Take her and dress her up a bit? You'd then
Have had a daughter-in-law to suit your taste.

MOTHER

You don't think so?   But that she would have been!
That stupid Lukash gave her up for you;
And yet she was obedient, kind, and good,
No matter what you did to her . . . You call
Her slattern, do you? and yet you yourself
Have taken that green dress of hers and made
It over and you're wearing it—for shame!

KILINA

Why not?   You've got to find your own clothes here! . . .
Here is my husband, gone off with the wind.
We're sinking into poverty the while.
I'm neither wife nor widow—just a waif!

MOTHER

Could any husband stick it out with you?
You greedy shark!   What we had, you've devoured,
You and your shameless brood—see, there they sit!
May famine take the lot of you some day!

KILINA

Starvation take her first who speaks the curse!
   At these words the door suddenly opens. The STARVELINGS
jump up and rush into the house while KUTZ *flees off into the*
marsh.
   KILINA *with a pail in her hands hurries to the forest stream*
nearby and with a splash fills the pail with water, then returns at
a somewhat slower pace.   She notices MAVKA, *her face covered*
with the grey veil, who is leaning weakly against the wall near the
doorway.

KILINA

(Stopping and putting down the pail)

Good Lord, who's this? . . . Hey, listen, are you drunk,
Or maybe frozen stiff?
   She shakes MAVKA *by the shoulder.*

MAVKA

(With difficulty, as though struggling with an overpowering
drowsiness)

                    Sleep conquers me . . .
The sleep of winter.

KILINA
(Throwing back the veil and recognizing her)
                Why have you come here?
Maybe they didn't pay you for your work?

MAVKA
(As before)
No one can ever pay me what is due.

KILINA
For what then did you come? He isn't here.
I know, you're after him! Come now, confess;
Is he your lover still?

MAVKA
(Still as before)
                  Once, long before
This gloomy day, there was a morning red . . .
               But now he's dead . . .

KILINA
You've gone insane!

MAVKA
               No, sane, and free again!
The cloud drifts slowly 'cross the sky,
Without a goal, to perish by and by . . .
           Where do those azure lightnings fly?

KILINA
(Plucking at MAVKA's sleeve)
Be off! Don't frighten me! Why stand you here?

MAVKA
(Now somewhat more aware, she steps away from the door.)
I stand to watch how happy you are here.

KILINA
I wish you stood amidst your charms and spells!

    MAVKA *is suddenly transformed into a willow with withered leaves and drooping branches.*

KILINA

(Recovering from her stupefaction, viciously)
Ah, 'twas a lucky hour when I said that!
Now you can stand and watch us all you want! . . .

BOY

(Running out of the house, to KILINA)
Hey, Mother! Where are you? We want to eat,
And Granny won't give us a bite!

KILINA

She won't?
(Bending down and whispering to the boy)
Behind the stove I hid a piece of pie—
When Granny goes outside, you eat it up.

BOY
(Pointing)
Who put that withered willow there? Did you?
What did you do that for?

KILINA

What's that to you?

BOY

I'll make a whistle from it.

KILINA

I don't care.
The boy cuts off a twig and goes back into the house.
LUKASH *comes out of the forest, emaciated, with long hair, ragged
and without coat or cap.*

KILINA

*(At first crying out joyfully, but immediately changing to
vexation)*
So here you are! Where've you been carrying on
For all this time?

LUKASH

Don't ask . . .

KILINA

I mustn't ask?
You run away, footloose, the Lord knows where!

You chase around and then you say: "Don't ask!"
But, dearie, I don't need to ask you where . . .
Some place where there's a tavern, where a fool
Can swill, and gamble all his clothes away.

LUKASH

It was no tavern . . .

KILINA
Who'll believe it, dolt!
(Striking up a song)
"I have been forced to spend a wedded life
With this sad drunkard . . ."

LUKASH
Shut your mouth!   Stop it!
(KILINA stops, gazing at him in fright.)
See here, let me ask you a question, too.
Where is my Uncle's oak, where that stump stands?

KILINA
(At first confused, but swiftly recovering)
Well, what were we to do?   Eat famine fare?
The merchants came, they bought, and that was all.
An oak is just a tree!

LUKASH
But Uncle Lev
Swore it should ne'er be felled.

KILINA
Your Uncle Lev
Is dead and gone, so what is his oath worth?
Did either you or I swear any oath?
I'd gladly sell the whole cursed forest too,
Or root it out entire.   Then we'd have land
Like other folk and not this bush bewitched.
When evening comes, it terrifies one's soul,
And what good do we ever win from it?
We grub here in the forest like the wolves,
And, really, soon we'll learn to howl like them.

LUKASH

Hush, hush! Don't talk like that! Shut up!
(His voice vibrates with a terrified apprehensiveness)
You say
To sell the forest . . . cut it down . . . and then
It won't be like . . . what you just said?

KILINA

Said what?
That like the wolves . . .

LUKASH

(Gripping her and covering her mouth with his hand)
No, don't say it!

KILINA

(Freeing herself from his grasp)
Good God!
You're drunk, or mad, or someone's put a spell
On you! Go in the house.

LUKASH

All right, I'll go . . .
I'll go at once . . . but first I'll take a drink.

He kneels down and drinks from the pail. He then stands up and stares moodily into space without stirring from the spot.

KILINA

What are you thinking of?

LUKASH

I? . . . I don't know . . .
(Hesitatingly)
Did someone come while I was gone?

KILINA

(Viciously)
Who would
Come here?

LUKASH

(Dropping his eyes)
I know not . . .

KILINA
(With a wicked smile)
                              You don't know?
But maybe I know who.

LUKASH
(In alarm)
You do?

KILINA
                              Why not?
I plainly see whom you expected here.
'Tis all in vain—too bad for what you'd hoped!
Whate'er was here, it's gone into that tree . . .

LUKASH
What's that you say?

KILINA
                    Just what you heard.

MOTHER
(She comes running out of the house and rushes to embrace
LUKASH. *He receives her embrace coldly.)*
                              My son!
My son! Oh dear! what have I suffered from
This wicked witch!

LUKASH
(Shuddering)
              What witch?

MOTHER
(Pointing to KILINA*)*
                    Why, this one here!

LUKASH
(With a contemptuous smile)
So, she's the witch? . . . Well now, it was your fate
To be a witch's mother-in-law for sure.
And who's to blame for it? You wanted her.

MOTHER
If I had known she could be such a slut,

And such a dirty idleback . . .

KILINA
(Breaking in)

Oy, woe!
Who would have thought it!   Never in the world
Was such a witch, a slattern such as she!
See what a mother, Lukash, you have got!
She's hard as iron, she will wear you down.

LUKASH

And you are just as hard as she is, too.

KILINA

No use expecting any help from you!
Like mother, so's the son, 'tis plain to see!
For what ill fortune did you bring me here?
To make a mock of me?

MOTHER

Why don't you, son,
Tell her to shut that mouth of hers?   Am I
A skittle to be knocked about by her?

LUKASH

Here, both of you, give me a moment's peace!
Do you want me to clear out of this house
And run away for good?   By God, I will!

KILINA
(To MOTHER)

You see, that's what you get.

MOTHER

I hope you get
The same from your son too.

*(Raging, she goes into the house again and on the threshold
she meets KILINA's son, who is running out with a willow pipe
in his hand.)*

Get out, you brat!
She slaps the boy and goes inside, slamming the door.

BOY

Oh, Papa, you've come back!

LUKASH

I have, my son.

He puts an ironical emphasis on the word "son."

KILINA

(Offended)

Well, tell the child how he should call you then.
It's "Uncle," isn't it?

LUKASH

(Somewhat ashamed)

I don't care which!

Come here, come here, my child!   Don't be afraid.

(He pats the boy's blond head.)

So, did you make that pipe yourself?

BOY

I did.

But still I don't know how to play.   Show me!

He holds the pipe out to LUKASH.

LUKASH

Eh, boy, my days for playing are all past!

He falls into a moody pensiveness.

BOY

(Persistently)

Ah, you don't want to show me!   Mother, hey!
Why doesn't Papa want to show me how?

KILINA

Who cares?   A lot of good that playing does!

LUKASH

Here, hand the pipe to me.

(He takes it.)

A fine one, too.

You made it out of willow?

BOY

That tree there.

He points to the willow into which MAVKA *has been trans-*
formed.

LUKASH

It seems to me I ne'er saw that before.
(To KILINA*)*
You planted it?

KILINA

Who'd ever plant it there?
Some willow branch fell down and sprouted roots;
The water made it grow . . . and all these rains . . .

BOY
(Eagerly)

Why don't you play a bit?

LUKASH
(Absently)
Eh? Play a bit? . . .
(He begins to play, at first softly, then more and more loudly
until he strikes into the spring song which he once played to
MAVKA. *As he does so the words begin to come out of the pipe:)*
"How lovely is the strain
Of mingled joy and pain;
It cuts deep in the breast
And cleaves the heart in twain."

LUKASH
(Letting the pipe fall out of his hands)
What sort of pipe is this? Black magic! Spells!

(The BOY *terrified, flees into the house.* LUKASH *seizes* KILINA
by the shoulder.)
Speak up, you sorceress! What tree is that?

KILINA

Here, take your hands off me! How should I know?
I don't associate with forest sprites
As your folks do. Now fell it, if you want to!
No one is stopping you. I'll get the axe.
She goes into the house and returns, bringing an axe.

LUKASH

*(Having taken the axe, he approaches the tree and strikes its
trunk once. It shrinks and makes a murmuring with its dry leaves.
He gets ready for another swing but his arms fall down powerless.)*
I cannot raise my arms at all; I can't . . .
There's something gripping at my heart . . .

KILINA

Let me!
She snatches the axe from LUKASH *and takes a violent swing
at the willow. At that instant, like the flying tail of a meteor,*
WILL-O-THE-WISP *swoops down from the air above and embraces
the tree.*

WILL-O-THE-WISP

I will deliver you, belovéd one!
*Suddenly the tree bursts into flame. Reaching the topmost
branches, the fire sweeps over on to the house, setting fire to its
straw roof. The flames speedily envelop the entire dwelling.*
MOTHER *and* KILINA'S *children come rushing out with cries of*
"Fire, fire!" "Save us, help!" MOTHER *and* KILINA *rush about,
snatching up whatever they can from the conflagration. They
carry out bundles and sacks on which the* STARVELINGS *are perched,
after which the latter creep into the bundles and sacks and hide
themselves inside. The children run with pails and vessels of all
sorts, pouring water on the fire, but it rages too fiercely to be
extinguished.*

MOTHER

(To LUKASH*)*
Why are you standing there? Help save your goods!

LUKASH

*(With his eyes fixed on the roof, from which innumerable
flowers of flame are now bursting out.)*
My goods? Maybe 'twill burn the evil, too?
*The rooftree cracks, pillars of sparks and flame fly up high,
the roof collapses and the whole house becomes a furnace. A
heavy dark cloud rises in the sky and snow begins to fall. Soon
nothing is visible through the heavy white blanket except the
crimson glow where the fire still burns. Gradually the red glow*

dies down and when the snowfall slackens, a blackened spot is visible where the fire had been, still smoking and hissing from the damp snow falling. MOTHER *and* KILINA's *children with the bundles and sacks are no longer to be seen. Through the snow flakes there loom indistinctly an undamaged shed, a cart, and some farm implements.*

KILINA

(Carrying the final bundle, she twitches LUKASH *by the sleeve.)*
Hey, Lukash, stir yourself!   Come, wake up now!
You might at least help me to carry this!

LUKASH

You carried all the Starvelings out with you.

KILINA

Come, pinch yourself!   What are you talking of?

LUKASH

(With a queer, quiet smile)
Ah, wife, I see that which you cannot see . . .
I've learned some wisdom now . . .

KILINA

(Frightened)
Oh, husband, how
Can you say such strange things . . . you frighten me!

LUKASH

Why be afraid? A fool you never feared;
Why fear a wise man now ?

KILINA

Come, Lukash dear,
Let's go back to the village.

LUKASH

I won't go.
I'll never leave the forest. Here I'll stay.

KILINA

What sort of work can you get here?

LUKASH

Why must

We work at all?

KILINA

But still we've got to live?

LUKASH

And must we live?

KILINA

For God's sake, husband, have
You gone completely off your head, or what?
Maybe what's happened here has been too much.
Come to the village. I can get a dame
Whose spells will break the charm.

She pulls at his sleeve.

LUKASH

(Looking at her with a contemptuous smile)
Who's going to stay
To keep a watch on this that still remains?

He points to the cart and farm implements.

KILINA

(Speaking like a thrifty housewife)
Oh, yes, that's right. They'd all be carted off!
Just let them learn our place has been burned down,
And every living soul would soon be here!
Yes, Lukash, maybe you had best stay here.
I'll run off somewhere, borrow me a horse—
For ours have all been roasted in the fire.
We'll load this on the cart and then we'll drive
To your folks—maybe they will take us in . . .
Oy, woe! We've got to save ourselves somehow . . .

She is already running into the forest while speaking these last words. LUKASH *follows her departure with a quiet laugh when she is finally lost to view.*

From the forest there approaches a tall female form wearing a robe descending to her feet and with a white headdress arranged in antique style. She walks with a hesitant motion as though swayed by the wind, stopping now and then and bending down

as though searching for something on the ground. When she has
drawn near, she stops beside the dewberry bushes growing close
to the blackened ruins, straightens up and reveals a female face
with wasted features but strongly like those of LUKASH.

LUKASH

Who are you? What do you here?

PHANTOM

I am your lost Destiny,
    Led into a labyrinth
    By unthinking villainy.
    Like a shadow through this grove
    Evermore I weave and rove,
Searching with sad eyes where the pathway lies
    Leading to lost Paradise.
    But the pathway I would trace
    By the snow is drifted o'er;
    Now in this blank labyrinth
    I am lost for evermore! . . .

LUKASH

    Break off, O my Destiny,
    From this dewberry a spray;
Though the snow be deep, through its thickness sweep
    Till you find that little way.

DESTINY

    Once in springtime in these groves
    Here I walked and planted there
    On the pathway guiding signs:
    Lovely flowers, rich and rare.
    But, unheeding, 'neath your feet
    You trod down those flowers sweet.
Now beneath the snow thorns and briers grow;
    Gone is every sign, I know.

LUKASH

    Search then, O my Destiny,
    With your hands beneath the snow,

If perchance a single stem
Of those flowers still doth grow.

DESTINY
Cold already are my hands,
And my strength is running low.
Though I weep and wail, nothing can avail.
Death approaches; I must go.
With a groan, the PHANTOM *moves on.*

LUKASH
(Stretching out his hands after the departing figure)
Tell me, how can one live on
When one's happiness is gone?

DESTINY
(Pointing to the ground at his feet)
Only like a twig that's found,
Cut off, lying on the ground!

LUKASH *bends down to the spot at which* DESTINY *had pointed and finds there the willow pipe he had let fall out of his hands.
He picks it up and goes across the white glade to the birch. He
sits down under its long branches heavy with snow, and turns the
pipe round and round in his hands, smiling at times like a child.*

*An ethereal, white, transparent form, with features recalling
those of* MAVKA, *appears from behind the birch and bends over*
LUKASH.

FORM OF MAVKA
O play, O play, give voice unto my heart!
'Tis all there is that now remains of me!

LUKASH
'Tis you? And have you as a vampire come
To suck my blood away? Come, drain it all!
(He bares his breast.)
Come, take new life from this my blood! You must,
For I have taken yours . . .

MAVKA
Nay, nay, dear heart,

You gave to me a soul, as the sharp knife
Gives to the willow twig a tender voice.

LUKASH

Your soul from me? Your body I destroyed!
For you are but a phantom now, a shade!
He looks at her with unexpressable pain.

MAVKA

Ah, for that body do not sigh!
'Tis now infused and glows with fire divine,
As clear and bright and glittering as good wine
Whose life in sparkling bubbles mounts on high.

Naught but an airy pinch of dust
Remains to mingle with the earth below.
Beside these waters shall a willow grow,
My end give life to something more robust.

And to me here shall many seek,
Both rich and poor, the joyful and the sad.
Their griefs I'll mourn, their joys shall make me glad—
To every one my soul shall gently speak.

And I shall find some word for all:
The quiet murmur of my rustling leaves;
The willow pipe that tender music breathes;
The melancholy dews that from my branches fall.

I'll give them back in mystic speech
All those dear tender songs you used to sing,
The tunes you played for me in that lost spring—
O play again, belovéd, I beseech!

LUKASH *begins to play. At first his music is melancholy,
like the winter wind, like a yearning for something lost and unforgettable, but soon the invincible song of love overcomes the
nostalgic tones. As the music changes, so winter all around under-
goes a transformation; the birches rustle their crinkly leaves, the*

sounds of spring are heard in the flowering groves, the dull winter day passes into a clear, moonlit, spring night. MAVKA *suddenly flashes out in all her former beauty with her starry crown alight.* LUKASH, *with a cry of ecstatic joy, rushes towards her.*

The wind lashes the white blossoms off the trees. The blossoms fall and fall until the pair of lovers are completely covered over, then the blossoms change into thick flakes of snow. When the snowfall ceases, the landscape is again a winter one, with snow clinging thickly on all the branches of the trees. LU-KASH *is sitting alone, leaning against the birch, with the pipe in his hands, his eyes closed and his lips set in a happy smile. He sits motionless. The snow falls over him like a thickening robe until his form becomes indistinguishable, and keeps on falling, falling endlessly. . . .*

Martianus the Advocate

Dramatic Poem in Two Scenes

DRAMATIS PERSONAE

MARTIANUS AEMILIUS, *an advocate*
AURELIA, *his daughter*
VALENTIUS, *his son*
ALBINA, *his sister*
LUCILLA, *her daughter*
CONSTANTIUS, Martianus' *clerk*
BROTHER ISOGENES, *an important member of the Christian clergy*
ARDENTUS, *a young Christian*
MOMUS, *a deaf-mute slave*
GERMANUS, *a doorkeeper*
CENTURION OF THE WATCH
GUARDS AND NEIGHBORS

The action takes place in the house of Martianus in Puteoli *near Naples during the third century, A.D.*

SCENE I

The peristyle or inner courtyard of MARTIANUS' *house. It is surrounded by a covered colonnade, plain, almost austere in style, and chambers, the doors of which open onto the colonnade. On one side the building rises in two stories, with steps leading to the upper one. The courtyard is strewn with sand and planted in places with evergreen shrubs, mostly aloes; plain benches of stone are placed here and there. In the center is a small pool without flowers or any ornamentation; beside it stands a sundial*

and a water-clock, together with a post with a gong hanging on it,
a mallet, and a lantern on a projecting hook. At the back of the
courtyard is a narrow double-leafed door with a small window in
one half and a wicket in the other. When the door stands open
a splendid view of the sea is visible. In the foreground between
two columns is MARTIANUS' *tablinum or office, a fairly large*
room, also very plain without any ornamentation, furnished with
shelves on which, arranged in good order, are tablets, codices,
rolls of parchments, and implements for writing. The rear wall
only of the tablinum is solid, the two other sides being made by
curtains which can be pushed back, while the front is open.
CONSTANTIUS, *a young man of modest appearance, is getting the*
tablinum ready for work: placing various documents on the small
table, pushing an armchair with a footstool up to the table, open-
ing a folding tabouret, smoothing the wax tablets and sharpening
styli for writing. MOMUS, *the deaf-mute slave, is brushing dust*
off the sundial and watching to see where the shadow falls. Sud-
denly he takes the mallet and beats the gong vigorously as though
sounding an alarm, but doing so with set features, perfectly calm,
like one who is living in a world of absolute silence. From one
side by a passage beyond the tablinum MARTIANUS *enters. He is a*
man of advancing years but not as yet old. He touches MOMUS
on the shoulder, smiles and makes a sign with his hand that fur-
ther beating is not necessary. MOMUS *stops, goes away to one*
side and, taking up a rake, begins to smooth the sand around the
shrubs. MARTIANUS *goes into his tablinum.*

MARTIANUS

Good day, Constantius.

CONSTANTIUS
Good day, my patron.

MARTIANUS
Our Momus is like fate, implacable.
The work will never lag on his account.
(Sits down in the armchair.)
Have you looked through these things to see what's first?

CONSTANTIUS
Yes, sir. The first is that case which concerns

The confiscated land which now belongs
Unto the local church.

MARTIANUS
     'Tis well. I have
Already something strong for the defence,
But look through all the laws and ascertain
How long a funeral society
May still maintain its rights unto the ground
Once granted to it as a burial place,
But which no longer serves for funerals.

  CONSTANTIUS *takes down a codex from a shelf, seats himself
on the tabouret and goes to work.* MARTIANUS *picks up one of
the rolls lying on the table and reads attentively.*

CONSTANTIUS
(Timidly, without lifting his head)
O patron, there is still one private suit.

MARTIANUS
Whose is it?

CONSTANTIUS
   Yours.

MARTIANUS
      I do not understand.
CONSTANTIUS
It is your wife's.

MARTIANUS
(Angrily)
You know I have no wife.

CONSTANTIUS
Forgive me . . . What I should have said is that
There's a report that Tullia's entered claim
Before the courts for half of your estate,
Alleging that it still is due to her
Since you two were divorced.

MARTIANUS
(Manifestly incensed, yet controlling himself)
Well, let her claim!

CONSTANTIUS

You do not wish me to make inquiry?

MARTIANUS

The court will notify us when 'tis called.

CONSTANTIUS

I heard that she has influence in the court;
Her husband, too . . .

MARTIANUS
(Acidly)
I do not care to hear.

Have you picked out that paragraph?

CONSTANTIUS

Yes, sir.

Both continue study in silence. Meanwhile there is a muffled sound of voices at the outer door which rises and then dies down. The door opens and the porter, GERMANUS, enters into the peristyle from the street and gives a tablet to MOMUS, making signs that it is for some one in the upper story. MOMUS takes the tablet and goes with it towards the tablinum. GERMANUS tries to hold him back, but MOMUS looks at him angrily and shakes his head. GERMANUS waves his hand in disgust and goes outside, closing the outer door behind him. MOMUS goes into the tablinum, hands the tablet to MARTIANUS, and remains standing on the threshold.

MARTIANUS

What have we here? From whom and unto whom?
Here are no names inscribed: 'I wait for you,
By day at any time, or even night.
It will be heaven for you. I kiss you, dear,
I love you so.'
(He shrugs his shoulders.)
I do not comprehend!
(With a smile)
Constantius, this may be meant for you?
Excuse my freedom, please.
(Tenders him the tablet.)

CONSTANTIUS
(Refusing it)
No, patron, no!
It is not meant for me, I am quite sure.

MARTIANUS
You needn't be alarmed. The note is well
Composed, polite, yet not without some fire.
(By signs he asks MOMUS *where the tablet came from. MO-
MUS points to the outer door and imitates the gestures made to
him by* GERMANUS. *At this* MARTIANUS *grows angry.)*
A piece of impudence!
He dismisses MOMUS *with a wave of his hand.*

CONSTANTIUS
Maybe a jest.

MARTIANUS
The First of April is already past!
(He goes into the peristyle, turns and speaks to CONSTANTIUS
from the threshold.)
That's all just now. I'll call you later on.
CONSTANTIUS, *picking up the codex, goes out at the left.*

MARTIANUS
(Lifting up his head and calling upstairs)
Aurelia!

AURELIA
(Answering from the upper chambers)
I come!
She runs down the steps to her father. AURELIA *is a young
and beautiful girl. Just now her voice shows signs of nervous-
ness.*

MARTIANUS
(Showing her the tablet)
Perhaps you know
Who wrote this thing.

AURELIA
(After a quick look)
Ah! . . .

She seizes the tablet, puts it in her bosom, and starts to run back upstairs.

MARTIANUS

Wait!

(AURELIA *stops.*)
                        How did you know
It was for you?   It has no signature.

AURELIA

I thought that it . . . well, really . . . I don't know . . .

MARTIANUS
(Severely)

I marvel, daughter, what it can be that
Should make you act like this.   You act as though
You were engaged in some impure intrigue.
This thing of secret letters . . . Someone dares
Invite you to a rendezvous with him;
Who waits 'at any time by day, or night.'
Why can he not come frankly to my house
And honorably ask me for your hand?
Is he ashamed of his unworthiness?

(AURELIA *remains silent.*)

Well, answer me!

AURELIA
                        It's not a 'he' at all . . .

MARTIANUS

What's that you say?   This is no time to jest.

AURELIA

I do not jest . . . 'Twas Mother wrote the note.

MARTIANUS
(Thunderstruck)

What's this I hear?   Well, what impertinence!

AURELIA

Don't speak of Mother thus!   How can it be
Impertinent of her when she loves me?

And I love her as well! Indeed, I do!
She calls me, wishes me to live with her,
And I should long ago have done what she
Requests, were I not so despicably
And shamefully afraid.

She bursts into tears.

MARTIANUS

Ah, now I see
How great an error I was guilty of
In hiding from you all the grievous wrongs
Committed by your mother against me.

AURELIA

(She stops weeping and speaks more calmly.)
No matter. 'Tis not mine to judge you two.
Though she be guilty in regard to you,
She never did the slightest wrong to me.

MARTIANUS

She left you when you were a helpless babe.

AURELIA

She had to leave me, quit this house as well;
And that I have remained in it till now,
'Tis you who are to blame.

MARTIANUS

Bethink yourself!
I'm to be blamed for giving you a home—
Not leaving you to your stepfather's grace?
To your mind, that is wrong?

AURELIA

I'd better hold
My peace, lest I should anger you the more.

MARTIANUS

Your silence now won't be of any help.
Your words have made me seem contemptible.
We'll talk this thing out to the bitter end.

If you desire so much to change this home
For your stepfather's house . . .

AURELIA

What's wrong with that?
If I got married, would I not exchange
Your house to share my husband's dwelling-place?
Would that seem like an insult then to you?

MARTIANUS

But there's a difference!

AURELIA

None that I perceive.
It might be so if daughters all got wed
For love alone. But everyone knows well
How many marry for no other reason but
To get away from their paternal homes.
Such marriages seem worse by far to me
Than what I plan. See, Father! you have turned
This house into a jail for me.

MARTIANUS

How so?

AURELIA

Why, Father, just behold how I live here:
Alone the livelong day; the household slaves,
If they are not deaf-mutes, are foreigners.
And these have all been chosen purposely
In order that they may not hear or talk,
Lest anyone should learn that in this house
The Christian rites are kept.

MARTIANUS

But you know well
That I must keep it secret.

AURELIA

Yes, I know.
But is it any easier for me?
No doubt you've had to keep me here immured,
Shut in, away from other Christian maids,

Lest I in their companionship might catch
Some of their warm devotion and perhaps
Unwittingly betray myself and you.
If I with pagan girls held intercourse,
That would have suited you still less, I know.
I live like hermit in the wilderness . . .

(With a bitter smile)

To make the likeness still more clear, our court
Is strewn with sand, and planted everywhere
With thorny shrubs.   A wilderness!

MARTIANUS
(Gently)

My child,

What reason can I give you in reply?
Perhaps just this: that in our fellowship
There's many another lovely, Christian maid
Who, of her own free will, lives just like you,
Renouncing worldly joys and luxury.

AURELIA

But they do so because of living faith,
While I must perish for a faith that's dead.

MARTIANUS
(Horrified)

A faith that's dead?   A dreadful thing to say!
It cannot be . . . You do believe in Christ?

AURELIA
(Sadly)

I do believe, but my belief seems dead.

MARTIANUS

What do you mean?   This is unnatural!

AURELIA

It seems to me that I do not belong
In any world, nor this, nor that to come.

MARTIANUS

Aurelia!   You pierce me to the heart

With talk like this.

AURELIA
Then, Father, I'll be still.
She hangs her head and folds her hands in meek obedience.

MARTIANUS
No, daughter, no!   Speak out your mind, I pray!
Tell me what burdens you that I may learn
The sickness of your soul.   Maybe, somehow,
We'll find a way to heal it.

AURELIA
'Twill be hard . . .
What has my faith to feed upon, I ask?
It's just like Momus, Father: deaf and dumb,
And all it has to do is quietly
To watch how life goes on like shadows cast
Upon the sunlit dial.   I dare not e'en
Go visit those who lie in bonds, nor serve
The poor, as those same maidens do
Of whom you spoke just now.

MARTIANUS
So that this house
May seem to you less of a wilderness
I'll tell you that in secret ways I help
The poor as far as in me lies.   And, too,
You do not visit those in bonds because,
As one who is not known to share their faith
And therefore has the judges' confidence,
I can the better plead their cause in court.

AURELIA
All this you could do just as well were I
Not here, or better still.   This simple dress
I'm wearing now you could give to the poor,
If I were dead . . .
(Nervously)
Much more, oh how much more
Could I be helpful to you, were I dead!

MARTIANUS

I have not merited such words from you.
'Tis merely vanity and petulance
Which now are speaking. If that 'simple dress'
Distresses you, I'll get you richer robes.

AURELIA

I've no desire for richer robes—for whom
And what should I go clothed in fine array?

MARTIANUS

Now see, you're talking like a pagan girl.
Why this 'for whom and what?' 'Twill not be long
Till Easter Day, when everyone will think,
Yes, e'en the poor, of getting garments new.

AURELIA

And they unto their temples go, a joyous throng.

MARTIANUS

Do we observe our feasts for human eyes?
'Tis only the idolaters do so.
For them a holy day means revelry,
A public orgy, but we Christians must
Observe our feasts in grateful quietness.

AURELIA

I do not know, maybe the thought is sin,
But when we thus observe our festivals,
In privacy, while others publicly
Assemble all together in their joy—
We seem to be a sort of outcast folk;
That God in heaven doth not acknowledge us,
When we do not acknowledge Him on earth
Before all men.

MARTIANUS

             I used to think so once,
But all our people, and the bishop too,
Assured me that my secret services
Meant more unto the Church than martyr's death.

AURELIA
I do not speak for you, but for myself.

MARTIANUS
Is it not possible for you to love
The Christ with fervent, e'en though secret, love?

AURELIA
My love to Christ is like my faith—it's dead.

MARTIANUS
Aurelia! Again those dreadful words.

AURELIA
What lies behind them is more dreadful still . . .
(After a pause)
Do you remember, Father, that first time,
One Christmas Eve, when you told me the tale
Of how God's Son was born in Bethlehem?

MARTIANUS
Ah, yes, indeed. How could I that forget?
I would that I once more might see the light
Which shone so brightly in your childish eyes;
To feel again the tremulous delight
Which thrilled from you to me and filled my soul
The while you sat there listening on my knee.

AURELIA *(Dreamily)*
It was a long time ere I slept that night . . .
I thought and dreamed about that Son of God,
Who came into the world with angels' songs,
With all the splendor of a new-born star.
In thought I travelled all the way to Him
With those three kings, and brought to Him my gifts.
But gold and frankincense and myrrh to me
Seemed all too small to offer to God's Son.
With purple I would fain have draped the stall,
The manger with choice blossoms would have strewn,
In daintiest fabrics would have swathed the babe,
And would have made his playthings out of gems.

MARTIANUS

Dreams such as those are sinless in a child,
But for adults such thoughts are far too close
Unto idolatry.

AURELIA

Be not afraid!
They've long since passed away . . . so soon as when,
The morning after, you said quietly:
'My child, speak not a word to anyone
About the tale I told you yester eve. . . .'
'Tis only now and then, with bitterness,
That I recall them—sometimes when I stood
At our scant household worship. Then I used
To think, 'O God, where are those gifts of mine!'

MARTIANUS

Christ wants no pomp and splendor from His flock.

AURELIA

But I have heard our churches are adorned
With splendid paintings; music there is heard.
Yet all those beauties are forbidden me.
But from my window I may freely look
Upon the pagan worship in the street:
The Saturnalia, the solemn march
Of Roma's priests, the Vestal Virgins' train.
And then I think, 'This faith is false, and yet
There is so much of beauty in its rites,
While our true faith appears so poorly garbed.'
It's thoughts like these that make my faith grow cold.

MARTIANUS

Aurelia! You, as a Christian. know
That there's a higher, purer beauty than
These idol worshippers can e'er conceive.

AURELIA

I do not see it round about me here! . . .
Ah, to be sure, I did discern it once;
But then you told me it was not for me. . . .

MARTIANUS

What, when?

AURELIA

Once when I to the circus went
With Mother . . . You were angry with her then . . .

MARTIANUS

Because I knew what drew her to attend
That vicious sport. Because I felt it shame
To take you there. The whole night long you tossed
About with nightmares, and you shrieked and wept. . . .

AURELIA

But none the less that was the only time
That ever I perceived with my own eyes
The higher beauty, vivid and alive,
Yet terrible . . .

MARTIANUS

And still you shudder now
When you recall it. No, it was not right
That you should have been taken there.

AURELIA

Perhaps . . .
Yet why should I have seen a vision there:
A maiden, young and beautiful and pure,
In garments white, who stood there on the sands
Of the arena, like a lily white
Upon a golden field. Why did I hear
A melody, like an Aeolian harp,
The alleluias she so sweetly sang?
Oh, why, oh, why, did I so clearly see
That living, crimson stream? . . . I understood
Then why those people, all beside themselves,
Came pouring from their seats and cried aloud:
'We, too, will follow Christ!'
Her voice rises hysterically.

MARTIANUS

Hush, not so loud.

Control yourself, my child.

AURELIA

What? Can they hear
Us in the street, while we within these walls
Confess ourselves aloud to Christ our Lord?

MARTIANUS

I must keep it a secret.

AURELIA

Yes, I know.
And you would have me lock my lips as well,
And only in my heart pray unto God?
'Tis so?

MARTIANUS

It is, my child.

AURELIA

That, Father, is
A thing I cannot do. I must forget,
If I am not to speak. And to forget
What I once in the arena saw and felt,
I must depart from you and leave this house.

MARTIANUS

Wherefore, my child?

AURELIA

I only can forget
The lily white by change and blossoming
Into a rose; though not a holy one,
Yet still a lovely one. In order to
Forget the golden sands there must be spread
Luxurious carpetings beneath my feet.
The sounds of the world's music must drown out
The sacred strains of that Aeolian harp.
If from my mind that crimson stream's to fade,
I must be clothed in silks of crimson hue,
And let the flower of youthful manhood flock
Around me with the cry, 'We are your slaves!'

MARTIANUS
(Looking at her with horror)
Aurelia!   Whence learned you such wild dreams?

AURELIA
They came from Mother.

MARTIANUS
Did she teach you them?

AURELIA
She passed them on to me with her own blood,
For I'm her child.

MARTIANUS
Are you not mine as well?

AURELIA
You have deprived me of that heritage.
By sealing up my lips, you also sealed
My heart, and I no longer wish to hear
Its pent-up sighings and its heavy groans.
Those sighs and groans must cease . . . Let me depart,
And to my Mother go.

MARTIANUS
So then you think
That your stepfather will at once provide
Those gold and purple robes?

AURELIA
Yes, Mother said
It should be done as soon as she receives
The money from somewhere.

MARTIANUS
Do you know whence?

AURELIA
I did not ask.   It matters not to me.

MARTIANUS
She is expecting that the courts will give
Her half of my estate.

AURELIA
(Disagreeably surprised)
Can that be true?

MARTIANUS
Maybe that is the reason that she calls
You to her now—to make a better case.

AURELIA
Don't say such things! I will not hear of them!
That Mother sues for part of your estate
Seems not quite right . . . and yet . . . if one reflects
A bit, it really may belong to her.

MARTIANUS
(Sharply)
You have reflected? Well, what then?

AURELIA
But, see!
In any case, my Mother gave to you
The younger, lovelier part of her whole life.

MARTIANUS
For shame! for shame! How can you talk like this?
How can you dream it is a seemly thing
To sell one's life for money, measured off
In portions, first to one, then someone else?
Away with you! You are no child of mine!

AURELIA
(Also flaring up)
No child of yours! I do not wish to be!
To be your child means blindly giving up
My youth, my beauty, yes! my very soul,
To be immured, sequestered from the world,
And all for what? To live in servile state
A tedious, stupid, passive semi-life.

MARTIANUS
But yet for money, it might be endured?
Is that your thought?

AURELIA
                I have already said
All that I think—and for my part, I need
To say no more.
                (*She starts to go, then stops.*)
                Tomorrow Mother will
Depart for Egypt, for, as legate there,
Her husband has by Caesar been assigned.
If I can go to her today, she'll take
Me with her unto Alexandria,
And there I'll live the life of a great princess
In Egypt.

MARTIANUS
            Cleopatra's daughter, eh?
    (AURELIA *flashes him a glance full of hatred and swiftly runs
up the steps to the upper story.* MARTIANUS *starts to follow her,
but stops.*)
No, no . . . what can I say to her?
    (*He sits down helplessly on one of the stone benches.*)
                                    Vile scene!
Disgraceful end!   How could I say such things?
    From a chamber at the rear of the peristyle, VALENTIUS *en-
ters.   He is a young man, resembling* MARTIANUS *not only in
appearance, but also in his movements, although he has not as
much reserve and self-control as his father.*

MARTIANUS
Ah, son, if you but knew what grief is mine!

VALENTIUS
I overheard all from the chamber there.

MARTIANUS
And so?

VALENTIUS
            In some respects my sister's right.

MARTIANUS
She is?

VALENTIUS
(Gently, but firmly)
Of course, just as a woman will,
She let her feelings carry her too far;
Yet 'twas no easy thing for her to speak.
I understand Aurelia. I, too,
Feel that I am a hindrance here at home.
And, truly, Father, what are we to you?

MARTIANUS
You wouldn't ask, if you a father were.

VALENTIUS
I know you love us. And, believe me too,
We love you in return.

MARTIANUS
                                    I cannot say
Your sister demonstrates that love.

VALENTIUS
                                    What then?
You cannot say we are to blame if you
Find neither joy nor helpfulness in us.
We merely vegetate in this our house,
And dare not fully live lest we become
A stumbling block to you upon the path
You needs must tread. Were it not better then,
If neither of us lived with you at all?
For if you love us, it must surely be
A burden to you that on your account
We waste and fritter our young lives away.

MARTIANUS
Why, son, do you say 'we'? I freely grant
That in your sister's training I have failed;
But I've had you brought up a different way:
You went to school, made friends—I never held
You back from outside social intercourse.

VALENTIUS
That, Father, was still worse. Aurelia

Has no idea how hard the world can be,
Or she'd not fret about this 'wilderness' . . .
In school, there were the daily irritants,
Real tortures!   All the pupils there were split
In two opposing camps—of 'Christ' or 'Rome.'
Fierce disputations constantly arose;
Both parties were as bitter enemies
As in real war. By both I was assailed
As bastard 'half-believer,' and today
The name still sticks among the younger set,
Because I—by your order, Father—showed
Indifference to questions of the faith.
I pass for an unfeeling nondescript
Amongst both Christians and idolaters . . .
Yet no one knows what seethes within my heart.

MARTIANUS

The Lord our God knows every secret thought;
He will reward you, son.

VALENTIUS

Reward, for what?

What have I done God's glory to promote?
What deed of mine can merit personal fame?

MARTIANUS

Where have you learned ambition, son?

VALENTIUS

From you.

How my soul felt exalted when you told
About Christ's entry in Jerusalem!
When all the thronging multitudes cried out:
'Hosanna to the Son of God!' and waved
The palms of victory above their heads!
A triumph, that!

MARTIANUS

But not the greatest, son.

By silent, patient suffering of abuse
The Son of God enhanced the crown of thorns
Above all earthly crowns. He triumphed then.

VALENTIUS

Still not the greatest; for, in heaven above,
He sat down on His throne at God's right hand
To wait the Judgment Day, when with the blast
Of trumpets He appears the second time.

MARTIANUS
(Devoutly)

That is our 'blessed hope.' But, see, my son,
The glory there belongs to God, not man!

VALENTIUS

But, Paul the Apostle, Father, was a man;
Yet he won glory over all the earth.
The wisest of the Greek philosophers
Acknowledged his supremacy; his name
Was honored by all peoples, in all tongues;
The churches are his shining lights. And I
Would suffer all to win a fame like that!

MARTIANUS

To all it is not given.

VALENTIUS
I know indeed
That such a fame is not for me to win,
For Martianus dare not have a son
Known as a preacher and evangelist.

MARTIANUS

A lawyer's son may take up law and help
His father in his work. . . . Of course, the task
Is not so glorious.

VALENTIUS
Don't think that I
Despise your work, but it has no appeal
For me, this work of studying laws and codes.
And cases touching Christians do not seem
To come up every day.

MARTIANUS
Thank God for that!

VALENTIUS

But, Father, let me speak quite openly . . .
Such glory as you win would be for me
A barren recompense. I was in court
When you were pleading last. I marvelled how
You could so speak. Before you stepped upon
The tribune, they had set the clepsydra,
That cold apportioner of measured time,
Which, drop by drop, implacably should mete
Out unto you the space of time so brief
Allotted to the advocate of truth.

MARTIANUS

Why not, Valentius?   The sun and moon
And stars are subject to the law of time—
When and how long they shine upon the earth.
I'm used to such restraint.   And was my speech
Attended by success?

VALENTIUS

            No.   Yet it seemed
To me your speech was finest of them all.
To what avail?   To whom did you pour out
Those pearls of wisdom?   To a few old men,
Who, dry as their own parchments, hunted through
The paragraphs in codices, while you
Addressed yourself to hearts and consciences!

MARTIANUS

The judges are the guardians of the law.
I rather aimed to move the people's souls,
And they, it seemed, did not remain unmoved.

VALENTIUS

But they did not applaud you when, I thought,
You stood upon the pinnacles of art;
But when you sank down to the commonplace,
I blushed for such vociferous applause.

MARTIANUS

Is it not always so?

VALENTIUS
                            Perhaps it is.
Yet, Father, for your sake I felt aggrieved.
The meanest country preacher has a fame
More brilliant, more enduring, more sublime
Than yours. The city's foremost advocate!
I couldn't stand such work!

MARTIANUS
                            Hear me, my son.
Are fame and glory greatest of rewards?
The laurel wreath the noblest crown on earth?
The cross of Christ, the olive branch of peace,
The sacred palms—are these not equal with
The laurel wreath of fame?

VALENTIUS
                            It may be so.
To each to whom they're due. My sister seems
To choose, if not the lily, then the rose;
But I prefer the laurel wreath for mine.
I've tried all avenues I know that seemed
To lead to fame: the drama, science, verse
And prose—I've failed in all. I have no skill
Or bent for literature. The vigorous deed,
Or else the living word—these are my gifts;
I am not made to be a lawyer's son.
'Tis caution' that has held me back so far.
Out of respect unto my father's work,
I have not tried to strike out my own way.
But now I've found a side-path for myself
Which will not traverse any course of yours. . . .

MARTIANUS
What path is that?

VALENTIUS
                            I'm going to enlist.

MARTIANUS
No, God forbid!

VALENTIUS
                    Why be so horrified?
Are there not Christians who as soldiers serve?

MARTIANUS
But they do so because they are compelled,
While you would volunteer to shed men's blood,
And march 'neath Caesar's eagles and accept
Rewards from unclean hands!

VALENTIUS
                    Because clean hands
Have no rewards to offer men like me.
If I may not defend poor human souls
Against the prince of darkness, I will go
And fight against the dark Barbarian hordes.
I'll hasten where the conflict is most fierce,
Where none will ever question me about
The faith I hold—where only courage counts
And one's good sword, and both of them I'll prove.
Today, the legion shall inscribe my name.

MARTIANUS
Today? . . .

VALENTIUS
                    Why put it off?   On what account?
The cohort on the morrow must set out.
I am prepared to leave.

MARTIANUS
                    My son! my son!

CONSTANTIUS
(Entering)
Forgive me, patron, for disturbing you.
Isogenes is here and must see you.

MARTIANUS
I'll come at once.
                    (CONSTANTIUS goes out.)
                    Valentius, later on
I'll talk to you. Don't go away as yet.

VALENTIUS

I've still about an hour or so to stay.

VALENTIUS *goes through the peristyle to his chamber.* MAR-
TIANUS *goes into the tablinum, where* ISOGENES, *an elderly man,
grave and quiet, is awaiting him.*

ISOGENES

Peace, brother.

MARTIANUS

And may peace be yours.

MARTIANUS *indicates the chair for* ISOGENES *to be seated. He
then sits down on the stool opposite his visitor.*

ISOGENES

You seem

Like one o'erwhelmed with grief.

MARTIANUS

Oh, my good friend,

They'll perish, both my children.

ISOGENES

Why, how's that?

When I just saw them, they were looking well.

MARTIANUS

They are not sick in body, but in soul.
I'm losing both of them. My daughter leaves
To join her mother and my son enlists—
Perdition sure for both.

ISOGENES

What's this? Why do

You let them rush into perdition thus?
You are their father—exercise your rights?

MARTIANUS

I dare not, brother. I have talked to them,
Not as one having rights, but one who feels
Deep in his soul that he's committed wrong.

ISOGENES

What wrong?

MARTIANUS

Like an idolater, I fear
I've offered them up as a sacrifice
Upon an altar's all-consuming flame—
And now they're bound to perish.

ISOGENES

Brother, this
Is something I don't altogether grasp,
Or otherwise I might give you advice.

MARTIANUS

(With a sudden hopefulness, he takes ISOGENES *by the hand.)*
Oh, brother, help me! Give me your advice!
Assist me, pray, to see my children saved!
Oh, help me, brother, for the love of Christ!

ISOGENES

You would not like, perhaps, what I might say.

MARTIANUS

Plead with the bishop; ask him to permit
My children publicly to join the church.
I'll ask him first, then you give your support.

ISOGENES

Can you not wait?

MARTIANUS

No, brother, I can't wait
Or waste a moment.

ISOGENES

Nothing can be done.
The bishop's been arrested; he's in jail.

MARTIANUS

Since when?

ISOGENES

Today. Tomorrow he'll be tried.

MARTIANUS

Is this not unexpected?

ISOGENES

Don't you know
That tribulation has arisen again,
When law becomes a scourge and not a friend
For all the Christians. I've now come to you
To ask you to prepare without delay
A sound defence by morning.

MARTIANUS

'Twill be hard.
The time is short. I do not know the charge.

ISOGENES

I've brought along all papers that relate
To the affair. Look through them. Let us know
How much there can be done.

He gives MARTIANUS *a roll of papers. The latter begins
to peruse them attentively. Meanwhile* AURELIA *comes running
down the steps and moves towards the outer door. In the middle
of the peristyle she stops and turns as if to go to the tablinum,
but stubbornly shaking her head, she continues on her way out.
In passing she tears a leaf from an aloe shrub, pricks herself in so
doing, but repressing a cry of pain, she conceals it in her dress
and without looking backwards, runs out into the street through
the wicket in the outer door.*

MARTIANUS
(Still perusing the documents)

It's difficult,
But possible—and with the help of God.
(Thoughtfully)
Yes, brother, I'll do all that can be done.
I'll work upon it all night through till dawn,
And do all possible that lies in man.
Now, give me just a moment of your time.
Permit me now to call my children here.
Then question them yourself about the faith—
For I have taught them as the Church requires—
And afterwards, if you deem them prepared,
Receive them into church this night.

ISOGENES

                                        I can't.

This is a crisis when you must appear
Most worthy of the pagan crowd's esteem.

MARTIANUS

But I myself will not be present there!

ISOGENES

Do you imagine that 'twill not be known
Whose children I've received into the Church?
The news of what I've done will fly all through
The place with lightning speed. As soon as you
Step on the tribune, all the crowd will roar
In thunder tones: "His children go to church!"
They won't give you a chance to speak a word.
And then where shall we find an advocate?
You know quite well we have no other one;
There's none else in the city whom we dare
To call—none who is Christian—and besides,
Not one of them can equal you in skill.
The time's too short to send away for help.
Moreover you have influence at Rome;
You've friends both in the Senate and at court.
Whom else can we rely on, saving you?

MARTIANUS

But, think a moment, brother—I'm a man,
A father. How then can I let my own
Dear children in the outer darkness die?

ISOGENES

You've planted in their hearts the seed of truth.

MARTIANUS

The seed sprang up and promises rich fruit,
Because it fell upon a generous soil—
If it's not garnered now, 'twill fail and rot.
My children, having learned the blessed Word,
Demanded deeds. My brother, you know well
That where there is no spring of water clear

To slake the thirst, a person needs must dip
The water from a slimy pool and drink,
Or else he dies. My children, brother, are
No lukewarm characters. The Lord has not
Yet spewed them out. My daughter is a girl
Who can be fired by a holy dream—
The stuff of which the martyrs are composed.
My son is of a bold, firm temperament;
He'd make a preacher—and a good one, too.

ISOGENES

It may be so. But now the Church no more
Depends on such supports as once it did.
When babes are born, of course, some blood is shed
And cries of pain are raised, but that's all past.
At present, Holy Church must save her blood
And turn it into milk to feed her young,
And change her voice to speak in tranquil tones
As a wise mother does. The bishop now
Warns all our maidens urgently against
The seeking of the martyr's crown—instead,
To seek to serve the Lord by quiet lives.
And as for preachers, we've no lack of them.
Your children cannot be exchanged for you.
You are at present our strong cornerstone;
You are the one sustainer of our house,
Although invisible. If you should fail,
The keystone gone, the structure will collapse.
The bishop they'll condemn to banishment;
The Church's goods they'll confiscate. With what,
Then, shall we feed our bodies and our souls?
The foe well knows by what the Church exists;
No longer does he heed the sheep, but strikes
First at the shepherd to destroy the flock;
He does not sweep the faithful from the face
Of earth, but mines the ground beneath their feet.
In this case, what you speak of won't avail:
Not all the blood in the arena shed,

Nor preacher's thunderings.

(He pauses a moment.)   Who knows, perhaps
It might be dangerous for your children, too . . .

MARTIANUS
(Offended)

Why so?

ISOGENES
        It's difficult now for the young.
Like untamed horses, they resist the reins
And will no longer run with blinkers on.
There was a tempest in our church last night:
The bishop struck Ardentus from the roll.

MARTIANUS
Ardentus! He excluded! And for what?

ISOGENES
For disobedience. You must have heard
That on the confiscated property,
Where we had planned to build a church at last,
There has been set up for the imperial cult
An altar and a statue.

MARTIANUS
                        Yes, I know.

ISOGENES
Ardentus vows he'll tear the statue down.

MARTIANUS
O God! An awful penalty for that!

ISOGENES
He dreads no punishment. It's fearful, though,
What tragedy he'll bring upon the flock.
The clergy prayed him not to do the deed,
But you know his bold, stubborn character.

MARTIANUS
He's brave and valiant as his father was—
In school we used to call him 'Hurricane'—
But my old fiery friend as legacy

Left to his son a true and loyal heart.
I scarce can comprehend it that the Church
Could e'er exclude Ardentus from the fold.

Isogenes
There was no other way to act unless
He'd promise to desist from his design.
But, having very little hope of that,
I meanwhile had the letters all prepared,
Containing notice of the bishop's act,
To send to all the churches round about,
To local courts and to the government
The self-same day on which he planned his deed.
And so I also come with this request
From all the clergy: do not undertake
In any way to act as advocate
In case Ardentus should be caught and tried.
Still better—publicly you ought to act
As though you'd never known him in your life.

Martianus
But, look! His father was my closest friend,
And ere he died, he gave his son unto
My guardianship.

Isogenes
                    Your guardianship was not
A legal one. Ardentus never lived
With you. You easily can stand aloof,
If you but will . . . My brother, you must needs
Obey us, if you are a slave of Christ
And Mother Church's true and loyal son.
                    Silence

Martianus
(With deep concern)
Are not such sacrifices overmuch
For human strength? Renounce a friend . . . and let
One's children perish both in soul and body . . .
Did ever human being do the like?

ISOGENES

Suppose a friend of yours should burn your home,
Would he continue still to be your friend?
In times of siege has it not oft occurred
That to their children fathers barred the gates—
Refused to let them go to springs outside
Lest they admit the enemy inside,
E'en though from thirst those children were destroyed?

MARTIANUS

My brother, precious souls are here at stake.

ISOGENES

Commend their souls to God, leave them to Him—
He can deliver from the lions' den
And from the flaming sword . . .

MARTIANUS *sighs deeply and bows his head.*

ISOGENES
(After a moment's silence)
My brother, then
You will defend the bishop's case in court?

MARTIANUS
(Tonelessly, almost indifferently)
Of course; there is no question as to that.

ISOGENES
(Rising)
So then, I will no longer take your time.
God's peace be with you, brother.

MARTIANUS
And with you.
(When ISOGENES *has left, he pulls back the curtain and calls.)*
Valentius!
VALENTIUS *enters the tablinum and stands before his father.
The latter gazes silently down on the ground without lifting his
eyes to his son.*

VALENTIUS
What were you going to say?

MARTIANUS

I'd hoped that I might find a remedy . . .

VALENTIUS

What sort?

MARTIANUS

I begged Isogenes that he
Might let you be received in church.

VALENTIUS

(Joyously) You did?
Oh, Father!

He kisses his father's hand.

MARTIANUS

Don't rejoice so soon, my son.
Isogenes declines.

VALENTIUS

We'll go alone
To church, provided you approve of it.

MARTIANUS

The church won't take you in.

VALENTIUS

Isogenes—
Has he alone the power to bind or loose?

MARTIANUS

He knows the clergy's mind in such a case.

VALENTIUS

(Flaring up)

If it's the clergy who would stifle souls,
Then we will testify before the church!
Let all the congregation judge the case!
I'll preach a sermon to them—You'll see then
Your son will bring no shame upon your name.

MARTIANUS

Nay, son, don't cause a rift within the church,
Or else I've lived my life on earth in vain.

VALENTIUS

Why, Father, this is moral slavery!

MARTIANUS

No, son, it's not from blind obedience
That I ask your submission to their will.
Isogenes brought such conclusive proofs
For sacrifice that I myself felt bound
To bow the head.

VALENTIUS

What is that which he fears:
New troubles for the Church?

MARTIANUS

Believe me, son,
I wouldn't think of risking my own life or yours—
The brightest flowers of this life of mine—
Unless I knew that it would serve the Faith.
The ways of God are dark, mysterious,
And past man's finding out. Perhaps the Lord,
As I, needs that his slaves be deaf and dumb . . .

VALENTIUS
(Gloomily)

Must I find gladness, too, in this?

MARTIANUS

My son,
Rejoice in this, that you are still so young—
When God has taken me back to himself
You will be free . . .

VALENTIUS

There may be sons, perhaps,
Whom such a thought might please—but I'm not one.
(A pause)
My father, it's now time to say farewell.
Give me your blessing.

He kneels down before his father.

MARTIANUS
(Making a strong effort at self-control)

Call your sister first;
I fain would bless her too along with you.

VALENTIUS
(In a low voice)

She's gone.

MARTIANUS
She's gone? Without a parting word!
He covers his face with his toga.

VALENTIUS
(In a still lower tone)

You're weeping, Father?

MARTIANUS
Would that I could weep!

Yet no tears come.

VALENTIUS
Father, forgive, forgive!
Alas, how have we wounded your kind heart!

MARTIANUS
(Lifting his son up)

Nay, I am more to blame. I've slain your souls.
May God have mercy on all three of us!

A last farewell in silence. VALENTIUS, *wiping his eyes, goes
across the peristyle and out of the outer door.* MARTIANUS, *pulling
back the side curtain of the tablinum, follows him out with his
eyes.*

SCENE II

The same place, the same day, only later. MARTIANUS *is
working alone in his tablinum. At times his eyes wander off into
space and become clouded with deep melancholy, but with a
violent effort of will he recalls himself and bends again over his
parchments. Suddenly beyond the outer door a confused sound
of voices is heard, low at first but gradually getting louder. Then
all at once the tremulous voice of a frightened young girl rings*

out: "Oh, Mamma, I'm afraid! What's this? Where are we coming to?" *Another voice, a woman's, deeper and steadier, replies:* "Just wait!" *Following this there is a knocking at the door which suddenly breaks off.* MARTIANUS, *hearing the voices and the knocking, starts up, looks out of the tablinum, then walks to the gate, passing* MOMUS *who is stooping over the clepsydra, ard pushes back the loophole in the door.*

MARTIANUS
(Looking through the loophole into the street)
Albina! Sister!

He immediately opens the wicket and steps outside. The sound of joyous greeting is heard. Then GERMANUS *opens the door wide and makes a sign to* MOMUS *to come, after which they both re-enter carrying a curtained four-legged litter. In the litter, lying back on a pile of cushions is* LUCILLA, *a slender, very sickly-looking young girl. Following the litter, with* MARTIANUS *comes* ALBINA, *middle-aged, very pale, with graying hair, and sad worn-out eyes. At a sign from* MARTIANUS *the slaves set down the litter close by the pool, then bring in the baggage of the new arrivals and put it in a chamber on the ground floor of the dwelling.* MOMUS *remains inside while* GERMANUS *goes back to his post, closing the door behind him.*

ALBINA
Oh, Martianus, what
A strange outlandish doorkeeper you have!
Not only would he not undo the door,
He wouldn't even let us knock.

LUCILLA
And he
Yelled in a barbarous tongue and frightened me.

MARTIANUS
He's German—doesn't understand our speech.
He wouldn't let you in because he knows
That I receive no guests when I'm at work.
I do not like the knocking—clients come
In through the vestibule.

MARTIANUS *and* ALBINA *sit down on a bench near the litter*
but not beside it.

LUCILLA

My Uncle, where is

Aurelia?

MARTIANUS

(Stooping down as if to pick up something)
She's not at home.

LUCILLA

Too bad!

I did so wish to see my cousin here.

ALBINA

You'll see her soon; 'twill not be long before
She's here.

(To MARTIANUS*)*

That's so?

MARTIANUS

I do not know.

ALBINA

As we were coming here along the hill
We met a young man—oh, so very like
To you. Maybe it was Valentius?

MARTIANUS

Undoubtedly.

ALBINA

Oh, had I known for sure,

I would have stopped and questioned him, but then
I hardly dared.

LUCILLA

(To MARTIANUS*)*
And will he soon return?

MARTIANUS

I don't think so.

ALBINA

(Looking sharply at her brother, then in a whisper)
There's something wrong . . .

MARTIANUS
(Also in a whisper)
                              Just wait;
I'll tell you later.

LUCILLA
                    Uncle, tell me, pray,
Is this a lucky day?

MARTIANUS
                         Lucky for me,
Because you came.

LUCILLA
               You don't quite understand . . .
I always dread the evil-omened days.

ALBINA
I told you, daughter!   Don't you still recall?

LUCILLA
Oh, Uncle, we let three ships sail away
From Alexandria, because they sailed
On evil-omened days.

ALBINA
                          We let them go
For better weather, for a smoother sea.

LUCILLA
So now, you see, we have arrived quite safe,
Or else, who knows, our ship might have been wrecked!

MARTIANUS
(In a whisper to ALBINA*)*
She sounds to me like an idolatress.

ALBINA
(Also in a whisper)
May God forbid!   It is her sickness that
Has left her weak in mind.

LUCILLA
                         O Mother, Uncle!
Why are you whispering?   Tell me the truth:
Is this an evil-omened day?

ALBINA

No, no!

LUCILLA

The calendar!   Get me the calendar!
She writhes in pain, her hand pressed to her heart.

ALBINA
(Dashing to her, greatly alarmed)
Go get it for her, Martianus, please!

MARTIANUS *goes into the tablinum and returns thence with
the calendar, a small marble cube with the names and dates in
three columns on each side.*

LUCILLA
(Running her finger down one of the columns)
Ah yes, it's Venus' day . . . may God be thanked!
*(Satisfied, she lies back in the cushions again, but suddenly
starts up once more and feverishly begins to search for some-
thing in her clothing and in the litter.)*
The locket, where is it?

ALBINA
*(She takes a small medallion attached to a ribbon out of the
purse hanging at her waist.)*
Here.
She is about to put it back again.

LUCILLA

Give it to me;
You'll lose it else.
(She takes the locket and hangs it round her neck)

MARTIANUS
What's in the locket there?

LUCILLA
A stone—it's called "the serpent's eye."   It's from
An Aesculapian priest in Syracuse,
When Mother visited the temple there.

MARTIANUS
(To ALBINA as well)

Is this the truth?

ALBINA

(Unobserved by LUCILLA, *she shakes her head in denial at*
MARTIANUS.*)*

What can one do with her?

LUCILLA

We'll go together to Lavinium's shrine
When I am rested.   Mother doesn't want
To go, but on the ship a woman said
That sickness can be healed there in a wink.

MARTIANUS

Lucilla, you'll get better here with me.

ALBINA

That's just the reason that I brought her here—
To gain some strength.   The spring in Egypt is
A trying time.   The burning winds that blow
Make it unbearable.

LUCILLA

It's heaven here—

I breathe so easily . . .

She draws a deep breath and smiles with pleasure.

ALBINA

(Smiling back)

My Daughter, see—
I said you would improve in Uncle's home.

MOMUS, *seeing that the sundial is almost in shadow, takes
down the mallet to strike the gong, but* MARTIANUS *gives him a
sign not to do so and points to the outer door.* MOMUS *goes
thither, opens the wicket, touches* GERMANUS *on the shoulder
and points to the side entrance.   The latter comes inside, closes
the wicket, bolts the door and crosses the peristyle to the side
entrance.* MOMUS *returns and begins to pour water out of a
ladle into the clepsydra.*

LUCILLA

*(Feverishly groping in her bosom and searching all about her,
suddenly cries out in desperation.)*

Oh, Mother dear!   I think I've lost my fish!¹

ALBINA

How's that, my child?   You had it round your neck.

LUCILLA

The ribbon must have snapped. . . .
(She wrings her hands.)
O Lord, my God!
Forgive me, O forgive me! . . . Mother, oh!

Why did I send you to that heathen shrine?
The Lord is wroth with Aesculapius,
And took away my fish.   He won't permit
An unclean girl to wear a Christian charm.
O Mother, now I know I'm going to die! . . .
Why did you go to Aesculapius? . . .
ALBINA looks helplessly at MARTIANUS.

MARTIANUS
(In a whisper to ALBINA)
Tell her you didn't go.
ALBINA
(Also in a whisper and shaking her head)
'Twill make things worse.

LUCILLA
(She suddenly notices that MOMUS has her fish in his hands
and is examining it.   Joyfully)
Here, give it me!   Where did you get it from?
It's mine, it's mine!
(Vexed, to MARTIANUS)
Why doesn't he obey?
Barbarian, too?

MARTIANUS
No, he is deaf and dumb.
He takes the fish from MOMUS and gives it to LUCILLA. She

---

1. The well-known early Christian mystic symbol.   The Greek word
   for fish, *ichthys*, furnished the initial letters of the words in the
   phrase, "Jesus Christ, God's Son, Saviour."

takes it with great gladness, presses it to her heart, kisses and
fondles it.

LUCILLA
(Looking at MOMUS*)*
A dreadful-looking man!

MARTIANUS
                              Why, not at all.
He's good and most submissive. He would take
And bear you in his arms if you would like.
     He makes signs to this effect to MOMUS*. The latter nods his*
head and gives LUCILLA *a friendly smile. She smiles back at him.*

LUCILLA
(To MARTIANUS*)*
Tell him to have the gate thrown open wide.
I think the sea is visible from here—
I'd like to look. . . .

MARTIANUS
                              It opens on the street,
My child; the people pass and they would stare.

LUCILLA
(Frightened)
And you're afraid?   Do all the people here
Throw stones at all the Christians whom they see?
(To ALBINA*)*
Oh. Mother, don't you ever dare go out
Into the street. You musn't go to church.
Don't ever let a soul come inside here
To hide away! I couldn't stand it, hear!
'Twould only make me still more sick and die!

ALBINA
May God forbid!   But don't get so alarmed.
Why should I go out here? Who'd come to hide?
I'm not acquainted here with anyone.

LUCILLA
At church you'd soon make friends with everyone.

(Nervously to MARTIANUS *and growing more and more agitated)*
Oh, Uncle, do you know . . . long time ago . . .
When I was small . . . my father always went,
And went to church . . . and people used to come
And hide in Father's house . . . and once . . . at night . . .
The city watch came in . . . arrested them . . .
And Father, too . . . and in a prison cell . . .
They threw him . . . with hot irons tortured him . . .
And then . . . they nailed him to a . . . wooden post . . .
And . . . and . . .
    Breathless, she clutches at her breast and groans.

ALBINA
(Darting to her)
Lucilla dear!

LUCILLA
Some water,
*(*MOMUS *at a sign from* MARTIANUS *brings her water to drink.*
    After having drunk, she lies back again quietly. Then to her mother)
So you won't go?

ALBINA
I will not go, my child.
I won't go anywhere. I'll stay with you.

LUCILLA
Those people? Maybe Uncle lets them hide?

MARTIANUS
No, none will seek a hiding place with me.
Don't worry—here there will be no arrests.
I am respected here.

LUCILLA
(Sighing with relief)
Ah, that is good!
(Covering her eyes)

If I could only spend a year here quietly,
I should get better, Mother.

MARTIANUS

                              Grant it, Lord!
Another year, and we shall see you wed.

LUCILLA

Oh, Uncle, you are kind . . . Aurelia
Is blest to have a father such as you. . . .
                    Her voice becomes tearful.

ALBINA

                    (To MARTIANUS*)*
Allow her to be carried to her room.
The evening falls.

MARTIANUS

                    Of course. By now the room
Will be arranged and supper be prepared.
Will you eat in your chamber, or perhaps
In our triclinium?

ALBINA

                    With you, of course.

MARTIANUS

I do not eat at night. Besides, I have
Some pressing work. So shall I call at once
And have them carry in Lucilla?

LUCILLA

                                        No!
I'll go myself. It prophesies bad luck
When one is carried into a new house.

ALBINA

Whoever told you that?

LUCILLA

                    No one. I know—
They only carry brides into their homes,
And dead out to the tomb.

ALBINA

God save you, dear!

MARTIANUS

If you with suchlike superstitions hold,
Then think that you are going to be wed
While staying here with me.

LUCILLA

It isn't that.

For Christians do not carry in their brides
As pagans do—and I'm a Christian girl.

MARTIANUS

Then to their superstitions pay no heed.

LUCILLA
(Stubbornly)

Yet, all the same, I'll go myself.
(She gets out of the litter, ALBINA *assisting her. After taking
a few steps, she stops and cries out.)*

O God!

ALBINA

Now, what is wrong?

LUCILLA

Why did I let myself
Be carried through the door unto this spot!

ALBINA

That's just into the courtyard, not the house.

LUCILLA
(Calmer, but still somewhat incredulous)
You really think that's so?

ALBINA

Of course, my love!

I do not merely think, I know it's so.
In Egypt all the structure's called the house.
Here, court and house are two quite separate things
   Quietly talking to her daughter, ALBINA *leads her by a side
passage into the inner rooms.* MARTIANUS, *having escorted them,*

now returns and gives orders by signs to MOMUS *to have supper served to his guests, and then enters his tablinum to resume work. Noticing that it is dark in there and that there is no oil in the lamp, he comes out into the peristyle again. While* MOMUS *is busy carrying the food across the peristyle,* MARTIANUS *seizes a moment when he is absent to slip into his children's room; from* AURELIA'S *he takes a ribbon and a flower—a lily, and from* VALEN-TIUS' *a few tablets, and hiding them under his toga, he enters the tablinum again and hides them in a drawer there.*

ALBINA
(Coming to the curtain of the tablinum; she is carrying a dish of food and a cup of wine.)
Do I disturb you, brother?   Then, forgive—
Just for a moment.   Have you any oil
Of aloes here?

MARTIANUS
I think there must be some.
Just wait—we'll make a light and look.
He goes out and touches MOMUS *to whom he gives orders for light. The latter brings oil, fills up* MARTIANUS' *lamp and the lantern beside the clepsydra, then gets a burning taper and lights up both in the tablinum and in the peristyle. Meanwhile* MAR-TIANUS *and* ALBINA *are talking together.*

MARTIANUS
(Perceiving the food and wine which ALBINA *is holding)*
What's this?   Some supper!   But I do not eat.

ALBINA
(Embarrassed, sets both cup and dish on a bench.)
You see . . . Lucilla urgently desired
That your Penates should receive a share.

MARTIANUS
I keep no altar and no household gods.

ALBINA
I told her so—but she would pay no heed.
She said, "Just set them in the atrium;

They'll find it there."

MARTIANUS

Oh, sister, this is sad!
A child of yours and Festus—she regards
These vanities more than the living God!

ALBINA

She does believe in Christ and worships Him,
But she's afraid—nay, downright terrified
Of anything that seems mysterious
Or threatening. This, Martianus, is
A throbbing, festering wound in my poor heart—
Her superstitious fears! What can I do?
You've seen it for yourself . . . Mothers there are
Who can give up their children for the Faith,
But I am weak . . . Perhaps, my brother, you're
Condemning me?

MARTIANUS

Not I, Albina, I
Am judge of no one's deeds.

ALBINA

It's easier
For mothers such as those. Their children die
But once—they suffer once—but I each day . . .

MARTIANUS

Since when did it begin?

ALBINA

Since Festus died.
I've been chastised already six long years.
She came into the world a sickly babe,
For I was leading then a feverish
And strenuous life. At times it seems to me
That I'm to blame for poor Lucilla's state—
I gave more strength and service to the Faith
Than to my sickly babe. I poisoned her
With milk that came from my o'erheated breast.
Nay, I infected her while in the womb
With blood that only burned with ardent flame

For supernatural ecstasies. Before
Her father died, in dreadful agonies,
A martyr's death—it seemed to me—O Lord,
Forgive!—my family had paid a debt
Most bloody. Then I could no longer see
My child live on in torments—O my brother!
Don't think my burdened soul found peace thereby.
Far from it! On the contrary I found
Myself bound in a lifelong slavery
Of duty, but alas! I did not die.

MARTIANUS

Why "lifelong?" Sister, do you not expect
To win to liberty?

ALBINA

Yes, when I die!

MARTIANUS

No, in this world, right here and now.

ALBINA

My Brother,
Cold comfort isn't it you're offering me?
Should I not long for death for my poor child?

MARTIANUS

For healing, not for death. Lucilla will
Recover; then you'll get her married off.
You'll feel yourself free after that, I'm sure.

ALBINA
(Heaving a deep sigh and with a hopeless wave of the hand)
God grant, my Martianus, that you ne'er
Experience such grief with child of yours!

MARTIANUS
(In a hollow voice)
Perhaps I know still worse.

ALBINA
What's that you say?

MARTIANUS

You've sacrificed the Faith for your one child.
I—on the contrary.

ALBINA

You've turned them out
Of home, your children, for idolatry?

MARTIANUS

No, both were Christians, but 'twas hard for them
To live in such a home where none can live
Except the deaf and dumb.

ALBINA

What do you mean? . . .

MARTIANUS

You may with easy mind the promise keep
You made just now not to attend the church
As long as you stay here, for I myself
Do not attend.

ALBINA

You have apostatized? . . .

MARTIANUS

No, I'm a secret Christian now, and by
The Church's will. So long as I shall live
I may not put these fetters off from me.
Silence for a moment. ALBINA *presses her brother's hand.*

LUCILLA

(From within)

Oh, Mother, where are you?

ALBINA

(Replying to her)

I'm coming, child.

(Then hurriedly to MARTIANUS*)*

Give me the oil of aloes. I must go.

MARTIANUS *gets a vial out of the tablinum and gives it to*
ALBINA, *who hurries back to her daughter. He then makes signs
to* MOMUS *to take away the food and wine which* ALBINA *had
brought.* MOMUS *does so. Complete silence now reigns. In the*

peristyle the light cast by the lantern battles feebly against the
invading darkness which seeps in from every side. MARTIANUS
sits in the tablinum bent over his work. Suddenly an urgent
knocking is heard at the outer door. MARTIANUS *springs up and*
walks toward it.

MARTIANUS

(Still on his way)

Who's there?

(A VOICE *from outside)*

It's I—Ardentus—let me in!

*(*MARTIANUS *opens the loophole in the door and peers out.*
Outside in the gloom he sees the pale, sweat-bedewed and blood-
stained face of ARDENTUS.*)*
What's happened now?

ARDENTUS

I tore the statue down.

*(*MARTIANUS *makes a gesture of dismay.)*

They saw me . . . they are chasing me . . . for God's sake,
Conceal me!

MARTIANUS

I cannot. I wouldn't dare.

A doctor lives nearby. Run to his place—
That will be safer both for me and you.

ARDENTUS

I cannot do it . . . I've lost too much blood . . .
I'm badly hurt . . . with stones . . . for God's sake help!
Deliver me! Think on the wounds of Christ!

MARTIANUS

My son, I dare not.

ARDENTUS

Ah, I am your son!

My father left me to your care, it seems.
(He stops, listens. The roar of a crowd and the patter of feet
can be heard approaching.)
Oh quick, let me come in!

CONSTANTIUS

(Coming out of his room, which is just beside the door)

Sir, I can hide

Ardentus in my room.

MARTIANUS
It can't be done.

Your room is in my house.

CONSTANTIUS
For God's sake, aid!
He'll perish on your very threshold here!
Oh, let him in!   I cannot bear the sight!
They'll tear him, slaughter, trample him to death.

MARTIANUS *in silence grips* CONSTANTIUS' *hands to keep him from pulling back the bolt of the door.* CONSTANTIUS *struggles to release his hands to get at the bolt.*

ARDENTUS
Oh, let me in!

MARTIANUS
I dare not let you in.

ARDENTUS
Then may God from His kingdom shut you out!
Accurséd Pilate, you!

He darts away and disappears. The roar of the crowd draws nearer.

MARTIANUS
Ardentus, son!

(He looses CONSTANTIUS *and is about to push back the bolt himself when a violent pounding of fists on the door arrest him. He stops.)*
Who's there?

SEVERAL VOICES
The city watch!   The people, too!

MARTIANUS
(Striving to regain his self-control)
What do you want?

A ROUGH VOICE
The felon who's in there!

MARTIANUS

Who's that?

THE SAME VOICE
You know him! Open, let us in!

ALBINA
(Running hither)

What's happening?

MARTIANUS
Back to Lucilla! Go!
I must somehow avert calamity.

*(ALBINA goes back. Now fully self-possessed, he speaks
firmly.)*
I need not open up to anyone,
Save to the law.

A DIFFERENT VOICE
Then let the watch come in.

MARTIANUS
But who gives me assurance that the crowd
Won't rush in too?

THE VOICE
I, the centurion
Here in command.

MARTIANUS
You do?

THE VOICE
Yes.
(Then to the crowd)
All you there,
Don't follow in. You'd better search around
And see if he's fled down some other street.
(After a little while, to MARTIANUS*)*
It's quite safe now to open up.

MARTIANUS *now opens. The watch, headed by the centurion, marches into the peristyle.*

MARTIANUS
I beg

That you will do your duty without noise,
For there is sickness here.

The soldiers scatter searching the rooms around the peri-
style, including the tablinum. They then go to the left where
the slaves live and return, bringing MOMUS *and* GERMANUS.
Other soldiers seize CONSTANTIUS.

CENTURION
(Pointing to the arrested)
Martianus, who

Are these?

MARTIANUS
These two are slaves of mine, and this,

My secretary.

CENTURION
(To his men)
None of these are like

The fugitive?

A SOLDIER
Not a bit! He was bruised

And bloody—not a bit like these men here. . . .

The CENTURION *waves his hand to let the prisoners go. He*
then goes toward the right-hand passage. MARTIANUS *overtakes*
him.

MARTIANUS

I beg of you to leave one room unsearched—
The one in which my niece is lying ill.

CENTURION

We know these sick folk!
(To his men)
Watch! Search everywhere!

The soldiers go into the passage, pressing MARTIANUS *aside*
so that he cannot precede them. A moment later a piercing
shriek is heard. LUCILLA, *in a white sleeping tunic with wide*
sleeves, runs out into the peristyle, followed frantically by ALBINA.
MARTIANUS *hurries after them.*

ALBINA

Where are you going, child?

LUCILLA
(Rushing hither and thither)
Where can we hide?
(She stumbles over the litter and jumps into it.)
Here, Mother, hide!   Come here inside with me!

ALBINA

What for?

LUCILLA
The watch—they'll get you if you don't!

ALBINA
That's not the watch . . . it's . . . Martianus, say!
What shall I tell her?

MARTIANUS
Say . . . some soldier friends . . .
To see my son. . . .

LUCILLA
(In a muffled voice)
No, no, it isn't true!
*The jingle of accoutrements is heard as the watch returns
into the peristyle.* LUCILLA *hastily pulls the curtains close.*

CENTURION
You've searched in every place?

A SOLDIER
Yes, sir.
LUCILLA *utters a dull groan. The* CENTURION *runs to the
litter.*

CENTURION
Who's here?

ALBINA
(Seizing him by the arm)
I beg—beseech you—do not look!

CENTURION
I must.
(He pulls back the curtains and looks into the litter. LUCILLA,
with a hoarse cry, sits up and then falls back in a swoon.   Then,

somewhat perturbed, he turns to ALBINA.)
O Matron, pardon, I knew not . . .

A VOICE *from outside*
Hey, watch!
They've found him, found him!   Here he is, outside!
CENTURION
(*To* MARTIANUS, *apologetically*)
Forgive me, sir, for these disturbances.
But then, you know, sir . . . duty . . .

MARTIANUS *remains silent. The* CENTURION *gives a sign to
his men and all together they pass out through the outer door
into the street.*
ALBINA
(*Who, meanwhile, has been busy with* LUCILLA)
O my God!
She's cold!   She's dead!

MARTIANUS *also bends over* LUCILLA *and touches her. He
shudders and quickly removes his hand from her body.*

MARTIANUS
No, sister; in a swoon,
That's all . . .
He makes signs to the slaves to carry LUCILLA *with the litter
back into the house.*
ALBINA
(*Struggling with* MARTIANUS)
Oh, loose me!   Let me go to her!

MARTIANUS
Of course, Albina.   I will go with you.
They go out at the right. The slaves return, GERMANUS
goes out by the left, MOMUS *remains in the peristyle. Then* AL-
BINA's *loud weeping is heard.* MARTIANUS *comes and knocks at
the door of* CONSTANTIUS' *room. The latter comes out.*

MARTIANUS
Please go and call some neighbor women in.
I cannot leave her with the corpse like this.

CONSTANTIUS

Can it be true your little niece is dead?

MARTIANUS

She is.

CONSTANTIUS

God rest her soul! I go, my patron.

He goes out while MARTIANUS *returns to* ALBINA. *Meanwhile* MOMUS *calmly attends to the lights in both tablinum and peristyle, looks at the clepsydra, and smooths the sand around it, which has been trampled by many feet.* CONSTANTIUS *re-enters, leading two women across the peristyle into the passage on the right, talking to them in whispers as they walk; they shake their heads in sympathy and sigh. Having escorted the women,* CONSTANTIUS *returns to his room.*

MARTIANUS

(He comes in, leading his sister by the arm, and seats her on a bench away from the light.)

Sit here, my sister. Mothers should be spared

The sight while others do such mournful work.

She weeps on his shoulder.

ALBINA

(Ceasing her weeping for a moment)

She spoke the truth. . . .

She begins to weep again.

MARTIANUS

(Quietly)

What do you mean?

ALBINA

Why did

We let them carry her into the house!

She bursts out weeping more violently.

MARTIANUS

You should not brood on things like that, my dear.

It was the will of God.

ALBINA

Oh yes, it's true.
The Lord has punished me as I deserved.
I've been a renegade! A recreant!

MARTIANUS

The Lord is kind. This is no punishment.
In mercy he has put his child to sleep
So that from tribulations she might rest.

ALBINA

*(After a moment's subsidence, she again breaks out into loud
weeping.)*
My daughter! . . . Why hast thou chastised me, Lord,
So much?
(Suddenly leaning back from MARTIANUS, *she takes his hand
and whispers to him.)*
How well she could discern and read
My secret thoughts . . . the innermost of all . . .
One time she said to me: "You hate the love
You bear to me."
She knits her brows in deep musing.

MARTIANUS

Pray, don't torment yourself
With vain regrets. The Lord recalls you back
To work for him once more. Be humble. Go.

ALBINA

(Without changing her expression)
Where to?

MARTIANUS

Where you and Festus worked before.
You'll be with brethren there.

ALBINA

(Now aroused)
My brother—you
Would send me hence, drive me away from you?
They would reject me, call me "renegade."

MARTIANUS
No, sister. None who has a heart would cast
A stone at you.
(Quietly but with a penetrating sadness)
But I—I can no more
Subject my kindred to the chains I bear.
I must forever stay just what I am;
Remain aloof from every tie of blood,
And never call a human soul my friend.
You needs must travel far enough away
So that my shadow never reaches you,
And walk there—not in darkness, but in light.

ALBINA
But how can I abandon my Lucilla?
Who is there who will tend her tiny grave?

MARTIANUS
A relative deceased may still abide
Within my dwelling-place, and your dear child
Shall rest forever in my garden here.
So far I've grown no flowers—but for her
I'll plant the richest blooms.

ALBINA
(Weeping, she falls into his arms.)
Oh, brother, thanks!

(MOMUS *approaches the clepsydra, looks at it, picks up the mallet and begins to pound vigorously on the gong.* ALBINA *leaps up, startled.)*
What's that?

MARTIANUS
It's only Momus at his task
Of telling us it's time to go to rest.

ALBINA
(Rising)
Ah, you need rest and sleep.

MARTIANUS
No, I must work

Until the morning comes.

ALBINA

Well, I will go . . .
I'll go . . . to look the last time on my child.
Oh, daughter!   Freedom will be bitter now
That you are gone!

She goes out weeping.

MARTIANUS
(Going to the door of CONSTANTIUS' *room)*
You are not sleeping yet,

Constantius?

CONSTANTIUS
(Appearing in the doorway)
How could I go to sleep
With all that's happened here?

MARTIANUS
Well, come to me.
We've got to work the whole night through till dawn.

CONSTANTIUS

What!   After this, you still can work?

MARTIANUS
I must.

They go into the tablinum, CONSTANTIUS *first, who sits
down at the table and gets ready his tablets.*

CONSTANTIUS

I fear my writing may be bad—my hand
Is trembling.

MARTIANUS
Have no fear; I'll make it out.
No doubt, I'll say it all in other words,
But this will help to make the points all clear.
It helps to think aloud.

He sits down in the armchair.

CONSTANTIUS
Good God, Oh, sir,

Your hair's completely white!

MARTIANUS
That's nothing much.
Now I'll dictate.
(He begins his dictation as CONSTANTIUS *writes.)*
"O honored justices,
I beg of you to judge this simple case
According to calm reason, most deliberate.
It is as lucid as a crystal clear,
Provided it's not clouded by the breath
Of passion or of prejudice.   One can
Examine best a crystal by cold light. . . ."

CONSTANTIUS
(Letting the stylus fall from his hand)
Forgive . . . I cannot . . .

MARTIANUS
Here, I'll finish it.
He takes the tablet and stylus from CONSTANTIUS *and writes
slowly but with a steady hand.*